Praise for Jennifer Worth

'These are powerful stories delivered with sweet charm and controlled outrage' *Times Literary Supplement*

'Worth is indeed a natural storyteller − in the best sense of the term, with apparent artlessness in fact concealing high art and her detailed account of being a midwife in London's East End is gripping, moving and convincing from beginning to end ... *Call the Midwife* is also a powerful evocation of a long-gone world ... and in Worth it has surely found one of its best chroniclers' *Literary Review*

'A chilling insight into life for the average mother [in the 1950s]' *Sunday Express*

'Sheer magic' *The Lady*

'Worth's book made me cry in a railway carriage' Matthew Parris, *Spectator*

'Worth is a vivid writer with a talent for the sting in the tail ... a highly readable book − and a must for social planners' *Evening Standard*

'Jennifer Worth has a gift for storytelling and a keen eye for the evocative' BBC TV's *Who Do You Think You Are*

'Jennifer Worth's entertaining and moving account of her experiences among the Docklands people balances sentiment with gritty realism' *Docklands News*

'A candid, poignant memoir ... this gripping narrative includes breech babies, adulterous relationships, urban pig-breeding and a surreal strip show in a brothel' *Townswoman*

'Worth's talent shines from every page' *Sainsbury's Magazine*

'In her marvellous new book ... [t]here are desperately sad stories here, but tales of great hope too. Of ordinary people living, giving birth and building their families despite enormous hardship and poor sanitation. And of midwives delivering superb care in the toughest conditions' *East End Life*

'Nobody who reads *Call the Midwife* will ever forget it' *The Woman Writer*

'The Docklands in London' ... ... e like the nineteenth cent

Jennifer Worth trained as a nurse at the Royal Berkshire Hospital, Reading, and was later ward sister at the Elizabeth Garrett Anderson Hospital in London, then the Marie Curie Hospital, also in London. Music had always been her passion, and in 1973 she left nursing in order to study music intensively, teaching piano and singing for about twenty-five years. Jennifer died in May 2011 after a short illness, leaving her husband Philip, two daughters and three grandchildren. Her books have all been bestsellers.

By Jennifer Worth

Eczema and Food Allergy
Call the Midwife
Shadows of the Workhouse
Farewell to the East End
In the Midst of Life

Farewell to the East End

JENNIFER WORTH

CLINICAL EDITOR
Terri Coates MSc. RN. RM. ADM. Dip Ed

PHOENIX

A PHOENIX PAPERBACK

First published in Great Britain in 2009
by Weidenfeld & Nicolson
This paperback edition published in 2013
by Phoenix,
an imprint of Orion Books Ltd,
Orion House, 5 Upper St Martin's Lane,
London WC2H 9EA

An Hachette UK company

1 3 5 7 9 10 8 6 4 2

This is the third work of non-fiction, of which the first two
were published by Merton Books. The events it recounts are
true. However, certain names and identifying characteristics
of some of the people who appear in its pages have been
changed. The views expressed in this book are the author's.

A CIP catalogue record for this book
is available from the British Library.

ISBN 978-1-7802-2447-3

Typeset by Input Data Services Ltd, Bridgwater, Somerset

Printed in Great Britain by Clays Ltd, St Ives plc

The Orion Publishing Group's policy is to use papers
that are natural, renewable and recyclable products and
made from wood grown in sustainable forests. The logging
and manufacturing processes are expected to conform to
the environmental regulations of the country of origin.

www.orionbooks.co.uk

Dedicated to Cynthia
for a lifetime of friendship

ACKNOWLEDGEMENTS

My thanks and gratitude to:

Terri Coates, the midwife who inspired me to write these books, Kirsty Dunseath for her editing skills, Dr Michael Boyes, Douglas May, Jenny Whitefield, Joan Hands, Helen Whitehorn, Philip and Suzannah, Ena Robinson, Mary Riches, Janet Salter, Maureen Dring, Peggy Sayer, Mike Birch, Sally Neville, the Marie Stopes Society.

Special thanks to Patricia Schooling of Merton Books for first bringing my writing to an audience.

All names have been changed. 'The Sisters of St Raymund Nonnatus' is a pseudonym.

CONTENTS

In 1855 Queen Victoria wrote to her daughter Vicky, the Crown Princess of Prussia, who was expecting a baby:

What you say about the pride of giving life to an immortal soul is very fine, but I own I cannot enter into all that. I think very much more of our being like a cow or a dog at such moments, when our poor nature becomes so very animal and unecstatic.

'YOUTH'S A STUFF WILL NOT ENDURE'

Someone once said that youth is wasted on the young.* Not a bit of it. Only the young have the impulsive energy to tackle the impossible and enjoy it; the courage to follow their instincts and brave the new; the stamina to work all day, all night and all the next day without tiring. For the young everything is possible. None of us, twenty years later, could do the things we did in our youth. Though the vision burns still bright, the energy has gone.

In the heady days of my early twenties I went to work in the East End of bomb-damaged London as a district midwife. I did it out of a yearning for adventure, not from a sense of vocation. I wanted to experience something different from my middle-class background, something tough and challenging that would stretch me. I wanted a new slant on life. I went to a place called Nonnatus House,† which I thought was a small private hospital, but which turned out to be a convent run by the Sisters of St Raymund Nonnatus. When I discovered my mistake I nearly ran away without unpacking my bags. Nuns were not my style. I couldn't be doing with that sort of thing, I thought. I wanted adventure, not religion. I did not know it at the time, but my soul was yearning for both.

---

* 'Youth is such a wonderful thing. What a crime to waste it on children.' George Bernard Shaw. The quote in the chapter title is from Shakespeare, *Twelfth Night*, act 2, scene 3.
† The Midwives of St Raymund Nonnatus is a pseudonym. I have taken the name from St Raymund Nonnatus, the patron saint of midwives, obstetricians, pregnant women, childbirth and newborn babies. He was delivered by Caesarean section ('*non natus*' is the Latin for 'not born') in Catalonia, Spain, in 1204. His mother, not surprisingly, died at his birth. He became a priest and died in 1240.

The nuns generated adventure. They plunged headlong into anything, fearlessly: unlit streets and courtyards, dark, sinister stairways, the docks, brothels; they would tackle rogue landlords, abusive parents – nothing was outside their scope. Sparky, saintly Sister Julienne with her wisdom and humour inspired us all to dare the impossible. Calm Novice Ruth and clever Sister Bernadette inspired respect, even awe, with their vast knowledge and experience of midwifery. Gruff and grumpy Sister Evangelina shocked and amused us with her vulgarity. And naughty Sister Monica Joan! What can be said of this wilful old lady of fey and fascinating charm who was once prosecuted for shoplifting (but found not guilty!)? 'Just a small oversight,' she said. 'Best forgotten.'

We took our lead from the Sisters, and feared nothing, not even getting our bikes out in the middle of the night and cycling alone through some of the toughest areas of London, which even the police patrolled in pairs. Through unlit streets and alleyways, past bomb sites where the meths drinkers hung out, past the docks where all was silent at night but for the creaks and moans as the ships stirred in their moorings, past the great river, dark and silent, past the brothels of Cable Street and the sinister pimps who controlled the area. Past – no, not past – into a small house or flat that was warm, bright and expectant, awaiting the birth of a new baby.

My colleagues and I loved every minute of it. Cynthia, who had a voice like music, and a slow, sweet smile that could calm any situation, however fraught. Trixie, with her sharp mind and waspish tongue. Chummy, a misfit in her colonial family because she was too big, too awkward, to fit into society, and who totally lacked self-confidence until she started nursing and proved herself a hero.

Youth, wasted on the young? Certainly not for us. Let those who waste their youth regret the passing of the years. We had experience, risk, and adventure enough to fill a lifetime. And to remember in old age is sweet; remember the shaft of sunlight piercing the black tenements, or the gleaming funnels of a ship as it left the docks; remember the warmth and fun of the Cockney people, or the grim reality of too little sleep and yet another call out into the night; remember the bicycle puncture and a policeman fixing it, or jumping barges with Sister Evangelina when the road was closed; remember the London smog, yellow-grey and choking thick, when Conchita's premature baby was born, or Christmas day, when a breech baby, undiagnosed, was delivered; remember the brothels of Cable Street, into which the child Mary was lured, and where old Mrs Jenkins lived, haunted by hallucinations of life in the workhouse.

I remember the days of my youth when everything was new and bright; when the mind was always questing, searching, absorbing; when the pain of love was so acute it could suffocate. And the days when joy was delirious.

THREE MEN WENT INTO
A RESTAURANT . . .

Carters used to say that a working horse knew the way back to his stable and would pick up his feet and pull his cart with a lively step at the close of day, knowing that soft hay, food and water were at the end of the journey. That was how we midwives felt as we headed home after evening visits.

A cold but kindly west wind blew me all the way down Commercial Road and the East India Dock Road towards the welcome of Nonnatus House, the warmth of the big kitchen and – most important of all – food. I was young, healthy and hungry, and the day had been long. As I pedalled along, Mrs B's home-made bread was foremost in my mind. She had a magic touch with bread, that woman, and I knew she had been baking that morning. Also in my mind was the puzzle Fred had presented us with at breakfast. I couldn't work it out – three nines are twenty-seven, plus two makes twenty-nine – so where was the other shilling? It was nonsense, didn't make sense, it must be somewhere. A shilling can't vanish into thin air! I wondered what the girls had made of it. Had they got any closer to solving the riddle? Perhaps Trixie had worked out the answer; Trixie was pretty sharp.

With the wind behind me the ride was easy, and I arrived at the convent glowing. But Trixie had come from the east, had cycled two miles into a strong head wind, and was consequently a bit ratty. We put our bikes away and carried our bags to the clinical room. The rule was that equipment must be cleaned, sterilised, checked and the bag repacked for immediate use in the middle of the night, should it be needed. Chummy – or Camilla Fortescue-Cholmeley-Browne – was ahead of us.

'What-ho, you jolly swags,' she called out cheerily.

'Oh no, spare me!' groaned Trixie, 'I really can't stand it just now. I'm not "jolly", and I'm not "what-hoing" anyone. I'm cold, my knees ache, and I'm famished. And I've got to clean my bag before I get a bite.'

Chummy was all solicitude.

'Sorry, old bean, didn't mean to sound a wrong note, what? Here, I've just finished folding these swabs. You have them; I can quickly do some more. And the autoclave is at 180 degrees; I put it on twenty minutes ago when I came in. We'll get these bally bags done in a jiff. Did you see Mrs B making bread this morning?'

We had. Mrs B not only made the best bread north of the Thames, she made jams and chutneys, cheesy scones and cakes to die for.

Our bags packed, we emerged from the clinical room and headed towards the kitchen, hungry for supper, which was a casual meal that we prepared ourselves. Lunch was the main meal of the day, when we all gathered around the big dining table, usually about twelve or fifteen people including visitors. Sister Julienne presided, and in the presence of the nuns and, frequently, visiting clergy, it was a more formal affair, and we girls were always on our best behaviour. Supper was different; we all came in at different times, including the Sisters, so we took what we wanted and ate in the kitchen. Standards were relaxed and so was conversation.

The kitchen was large, probably Victorian, and had been modernised in Edwardian days, with bits and pieces added on later. Two large stone sinks stood against the wall beneath windows that were set so high no one could see out of them, not even Chummy, who was well over six feet tall. The taps were large and stiff, fed by lead pipes that ran all the way round the kitchen and were attached to the wall with metal fixtures. Whenever you turned a tap on, the pipes gurgled and shook as the water made its way along its course, sometimes coming out in a trickle, sometimes in vicious spurts – you had to stand well back to avoid a soaking. Wooden plate racks were fixed above each sink which was flanked on either side by a marble-topped surface. This was where Mrs B did all her mixing and kneading of dough, covering the mixture with a cloth for it to rise, and all the other magic rituals necessary for making bread.

Against the second outside wall stood a double-sized gas stove, and the coke stove, which had an oven attached and a flue which ran up the wall and disappeared somewhere near the ceiling about fifteen feet above. The hot water for the whole convent was dependent upon this boiler, and so Fred, the boiler- and odd-job man, was a very important person indeed, a fact even Mrs B was obliged to concede. Fred and Mrs B were both Cockneys, and a guarded but fragile truce existed between them, which now and then erupted into a slanging match, usually when Fred had made a mess of Mrs B's nice clean kitchen, and she would go for him hammer and tongs. She was a large lady of formidable frontage, and Fred was undersized even by Cockney standards, but he stood his ground and fought his corner manfully. The exchanges between them were rich, but Mrs B knew that the Sisters couldn't do without him, so reluctantly they settled down to another period of truce.

Mrs B certainly had a point. Fred certainly was messy. The main problem was his squint, the most spectacular you have ever seen. One eye pointed north-east, the other south-west, so he could see in both directions at once, but not in the middle. Not infrequently, when he was shovelling his ash, or tipping his coke, it would go in the wrong direction, but he would sweep it up willy-nilly, and often whatever he was sweeping, par- ticularly the ash, would go the wrong way also. Ash could be flying all over the place, at which point Mrs B ... well, I need not go on!

We settled down to our bread with cheese and chutney, and dates and apples, with a few pots of lemon curd, jam or marmalade. We really appreciated our food because we had all been war-time children, brought up amid strict rationing. None of us had seen a banana or chocolate until we were in our mid to late teens, and had been brought up on one egg and a tiny bit of cheese that was to last a whole week. Bread, along with everything else, had been strictly rationed, so Mrs B's delectable provender brought murmurs of delight.

'Bagsie the crust.'

'Not fair, you had it last time.'

'Well, we'll split it, then.'

'How about cutting the crust off the other end, as well?'

'No, it would go stale in the middle.'

'Let's toss for it.'

I can't remember who won the toss, but we settled down.

'What do you make of Fred's puzzle?' I asked.

'Don't know,' said Chummy, her mouth full. She sighed with contentment.

'It's a load of rubbish if you ask me,' said Trixie.

'It can't be rubbish, it's a question of arithmetic,' I replied, cutting another wedge of cheese.

'Well, you can think of arithmetic, old sport, I've got better things to think about. Pass the chutney.' Chummy had a large frame to fill.

'Leave some for Cynthia,' I said. 'She'll be coming in any minute, and that's her favourite.'

'Whoops, sorry,' said Chummy, spooning half back into the jar. 'Greedy of me. Where is she, by the way? She should have been back an hour ago.'

'Must have been held up somewhere,' said Trixie. 'No, it's not arithmetic. I passed my School Certificate with merit, and I can assure you it's not arithmetic.'

'It is. Three nines are twenty-seven – that's what they taught me at school – plus two makes twenty-nine.'

'Correct. So what?'

'So where's the other shilling?'

Trixie looked dubious. She didn't have a quick answer, and she was a girl who liked quick-fire repartee. Eventually she said,

'It's a trick, that's what it is. One of Fred's low-down, wide-boy Cockney tricks.'

'Nah ven, nah ven, oo's callin' me a low-down Cockney wide-boy, I wants to know?'

Fred entered the kitchen, coke-hod in one hand, ash bucket in the other. His voice was friendly, and his toothless grin cheerful (well, not quite toothless, because he had one tooth, a huge yellow fang right in the centre). From his lower lip hung the remains of a soggy Woodbine.

Trixie didn't look abashed at having insulted the good fellow; she looked indignant.

'Well, it *is* a trick. It must be. You and your "three men went into a restaurant" yarn.'

Fred looked at her with his north-east eye and rubbed the side of his nose. He rolled the Woodbine from one side of his mouth to the other and sucked his tooth, then gave a sly wink.

'Oh yeah? You reckons as 'ow it's a trick. Well you work i' ou' Miss Trick – see? You jest work it out.'

Fred slowly kneeled down at the stove and opened the flue. Trixie was furious, but Chummy came to the rescue.

'I say, old sport, go and look in the big tin, see if there's any of that cake left. She's a gem, that woman Mrs B, a jewel. I wasted two years at the Cordon Bleu School of Cookery, fiddling about stuffing prunes with bacon and filling figs with fish, soppy things like that. But no one there could come up with a fruit cake like Mrs B's.'

Trixie calmed down as we tackled the cake.

'Leave some for Cynthia,' said Chummy. 'She'll be here in a minute.'

'Aint she come back yet? Ve quiet one? She should be 'ere by now.'

Fred, as well as being a tease, frequently showed a protective instinct towards us girls. He rattled the rake in the flue.

I still wasn't satisfied that Trixie was right about Fred's story being a trick. I had been puzzling about it on and off all day, and now that Fred was here I wanted to get to the bottom of it.

'Look here, Fred. Let's get this straight. Three men went into a restaurant. Right?'

'Right.'

'And they bought a meal costing thirty shillings?'

'Straight up.'

'So they paid ten shillings each. Correct?'

'You're a smart one, you are.'

I ignored the sarcasm.

'And the waiter took the thirty shillings to the cashier – yes?'

'Yes.'

'. . . who said the men had been overcharged. The bill should have been twenty-five shillings. Have I got it?'

'You 'ave. Wha' 'appened next?'

'The cashier gave five shillings change to the waiter.'

'No flies on you, eh? Musta been top of ve class a' school.'

'Oh, give over. The waiter thought, "The customers won't know," so he trousered two shillings and gave the men three shillings.'

'Naugh'y naugh'y. We all done it, we 'as.'

'Speak for yourself.'

'Ooh, 'ark at 'er. Miss 'oity-toity.'

Trixie intervened.

'That's where I don't get it. Each man took a shilling change, so that means each one had paid nine shillings instead of ten.'

We all chorused, 'And three nines are twenty-seven plus two in the waiter's pocket makes twenty-nine. So what happened to the other shilling?'

We all looked at each other blankly. Fred carried on raking and shovelling and whistling his tuneless whistle.

'Well, what happened to it, Fred?' shouted Trixie.

'Search me,' said Fred, 'I ain't got it, copper.'

'Don't be silly' – Trixie was getting irritated again – 'You've got to tell us.'

'You work i' ou',' said Fred provocatively as he gathered up his ash bucket. 'I'm goin' to empty vis, and you three smart girls'll 'ave an answer 'afore I gets back.'

Novice Ruth and Sister Bernadette entered at that moment. 'An answer to what, Fred?'

'Vem girls'll tell yer. They're workin' it ou'.'

While the Sisters attended to their supper, we told them the conundrum. Novice Ruth was a thoughtful girl, and she paused, knife in hand. 'But that's crazy,' she said, 'it doesn't work. Where's Cynthia, by the way?'

'She's not in yet.'

'Well she should be by now, if she had only her evening visits to do.'

'She must have been delayed.'

'I suppose so. This is delicious bread. Mrs B does have a magic touch when it comes to bread. The secret's in the kneading, I think. Knowing just when to stop.'

Trixie had got out pencil and paper.

'We've got to work this out. A shilling can't vanish.'

She started writing down figures, but it got her nowhere, and she began to get cross again. Then she had a bright idea. 'Let's use matches instead of shillings.' She took the box from the gas stove and emptied it out. 'We three will be the three men, and Novice Ruth can be the dishonest waiter, and you, Sister Bernadette, can be the cashier.'

She pushed a pile of matches towards Chummy and me.

'Now you, Novice Ruth, you're the waiter – put a tea towel over your arm. Come up to us with the bill, that bit of paper will do, and ask us for thirty shillings.'

Novice Ruth joined in with the spirit of things. We each counted out ten matches and gave them to her, and she collected them up.

Sister Bernadette had made herself a sandwich and was watching us quizzically.

'Now you're the cashier, Sister. Go and sit over there.'

THREE MEN WENT INTO A RESTAURANT ...

Sister Bernadette gave Trixie an old-fashioned look and moved her chair to the end of the table.

'No. That's not far enough – go and sit by the sink.'

Sister picked up her sandwich and moved her chair to the sink.

'Now,' said the stage director, 'waiter, you must take the bill and the money to the cashier.'

The waiter did as she was told.

'Cashier, you must add up the bill and find it is wrong, and say to the waiter ... go on, say it ...'

Sister Bernadette said, 'This is wrong. The bill comes to twenty-five shillings, not thirty. Here is five shillings change. Give it to the men,' and she handed five matches to Novice Ruth.

'Good,' said the director condescendingly, 'very good.'

Trixie turned to Novice Ruth.

'Now what do you do, waiter?'

'I see the chance to earn a bit on the side,' said the pious novice slyly as she tucked two matches into her pocket.

'Yes, that's correct. Proceed.'

Novice Ruth returned to the table and gave us three matches. We each took one.

'Good show,' cried Chummy. 'I've only paid nine shillings for my meal.'

'And so have I,' I said. 'What have you paid, Trix?'

'Well, I've paid nine shillings. I must have done, because, because ... oh dear, that's where it all goes pear-shaped,' cried Trixie in real anguish, because usually she had an answer for everything. 'Three nines are twenty-seven and ... look, we must have gone wrong somewhere. Let's start again.'

Once more we shook out a random pile of matches. 'You be the dishonest waiter again, Novice Ruth.'

At that moment Sister Julienne entered.

'What on earth are you doing with all those matches? And what did I hear about Novice Ruth being a dishonest waiter?

As Novice Mistress of Nonnatus House I cannot approve of that,' she said, laughing.

We sorted out the second lot of matches and told her Fred's riddle.

'Oh, that old chestnut! Fred comes out with that one for all the girls. He's just doing it to stir you up. No one's worked it out yet, so I doubt if you will be able to. I came here to see Cynthia. Has she gone upstairs?'

'She's not in yet.'

'Not in! Well where is she? It's nearly nine o'clock. She should have finished her evening visits by six thirty or seven at the latest. Where is she?'

We didn't know, and suddenly we felt guilty. We had been stuffing our faces and worrying over a silly old riddle, when really we should have been worrying over the fact that Cynthia was not with us, time was passing, and no one knew where she was.

Fred had come back into the kitchen and heard this last bit of conversation. He went over to the stove as we all looked anxiously at one another. His voice was reassuring.

'Don't choo worry, Sister. She'll be safe as 'ouses. Somefinks made 'er late, but she won't 'ave come to no 'arm, you'll see. You know ve old Cockney sayin', "A nurse is safe among us." Nuffink will 'appen to 'er. She'll turn up.'

Novice Ruth spoke. 'I think it's very likely that she was delayed at the Jessops, Sister. The baby is a fortnight old, and Mrs Jessop went for Churching today. The women always have a party afterwards, and I expect Cynthia was invited to join them.'

Sister Julienne looked somewhat relieved but nonetheless said, 'I feel sure you are right, but the bell for compline will sound any minute now, and it would ease my mind if you, Nurse Lee, would cycle round to Mrs Jessop's whilst we are saying our evening office.'

★

It was only a ten minute ride to the Jessops, and on the way I thought about this curious business of Churching. I had never heard of it before my stay at Nonnatus House. My grandmother, mother and aunts had never gone in for it, as far as I was aware, but many of the Poplar ladies would not go out after a child was born until they had been properly 'Churched' by the vicar. Perhaps it was a service of thanksgiving for a new baby, or more likely thanks for having survived the ordeal of childbirth, dating back to a time when giving birth was frequently attended by death. It occurred to me, though, that the origins of Churching could be even more ancient, stemming from the times when women were considered to be unclean after childbirth and needed to be ritually cleansed. As with many other pagan rituals the Church had merely adopted the practice and incorporated it into the liturgy.

There certainly was a party going on at the Jessop household – screams of female laughter could be heard all the way down the street (men were excluded from these occasions), and it took me some time to make myself heard. When the door finally opened I was all but dragged in and a glass was forced into my hand. I had to extricate myself and make my enquiry. Cynthia was not there. She had visited at 6.30 but, in spite of being pressed to stay, she had left at 6.45.

The Sisters were leaving the chapel after Compline as I arrived back at Nonnatus House. Normally this is the time of the Greater Silence, which is the monastic observance of quiet until after the Eucharist the following morning. But there would be no Silence that evening. Sister Julienne immediately rang the police, but no accident had been reported, and a nurse had not requested help for any other reason. She then instructed each of us, including three nuns, to go out on our bikes searching the streets. She marked out which areas, relating to the addresses of Cynthia's evening visits we were to search, on a plan and instructed us to enquire at each house what time Cynthia had arrived and left. Sister Evangelina, who was well over sixty, and had had a long working day, got her bike out and doggedly pedalled against the wind, searching for the missing girl. Fred, who couldn't ride a bike, went out on foot to search the streets nearest to Nonnatus House. Only Sister Julienne remained behind, along with Sister Monica Joan, because the House could not be left empty. We were a midwifery practice, and someone had to be on call at all times.

Subdued and anxious, we left Nonnatus House, each going in different directions, with instructions to ring Sister Julienne if we had any positive news. I do not know what was going through the minds of the others as we went around; I only know that I was fearful for Cynthia. The streets were narrow and unlit, filled with half-destroyed, boarded-up houses and areas marked for demolition. Bomb sites, in which the meths drinkers slept, were round every other corner. The possibility of danger was everywhere, yet I doubt if any one of us had ever felt under threat. Fred's reminder of the Cockney saying 'A nurse is safe among us' was perfectly true. We all knew that we were protected by our uniform, and that the Sisters were respected and even revered for their dedication to three generations of Cockney women. No man would attack a nurse – if he did it would be the worse for him, because the other men would make him pay for it.

And yet ... and yet ... Cynthia was missing, and as I cycled around looking for her the knowledge that this was a rough district which, in some areas, had been made virtually lawless by the Kray brothers, could not be shifted from my mind. A couple of policemen were approaching. Now why, I thought, do the police always go around in pairs, whilst we nurses go out alone, even in the middle of the night? I stopped and spoke to them, but no, they had not seen another nurse that evening, nor heard of one in trouble, but they would keep their eyes open. I called at a couple of houses that had been on Cynthia's list, but she had left them some three hours before.

The ride back to Nonnatus House was not pleasant. I went

through many side roads and back streets, even calling her name from time to time. But she was not to be found.

It was nearly ten o'clock and I was returning to the convent when I saw coming from the approach way to the Blackwall Tunnel two figures – a man with a distinctive hobble-de-hoi gait pushing a bicycle, and a female figure walking beside him. My heart leaped, and I quickened my pace, calling out, 'Cynthia, Cynthia, is that you?' It was, and I almost cried with joy.

'Oh, thank God you are safe. Where have you been?'

Fred answered for her.

'She's been froo ve Blackwall Tunnel – twice. Vat's where she's bin.'

'Through the Tunnel? On a bike? You can't have.'

Cynthia nodded dumbly.

'But you could have been run over.'

'I know,' she gasped, 'I nearly was.'

'How did you get there?'

She couldn't answer, so Fred did.

'I dunno as 'ow she got in. All I knows is I found 'er comin' out lookin' 'alf done for.'

'Oh Fred, I'm so glad you found her.'

'I ain't done much, really, all I done was push 'er bike.'

'Thank you, Fred,' murmured Cynthia gratefully.

We got her back to the convent. Most of the others had already returned with the bad news that she had not been found, so when she emerged the relief was almost overwhelming. In the light, we could see the state she was in. She was filthy, covered in oil and thick, greasy mud, and she stank of petrol.

When she had had a cup of tea she was able to answer some questions.

'I don't know how it happened, but somehow I got in the wrong lane of traffic, and then was forced into the entrance to the tunnel, and once I was there I couldn't stop and turn round, and then the tunnel closed over me, and started to go downhill, and I just went faster and faster, because the lorries kept me going on.'

Fred, who saw himself as the hero of the hour, finished off the story. None of us had been through the tunnel, but he told us that it was a mile long and zig-zagged all the way under the Thames from Poplar to Greenwich. It was narrow, having been built for Victorian traffic, and was far too narrow for twentieth-century freight vehicles. Two lorries going in opposite directions could only just pass each other if each of them drove as close as possible to the wall, sometimes scraping it. Cynthia could easily have been crushed. She could not have got off her bike because there was nowhere to stand; a concrete barrier about twelve inches high and the same deep was all that separated the road from the tunnel wall. She just had to keep cycling amid the noise, the dazzle of headlights, and the exhaust fumes. As she approached the other side, the tunnel started to ascend, and so she had to pedal uphill. To make matters worse, with the wind in a certain direction, the Blackwall acted as a wind funnel, as it had on that night. So poor Cynthia was forced to cycle uphill against a strong head wind – the worst possible combination.

And then, of course, she had to come back . . .

It is often surprising how quickly the young can recover from a nasty experience. Cynthia was not injured – she had been badly frightened and was physically exhausted, but she was not hurt. We made a big fuss of her. We sat her down near the stove, and Fred opened the vent and raked some hot coals onto the hearth to warm her. Novice Ruth boiled some water and poured it into a tin bowl, into which she put a spoonful of mustard, and instructed Cynthia to take off her shoes and stockings and soak her feet. The heat brought the colour back into her cheeks. Chummy cut the crust off the other end of the loaf and added a wedge of cheese with the last of Mrs B's chutney. Trixie brought out the cake. Sister Julienne made a large mug of steaming cocoa.

Cynthia leaned back in her chair and sighed.

'I don't know how it happened, I really don't, but once I had got into the situation I couldn't get out of it. It was a nightmare. But it's all over now, thank God, and Mrs B's bread is delicious.'

She sank her teeth into the buttered crust and giggled.

'I don't know if the police knew I was there. I'm sure I shouldn't have been.'

Sister Julienne said, 'It is probably illegal. I don't think even motor bikes are allowed through the tunnel, never mind a bicycle! I will have to inform the police you have been found, but I won't tell them where you have been.'

Fred interrupted. 'Best not tell the police nuffink. Wha' vey don't know vey can't do nuffink abaht.'

Cynthia looked steadily at him. 'Fred,' she said, 'I've been thinking on and off all day about that story you told us at breakfast and I can't work it out. Three men went into a restaurant . . .'

'Oh no, not that again,' wailed Sister Julienne. 'I'm going to bed.'

TRUST A SAILOR

Novice Ruth had the face of a Botticelli angel. None of the men of Poplar had the courage to speak to her as she passed by; they seemed to be in awe of her beauty, her clear white skin, her wide grey eyes, her perfect teeth and gentle smile. It wasn't that they were afraid of talking to a nun – they talked to the others. Perhaps it was her distinction, her quiet lady-like ways and above all her loveliness that left them tongue-tied. If any of them thought, 'a nun! What a pity, what a waste!' they would never have dared to say so.

She was about twenty-five, closer to the age of us young girls than to the other Sisters, but she was not one of us. No, she was firmly of the monastic order and, as she was still in her Noviciate, the rule was probably stricter for her than it was for her fully professed Sisters. Her profession filled her with a joy that was well-nigh tangible, and this happiness lent radiance to her beauty. She was also a fully trained nurse and midwife. After her training she had tested her calling to the religious life as an Aspirant and then a Postulant, before going on to the two years of her Noviciate. Yet still the monastic rule would require three more years of training, with solemn vows to be taken at the end of the first and second years, and final vows at the end of the third year. It was not a path to embark upon lightly, yet it seemed no burden to Novice Ruth. Holiness appeared to be her natural milieu.

But there was another side to Novice Ruth that I am not sure anyone, apart from we girls, knew about. Certainly the people of Poplar never saw it, and I doubt if her older Sisters did. She had a tendency to a giggly girlishness that was most unexpected and therefore all the more endearing. She would laugh at almost anything. This side of her came out mostly around the big kitchen table when we were sorting out our supper, especially if two or three of us were there before the Sisters came in. This was the time when we swapped yarns about the doings of the day. Anything would set Novice Ruth off: the simplest thing like a chain or a pedal coming off a bike, or losing your cap in the wind. She would literally curl up giggling and have to hold her sides as tears streamed from her eyes. Her laughter was most infectious, and we all enjoyed supper when Novice Ruth was around.

She was also a serious mimic and could take off anyone to perfection. Sister Monica Joan was one of her favourites: 'I see the shifting shades of the etheric ether descending into the slime of Planet Earth and illuminating ... oooh, jam *and* butter on these scones, how delicious.' And she'd have us all in stitches.

One evening we were in the kitchen enjoying cheese and chutney sandwiches with crumpets and honey to follow when the heavy tread of Sister Evangelina was heard. I was always nervous of Sister Evangelina as she had made it quite clear that she did not approve of me and, for her, I could do nothing right. The characteristic 'humph' assailed my ears, then the humourless voice: 'Nurse Lee, Nurse Scatterbrain, I want a word with you.' Every muscle in my body tensed, and I leaped to my feet, knocking over a pot of runny honey. 'Yes, Sister,' I said smartly and turned round, to find Novice Ruth. I got nasty indigestion from that one.

No one could mimic the Cockney dialect and accent better than Novice Ruth. Whether it was the whining of a child or the scolding of a mother or the raucous shout of a coster, she had them all down to perfection. After a hard day she was particularly fond of 'Nah ven, nah ven, le's 'ave a cup o' tea an' a bi' o' cake, ducky. Nice bi' o' sailor's cake, eh ducks?' And we would split our sides with laughter, though I am not at all sure that, if Novice Ruth knew what the last phrase meant, she would have repeated it so often. We had heard that remark many times in the homes around the docks, and I doubt that any of us knew what it meant. I suspect we all thought sailor's cake was a rich fruit cake with rum in it.★

The telephone rang at 1.30 a.m. Novice Ruth answered it.

'Nonnatus House. Can I help you?'

A soft Irish voice replied.

'I was given your number, and told to call you when I was in labour.'

'What is your name and address, please?'

'Kathleen O'Brian, 144 Mellish Street, the Isle of Dogs."

Ruth did not recognise either the name or the address from antenatal visits. Neither could she recall any expectant mother with an Irish accent.

'Are you booked with us?'

'I don't know.'

'Well, you must be booked with someone.'

'What does that mean?'

'It means that you have registered for antenatal care and delivery of the baby, and for postnatal care.'

'Oh.'

There was a long pause.

'Well, I'm not sure what that means, but I think I'm in labour, and I was told to call you. Can you come? The pains are getting quite strong, an' all.'

'How often are they?'

'Well. I don't rightly know, I don't have a clock, but quite often, and quite strong, and . . . oh, there's the click. The pennies are running out and I don't have any more . . . 144 Mellish Street, Isle of Dogs . . .'

The phone went dead.

Ruth put on her habit and went to the office to search through

★ The meaning is too rude to print, but those interested can consult *Rude Cockney Rhyming Slang* by Jade Janes, published by Abson Books, London, 1971.

the antenatal notes. She could find no Kathleen O'Brian. The woman must have booked elsewhere, but she would have to go to Mellish Street to see the woman and get the address of the correct midwifery service before she could refer her on. Ruth went to the shed and got out her bicycle. She was just about to cycle off, when she paused. Perhaps she ought to take her delivery bag. You never knew! She went back to the clinical room and fetched it.

The cold night air woke her up as she cycled through the quiet streets. She found Mellish Street without any trouble; it ran at right angles to the river. The houses were drab and tall, the street unlit, and she could see no house numbers. So she got off her bike and detached the lamp, shining it on the buildings in the hope that it would illuminate a number. It shone on number 20. She pedalled on, the cobbles making it a slow and painful ride.

Suddenly a female voice called out in the still night: 'Is that the nurse?'

'Yes, and I'm trying to find number 144.'

'It's me you are wantin', me darlin', and right glad I am to see you.'

The soft Irish accent was unmistakable, but the voice trailed away into a groan of pain, and the girl leaned against the wall, her head thrown back and her face contorted with agony. She suppressed the scream rising in her throat, giving a high strangulated sound, even though she pressed both hands to her mouth. The midwife took her body in both hands to support her – she was just a slip of a girl, barely more than eighteen, small and thin and heavily pregnant. The contraction was powerful and long, but eventually it subsided. The girl relaxed and laughed.

'Oh, that was a nasty one. Me mammy didn't ever tell me it could be as bad as that.'

'You shouldn't be standing out here in the street.'

'I didn't want you to miss the house.'

'Well, someone else could have looked out for me.'

'There is no one else.'

'What! You mean you are alone here, in labour?'

'What else could I be doing!'

'Oh, never mind. We've got to get you to your bedroom before the next contraction comes on.'

'I've got a room on the third floor, and I'm feelin' fine now.'

Ruth removed her delivery bag from the bike, took the girl's thin arm, and together they entered the house. It was completely dark inside, so she ran back to her bike to detach the cycle lamp. The torchlight illuminated the narrow stairway. They passed several closed doors, but there was not a sign of another human being. On the second-floor landing the girl started groaning and breathing heavily, doubled up with pain. Ruth was alarmed; it was possible that the girl was entering the second stage of labour. She took hold of the girl again to support her, and then suddenly felt a rush of warm fluid at her feet. The waters had broken.

'Quickly,' she said, 'upstairs. Only one more flight. You have to get to your room. We can't have the baby born on the landing.'

The contraction passed, and the girl smiled.

'I can get there. Don't trouble yourself, nursey. I feel fine now the pain's gone.'

With surprising agility the girl mounted the stairs, followed by Ruth, and they entered a pitch-dark room, cold as a coffin. She looked around her and said cheerfully, 'I'm so glad you brought a light with you, because the meter ran out, and I only had enough pennies either for the telephone or for the meter. I think it was the angels told me to use them for the telephone.'

The torch light revealed a bleak, barren room, devoid of any comfort. A rough wooden bedstead stood against one wall. A dirty, stained mattress and pillow lay on the worn-out springs. There were no sheets or pillow-cases; two grey army blankets were the only coverings. A small table and chair and a chest of drawers were the only other furniture in the room. There were no curtains, no rug or mat. An enamel bowl and a jug half full of cold water stood on the table. The electric meter was high on the wall near to the door. In those days the majority of houses and flats received gas and electricity through payment into a coin meter. When the coin ran out, the power supply cut off. Every midwife carried a shilling in her pocket, because meters running out were a constant hazard in our work. Ruth climbed onto the chair, inserted a shilling and turned the key. A dim electric light bulb hanging from the middle of the ceiling cast a gloomy light over the room, and now Ruth could see the girl more clearly. Her small face was delicately boned, and her mouth was beautifully shaped. Her eyes were cornflower blue, and her hair a glorious autumn brown. She sat on the edge of the bed, holding her stomach. Her eyes were laughing.

'Trust a sailor! This is what happens to a girl when she trusts a sailor! What's your name, nurse?'

'Novice Ruth.'

'Ruth. That's me mam's name. She always says . . .'

'Look here, Kathy, we haven't got time to chatter. You can tell me what your mother says after your baby is born. It won't be long now because I can see you are in advanced labour, and your waters have broken. Undress and get onto the bed. I must examine you. Where is your maternity pack?'

'What's that? I don't know.'

'Every expectant mother is given a box for her home birth containing sheets to protect the mattress, cotton wool for the baby, sanitary towels, that sort of thing. Where are they? Have you got them?'

'No.'

'You should have been given a maternity pack. Who did you book with?'

'I was just told to call you when I went into labour.'

'You've told me that. But which clinic did you go to for antenatal care?'

'None.'

'None! You mean you have had no antenatal care?'

'I didn't tell anyone I was pregnant. Me mam and me grandma, they would have killed me, they would. Never trust a sailor, they always say. And I did, silly me, and now look at me.'

The girl cheerfully patted her stomach. But then her face changed. 'It's coming again . . .'

She threw her head back as pain seared her body. Beads of sweat stood out on her forehead, and her whole expression seemed to be turning inwards as her mind and body focused on the tremendous force of the contraction.

There was no time to lose. Ruth took her stethoscope, gown, gloves and mask from the outer compartment of her delivery pack. She opened the box, and the sterile lid formed a tray on which she placed in readiness her kidney dishes, gallipots, sterile water, antiseptics, scissors, hypodermic syringe, needles, sterile cotton wool and gauze swabs, catheters and blunt forceps. She also carried chloral hydrate, potassium bromide, tincture of opium and pethidine for relief of pain. Cord clamps and cord dressings, powder for the baby and gentian violet or silver nitrate for sterilisation of the cord stump completed her equipment.

All her training and experience told her that a primigravida★ who had had no antenatal care should be transferred immediately to hospital. But to arrange this, she would have had to go down the road to a phone box, and birth was imminent. While she was gone the baby would probably be born. She looked at the thin, horsehair mattress on sagging springs. There were no sheets, no waterproofing, no brown paper, no absorbent pads. There was no cot, no baby clothes, nor any apparent provision for a baby. There was no fire, nor heating of any kind, and the room was cold. There was a jug of cold water, but she had no means of heating it. The light was quite inadequate for

---

★ A full glossary of obstetric terms is included at the back of the book.

24

delivery, and the only means of supplementing it was the bicycle lamp. But her midwife's training had been strict and uncompromising; whatever the circumstances, she must improvise, and cope.

The contraction passed, and the girl sighed with relief.

'Oh, that's better. I feel all right when the pain has gone.'

'I want to listen to your baby's heartbeat, and then to examine you. I need to know how near you are to delivery. Would you lie down, please?'

She palpated the girl's abdomen to determine which way the baby was lying. She listened for the heartbeat and heard it quite clearly. Satisfied that the baby was safe, she prepared to do a vaginal examination, saying as she gowned and gloved: 'You don't seem to be prepared for having a baby. There isn't even a cot or baby clothes here.'

'Well, I haven't really been here long enough to get anything. I only came over from Ireland yesterday.'

'What! You came on the ferry yesterday!'

'Yes.'

'But you might have gone into labour on the boat.'

'I might have, but I didn't. The angels must have been looking after me.'

'When you got to Liverpool, how did you get to London?'

'I got a lift with an overnight lorry driver.'

'I can't believe it! You might have had the baby on the lorry!'

'The angels again.' The girl shrugged cheerfully.

'When did you arrive?'

'This morning. I had been given this address and the landlord's name. That was the only good thing my charming sailor-boy did for me.'

She looked around the room and smiled contentedly.

'Just draw up your knees for me, please, and let your legs fall apart. I want to examine you internally. The waters have broken, and I want to feel how far you are dilated, and in what position the baby is lying.'

But there was no time for a vaginal examination. Another contraction was coming, and the girl winced in pain, throwing herself around the bed in an effort to escape it. The pain intensified as the uterine contraction became more fierce. Ruth admired the way the girl was coping with labour – she had already had a lot of physical exertion getting to London during the past twenty-four hours. She must have been tired and hungry, and there were no signs of food in the room. She had had no sedation or analgesic, yet she made no fuss nor complaint. The contraction became even more powerful, and suddenly Kathy spontaneously pulled her legs up, gave a prolonged grunt and pushed with all her strength. Ruth only got there just in time, pressing the palm of her hand firmly over the emerging head of the baby and holding it back to prevent an uncontrolled delivery.

'Kathy, don't push, not now, do *not* push. The baby mustn't be born too quickly. Pant, my dear, quick breaths: in, out, in, out. Don't push, just pant quickly, in, out, in, out.'

The girl did exactly as she was told, and Ruth breathed a sigh of relief as the contraction passed.

'With the next contraction your baby will be born. I know you feel as though you want to push, but don't, not until I tell you. I want the baby's head to be born slowly. If you push too soon, it will come too fast. Do you understand me Kathy?'

The girl smiled weakly and nodded.

'Is it possible for you to turn onto your left side to face the wall? It will make it easier for both of us.'

The girl nodded and turned over, and as she moved another contraction started.

Ruth was on her knees beside the low bed with its sagging mattress. The light was terrible, but she had no time to get her torch. The girl gave a low scream and buried her pretty face into the filthy pillow in order to stifle the sound. The baby's head was emerging fast, too fast. Again Ruth held it back.

'Don't push, Kathy, just pant in and out quickly. Keep panting – like that. Good girl.'

As the contraction subsided she eased the pressure on the presenting part and allowed the head to slide out a little, until it crowned. The perineum was stretched, but was still holding it back.

'Only one more contraction, and your baby will be born. Try not to push. Your stomach muscles are pushing hard enough. They don't need any help. The baby will come anyway.'

Kathy nodded, but was unable to speak because another contraction came almost immediately. Ruth slowly edged the perineum around the broadest part of the baby's head – 'Now you can push, Kathy.' The girl did so, and the head was born.

'That is the hardest part over, my dear. There will be a minute of rest, then another contraction.'

Ruth watched the head move about ten degrees clockwise as it aligned with the rest of the body. Another contraction came quickly.

'You can push now, Kathy – as hard as you like.'

Deftly she hooked her forefinger under the presenting shoulder. The baby's whole body slid out easily, Ruth guiding it upwards between the mother's legs, and over the pubic bone.

'You can turn over now, Kathy, onto your back, and look at your baby. It's a little boy.'

The girl rolled over and raised her head.

'Oh, bless him. A sailor's son. Isn't he tiny, nurse?'

The baby was indeed tiny, smaller than Ruth had expected from her admittedly brief abdominal examination. From appearances, he seemed to weigh no more than four pounds. 'No doubt due to malnutrition and overwork in the mother during pregnancy,' she thought bitterly. It was not uncommon. She clamped the cord in two places, and cut between the clamps. The baby was now a separate being.

But where should she put him? There was no cot, no blankets, he was small, and the room was cold. He must be kept warm.

She pressed him firmly under his mother's arm.

'Keep him warm with your body. Haven't you got anything I can wrap him in?'

The girl was contentedly cuddling her naked baby and paid no attention to what was being said. Ruth opened the chest of drawers. There was a towel in the top drawer. She opened the second drawer. There were a couple of jumpers in it. She opened the third drawer, which was empty. 'This will have to do,' she thought, taking up the towel and jumpers. They were all cold, but thankfully did not feel damp.

'Just lift your head and shoulders a minute, will you, Kathy? I want to put these things under your body to warm them, before I wrap your baby in them.'

She pulled the dirty grey blankets over the girl and baby to keep them warm and sat on the chair beside the girl to await the third stage of labour. A few minutes passed. She placed her hand on the abdomen to assess progress. 'Something's not right here,' she thought. The uterus felt hard and bulky, and a strong contraction was developing. Kathy grit her teeth and started to bear down. Ruth leaped into action.

'There's another baby coming! Don't push, whatever you do, don't push – just pant, like you did before.'

Kathy was tensing all her muscles, and the baby lying under her arm was in danger of being crushed. Ruth grabbed the towel and jumpers and pulled them sharply from under the girl's body, then took the baby from her. She wrapped him up quickly, and put him in the top drawer of the chest.

She returned to the bedside, pulled back the blankets and saw the head of the second baby emerging. She was just in time to control a rapid delivery.

With a twin birth, if the lie of the second baby is in a normal head-down position, if the uterine activity is normal, and especially if the baby is small, the birth can be fairly quick, because the birth canal has stretched, and there will be little resistance. Two or three good strong contractions may be sufficient to complete the birth. Kathy's second delivery was swift and easy, and within a few minutes the baby was lying on his mother's abdomen. She stretched out a hand to touch him. Her voice sounded incredulous. 'Another baby! It can't be true.'

'It is true, Kathy. You have another little boy.'

Kathy stroked his head. 'Another little boy,' she repeated vaguely. Her blue eyes were wide and dreamy, and her body was limp after the exertion. Her voice sounded far away.

'Another little sailor boy. Oh, you poor wet little thing. And where's your daddy, little sailor, where's your daddy? He sailed away on the deep blue sea. Sailed far away.'

Ruth took Kathy's pulse and blood pressure, which were slightly lowered, but not too much. She knew that she had been lucky in having no complications for which medical assistance, or at least another midwife, would have been necessary.

'You are a healthy girl,' she said aloud. "How did you get yourself into this pickle?'

Kathy smiled dreamily. "Oh, that sailor boy. His curling hair, his night-black eyes, and oh, his saucy smile! Somehow I knew he wouldn't be true. Never trust a sailor, they said, and silly me, I did. Now I've got two little sailor boys. What's me mammy going to say? And me grandma? She's the one I'm frightened of. A real terror, she is. If you knew her, you'd be frightened too, nurse.'

Kathy sighed sleepily, and closed her eyes 'I feel so tired now,' she murmured, and fell fast asleep.

Ruth had many practical duties to attend to, not least of which was to separate the baby from his mother – and she had only one set of cord clamps in her bag, which she had used for the first baby. So she cut a gauze swab in half, tied each piece firmly to the cord, and cut between the knots. 'Always improvise,' her midwifery tutor had taught.

The baby was small, but looked perfectly formed and healthy. Ruth picked him up, and he whimpered. She held him upside down, and he cried lustily. 'That's what I like to hear,' she thought, 'cry some more, little baby. Your lungs are only small, and this is the best way of inflating them.' The baby obliged by screaming. She nodded in satisfaction and laid him with his mother to keep him warm.

Then she began wondering what to do with him. Ideally both he and his brother should have been bathed, examined thoroughly, weighed and measured, and put into a clean cot near to a fire. But she had no hot water, no soap, no clean towels, and the room temperature was far too cold to expose his naked body. To wrap him up warm was the immediate challenge. She looked around the room for something – anything she might use. She saw a cupboard in the corner and opened it, hopefully, but all she found was a lot of broken mechanical equipment. Then she saw the clothes that Kathy had taken off – a skirt, a jumper and a thin, cheap jacket. 'That will do,' she thought, 'better than nothing, anyway.' The garments were still quite warm, so she wrapped the baby up in them, and tucked him into the second drawer. 'Phew!' she thought, 'this has been a night. What next?'

What happened next was more than she, or anyone else for that matter, could have imagined in their wildest dreams.

Ruth sat down once more on the chair beside the mother, to await the third stage of labour. She had time to reflect on the situation. After a twin birth the uterine muscles are stretched and tired and can take up to half an hour to contract again for the expulsion of the placenta. Kathy lay sleeping, her fragile yet strong young body exhausted from a twin birth, and soothed by the blessed relief from pain. Ruth sat beside her and leaned her head on the wall. She glanced at her watch. What had happened to the time? Less than an hour had passed since she had got out of bed to answer the telephone. She tried to recall the sequence of events: the cycle ride through the night, the girl standing out in the street, the race to get upstairs, the waters breaking on the landing, and the birth of one baby, then two. It had been like a speeded-up film. What did time mean, anyway? There were some who said that time does not exist, others who said that past, present and future are one and the same. What did anyone know about time? Least of all herself. And Kathy was sleeping, blissfully sleeping.

Ruth placed her hand on the fundus of the uterus to assess progress of the third stage and stiffened with shock. The uterus still felt full, hard and bulky. 'There's something wrong here,' she thought, 'this doesn't feel like a placenta.'

She carefully palpated the abdomen. 'It's definitely not a placenta. It can't be ... It's not possible ...'

She picked up her foetal stethoscope, applied it to the abdomen in several places and heard a rapid, regular heartbeat. Her mouth went dry, and she had to sit down again. Another baby! Undiagnosed triplets, no antenatal care, no assistance available, and apparently no one else in the building to summon help. She shivered as much from shock and fear as from the cold. Thoughts were racing through her mind. Would the delivery be normal? She had been lucky twice, but the third baby might be lying in any position. He might be a transverse lie, or a shoulder or a brow presentation ... or anything. She palpated the abdomen but could not feel a head or a breech. The foetal heartbeat was a steady 150 beats per minute, which was undoubtedly high, but might be normal for a third baby. She had never delivered triplets, nor even seen a triple birth. She felt numb with fear. Would he be healthy, like the others? There might be breathing problems, or other life-threatening difficulties derived from immature internal organs. Perhaps the placenta might come away first, leaving the baby with no maternal blood supply, or the cord might prolapse. She didn't know if there would be one, two or three placentae. She couldn't see inside, and she could not tell from external palpation.

Nearly half an hour had passed since the second birth, and there was no contraction. Kathy still slept quietly, but Ruth was trembling with anxiety. 'If this is uterine inertia, it is a serious condition, and the baby will die. Dare I risk leaving Kathy alone for ten or fifteen minutes while I go to a telephone to call the hospital?' she asked herself. She dithered. Should I? Shouldn't I? Which course of action would be the least dangerous?

The situation resolved itself. In her sleep Kathy groaned in pain, and in the same instant there was a click from the electric meter and the light went out. The room was in total darkness. Ruth knew the bicycle torch was on the chest of drawers, but in trying to locate it she knocked it onto the floor, and then had to crawl around trying to find it. She could hear Kathy groaning and straining and pushing, but there was nothing she could do until she had light. She found the torch and switched it on. Kathy now lay calm and apparently asleep. Ruth went over to the bed and pulled back the blankets. A baby lay in a pool of blood, between his mother's legs. She propped the torch on the end of the bed and picked up the baby. He was small, like the other two, but seemed perfectly formed, and even gave a little cry. She held him upside down, and he cried more loudly. 'This is a miracle,' Ruth thought. She cut another gauze swab into two pieces and ligated the cord, then cut the baby free from his mother. She lay him on his mother's abdomen and covered them both to keep them warm. There was no other clothing available in the room, so she took one of the grey army blankets off the mother, cut it into pieces, wrapped a piece round the baby, and tucked him into the bottom drawer. The other pieces of blanket she tucked under and around all three babies to ensure that they were warm. Then she closed, or rather nearly closed, the drawers to keep out any draughts.

Meanwhile, Kathy was sound asleep, her body exhausted. Ruth sat beside her and tentatively palpated the uterus – would there be another one inside? But no; the abdominal muscles and the uterus felt soft. Ruth breathed a sigh of relief, but at the same time reminded herself that labour was far from over. The third stage had to be completed, and she knew that this was frequently the most difficult and the most dangerous part of delivery. She leaned back in the chair and closed her eyes. Was this a dream? Could it really be happening? She had been out the night before, followed by a busy day, and had enjoyed very little sleep in the past twenty-four hours. She very nearly dozed off, but a warning bell sounded in her brain, and she jumped up and splashed her face with cold water from the enamel jug. The shock soon focused her mind again.

About twenty minutes had been spent wrapping and settling the babies, during which time there had been no contractions. Something had to be done. Ruth picked up the torch and shone the beam of light into the bed. The mess was quite indescribable; a great pool of blood and amniotic fluid was seeping into the uncovered mattress – and she could do nothing about it. Normally a midwife would have covered the mattress with brown paper, absorbent sheets, a rubber sheet, and on top of that more absorbents, which could be changed frequently – but she had none of these. The mess would have to stay where it was. She shone the beam of light onto Kathy's vulva. Three cords were showing. But how many placentae would she have to deal with? It could be as many as three, if the babies had developed from three separate ova. She did not know, and there was no way she could find out.

Ruth knew the risk of post-partum infection and in other circumstances she would have removed all soiled padding from beneath Kathy, washed her, cleaned the vulva with antiseptic, replaced the bedding with clean absorbent sheets and covered her legs with more clean sheeting. She would also have scrubbed her hands thoroughly, and put on sterile gloves. But none of this was possible. She also knew that warmth was essential, because a woman sweats during labour, losing a lot of body heat, and can become cold and shivery. Yet there was only one thin army blanket available.

She shone the torch despairingly around the empty room and saw her coat hanging on the back of the door. That would do. She took it off the hook and covered the girl with it for extra warmth. Kathy's breathing was deep and regular, her pulse and blood pressure were on the low side, which was a good sign, and her colour was fine. There had been no contractions, and the uterus felt as it should feel.

In those days the management of the third stage of labour was left entirely to nature, and midwives were taught not to meddle or interfere with the process which separates the placenta from the uterine wall and controls bleeding. Today an oxytocic drug may be injected immediately after the baby is born, and a powerful contraction develops, separating the placenta, so that the third stage is over in a few minutes. We did not have that advantage. Patience, experience, observation and masterly inactivity were our guides. We were taught that meddling with the uterus or attempting to hurry the third stage would usually give rise to partial separation of the placenta, causing haem-orrhage. We were taught never, never to pull on the cord, and only to knead or massage the fundus after uterine contractions had already developed, and only then if it became absolutely necessary.

Ruth sat quietly beside the bed, her left hand guarding the uterus, which she could clearly feel. The torchlight was growing fainter, so to save the battery she switched it off and sat in total darkness. Twenty-five minutes had passed with no sign of a contraction, and she was beginning to grow anxious. She might have to leave the girl alone while she summoned medical aid. But then she felt a distinct hardening of the uterus, and the fundus rose under her hand. Kathy moaned with pain and moved awkwardly.

'This is it.' Ruth stood up, switched on her torch and shook Kathy. 'Wake up. I want you to push as hard as you can. Wake up and push down. Draw your knees up to your chest so that you can push as hard as possible, as though you were going to open your bowels – go on, push – harder.'

Kathy did as she was told, and Ruth assessed from the feel of the uterus that the placenta had separated and was lying in the lower segment. The fundus had risen higher in the abdomen and was still hard and firm.

'Now relax, Kathy. Put your legs down and breathe in and out deeply. Relax as much as you can. I am going to press on your tummy. It will be uncomfortable, but it won't hurt.'

Using the fundus as a piston, and with firm but gentle pressure, she pressed her left hand in a downward and backwards direction. Her right hand took hold of the cords and lifted the emerging placenta from the vault of the vagina. Two cords were attached. One remained hanging from the vagina, indicating that one placenta remained in utero.

At this point Ruth massaged and kneaded the fundus vigorously, and another contraction developed. 'Start pushing again, Kathy, like you did before. We have to get this out with this contraction.'

'What's going on?' moaned poor Kathy.

'I'll tell you later. Just push with all your strength.' Kathy did so, and a few seconds later the other placenta slid out onto the mattress.

A huge gory mass of placentae lay on the bed. Ruth scooped them up into kidney dishes and placed them on the table. She had not the slightest chance of examining them, because the torchlight was dim and growing dimmer by the minute as the battery failed.

Kathy was wide awake now. 'What's been happening?' she asked. 'I've got twins. Where are they?' She looked around her.

'No. You're wrong. You've got triplets, and they are in the chest of drawers.'

'Triplets! You mean three babies?'

'Yes.'

'How?'

'Well, you were exhausted and fell asleep after the second baby was born, so the third baby must have slid out with hardly any pain worth speaking of. Not enough to wake you up, anyway. I didn't see it, because the meter had run out, and I'd dropped my torch.'

'And I've got three babies?'

'Yes. Three little boys.'

Kathy leaned back with an incredulous sigh.

'Holy Mary, Mother of God – what's me mam going to say? Oh be-Jesus, illegitimate triplets. Trust a sailor!'

Ruth cleared up and returned to the convent, where arrangements were made for Kathy and the babies to be admitted to the London Hospital. The girl had no one to look after her, and she was quite unable to look after the babies in the room where she was lodging. She had no money, no clothing, no heating, no food even, and the babies were small and vulnerable.

We did not find out what happened to them after they left hospital. If the sailor could not be traced and persuaded to marry Kathy and support his children, the prospects for them were bleak. Returning to the family in Ireland would have been the best thing, but in rural Ireland in the 1950s poverty and the shame of illegitimacy drove many families to reject their grandchildren. Places in a children's nursery in London would have been offered, with access for the mother, but she would have had to live separately and support herself. It is unlikely that she would ever have earned enough money to have the boys with her and to support them. Adoption would have been possible, if Kathy had agreed, but the chances of anyone wanting to adopt all three babies were slender, so the boys would probably have been separated and would have grown up not knowing they had brothers.

Whilst I cannot record a happy ending, Kathy was buoyant, cheerful and resourceful, and we cannot be sure that life treated her harshly. It might have been quite the opposite. So often in medicine we see and become deeply involved with people at the most intimate and dramatic time of their lives. But then, like ships, they pass in the night; they are gone and we see them no more.

CYNTHIA

I was cycling back to the convent after a morning's work, weaving my way in and out of the lorries on the East India Dock Road, singing to myself as I pedalled the old Raleigh, which was as heavy as lead with two of its three gears not working, and perfecting my no-hands-steer-with-knees-and-bodyweight technique, when I saw Cynthia ahead of me. She was cycling more slowly than me, and her bike was wobbling about on the road. I called out, 'Hi, there!' as I drew level; but my high spirits quickly changed to concern. She was crying.

'What's up? Oh, Cynthia dear, what's happened?'

She looked round, tears streaming down her face. A lorry screeched past, hooting noisily, its driver gesticulating obscenely.

'Here, we had better pull into the kerb, or we'll have an accident. Now what's up? Tell me. I've never seen you like this before.'

Cynthia was the peace-maker amongst us, a wise and mature influence. To see her crying in the street was a real shock. I gave her my handkerchief because hers was wet.

'The baby's dead,' she whispered.

'What? It can't be,' I gasped incredulously.

I knew she had been out all night. She had come into breakfast tired but happy, telling us of the delivery of a baby boy – a normal delivery, a healthy baby, and a contented mother. She had left them at 6 a.m., everything satisfactory. We were required to make a return visit within four hours. I had left to make my morning visits at 8.30, and Cynthia had remained behind to clean and sterilise her equipment and write up her notes before returning to the newly delivered mother and baby at 10 a.m.

'What happened?' I asked when I had recovered from the shock.

'I went back to the house as usual,' Cynthia explained. 'I never thought anything would have happened. The door was open, and I went in. Everyone was crying. They said the baby was dead. I couldn't believe them. I went and saw the baby. It was quite dead and cold.'

'But how? Why?'

'I don't know.'

She blew her nose and wiped her eyes. 'I don't know. I just don't know,' she whispered and started crying again.

'Look here, we'd better get back, but don't try riding that bike. You'll only fall off. I'll push it for you.'

We started walking along the pavement, with me pushing both bikes – a noble but futile gesture. Have you ever tried pushing two bikes along a pavement crowded with people and prams and children running around? Soon Cynthia's tears were mixed with tears of laughter.

'I'll take mine, or you'll do someone a nasty injury.'

We walked along without speaking for a while. I didn't know whether to ask more questions or to keep silent, but she said: 'They've taken him away.'

'Who? The doctors?'

'No. The police.'

'Police? Why? What for?'

'Post-mortem examination. The parents didn't want them to, but the police insisted, saying it was the law with a sudden, unexplained death.' Her voice faltered and she started crying again.

'I don't know if I did anything wrong. I've been going over and over it in my mind. I did everything we were taught to do. The baby cried soon after birth. I cleared the airways. I cut the cord aseptically. All his limbs moved independently. His spine was straight, his breathing was normal, and the sucking reflex was there. He was a perfect baby, I thought. I don't know why he died, or if I did something that might have caused his death.'

She shuddered and could hardly walk straight. The front wheel of her bike hit a bus stop, and the handlebars twisted and poked into her chest, making her groan with pain. We straightened out her bike.

'Of course you've done nothing wrong. You are the best of midwives. I just *know* it wasn't your fault in any way.'

'You can't be sure,' she whispered. 'That's why the police took him away.'

We continued for a while in silence. I did not like to intrude on Cynthia's thoughts but felt compelled to ask, 'What did you do?'

'Well, I tried mouth-to-mouth resuscitation, but it was hopeless. The baby was quite cold and stiff.'

She was shaking, and her voice was barely audible above the noise of the street.

'Let's get off this main road into a quieter one,' I said. 'All this noise is getting on my nerves. Then you can tell me more.'

We pushed our bikes round a corner and continued in a more peaceful environment. Children were playing in the street, women were scrubbing their doorsteps or shaking mats. Several greeted us.

'I went down the street to the phone box,' Cynthia continued, 'and rang Nonnatus House and spoke to Sister Julienne. She came straight away. It was wonderfully reassuring to see her. She christened the baby, even though he was dead, and prayed with the family and me, and then she went to inform the doctor and the police. I had to remain in the house with the baby's body.'

She started crying again. I leaned over and squeezed her hand.

'We didn't have to wait long. The doctor came. He examined the little body and said he could see nothing to suggest the cause of death, but that a post mortem would be necessary before a death certificate could be issued. The family were terribly upset at this, saying they didn't want to see their baby cut up, they just wanted him to have a quiet Christian burial. The doctor was ever so kind with them, but explained that a PM was unavoidable under the circumstances.'

We continued plodding along, circling around a group of little girls playing hop-scotch.

'Two policemen arrived. They took notes and spoke with the doctor. Then they questioned me. It was awful. They weren't nasty or bullying or anything like that ... it was just being questioned about a death, and seeing them write down everything I said that was so awful. I must have looked as white as a sheet, because the doctor was very kind and assured me that I was in no way at fault. I had been asked to tell them everything I knew, you see. They asked to see my records, and took my notes away with them. I think I had filled in everything correctly. I don't know. It's like a bad dream.'

She looked ill.

'You need a good hot cup of tea,' I said, 'We're nearly at the convent – good thing too. You look just about finished.'

'It's the shock, I suppose.'

'I'll say it is!'

'I'm cold, too.'

'Not surprising. You had no sleep last night?'

'A couple of hours, then I had to go out.'

By now we had reached Nonnatus House. I took both the bikes to put them away. Cynthia said she had to report to Sister Julienne as soon as she got in.

In the bicycle shed Sister Bernadette was putting her bike away.

'Ah, Nurse Lee. Just the person I wanted to speak to. Did I see you cycling with no hands down the East India Dock Road?'

Sister Bernadette was a midwife whom I both respected and admired, but she could be very sharp.

'Me? Oh, er, well perhaps ...'

'I am sure it was you. I can't think of any other midwife who would cycle in that nonchalant fashion down the main road. And were you whistling by any chance?'

'Whistling? Well, I'm not sure. I can't quite remember, but I suppose I might have been.'

'You certainly were. Now look here, Nurse Lee, you are not one of the local lads. You are a professional woman. They can do that sort of thing, but you can't. It's too casual, too lackadaisical. It gives the wrong impression. It simply won't do.'

'I'm sorry, Sister.'

'Don't do it again, Nurse.'

'No, Sister. I won't, Sister.'

But I did, and I'm sure she knew that I did!

Cynthia did not come in for lunch. She had been sent to bed with a couple of aspirins and some hot chocolate. Sister Julienne said grace and when we were seated told everyone what had happened.

'Humph,' grunted Sister Evangelina, 'alive and healthy at six o'clock. Dead at ten. Sounds like smothering to me.'

'Oh no, Sister. I am sure you are wrong. They are a nice family. They wanted the baby. They wouldn't do a thing like that.' Sister Julienne was shocked.

'Can't be sure. No one can. These secrets are well kept. There have been more unwanted babies smothered than I've had hot dinners. Desperation drives people to do it.'

'But these people are not desperate,' Sister Julienne replied. 'I agree with you that desperation might lead a starving family to smother a newborn baby, but those days are past.'

Chummy, Trixie and I were wide-eyed with interest. We had heard nothing like this before, coming as we did from middle-class backgrounds. But Sister Evangelina had been born into the slums of Reading in the 1890s and had experienced more poverty and deprivation than we could ever dream of.

'But wouldn't they be caught?' asked Chummy.

'Probably not.' Sister Evangelina glared at Chummy, and then at Trixie and me. 'You young girls! Ignorant! Don't know anything of the past! So many babies were born, and so many died, that the authorities would never have noticed a few smothered here or there – especially if a relative had assisted at the birth, and no one else. The family could just say the baby was still-born.'

'But why?' asked Trixie.

'I've told you: desperation. Poverty, starvation, homelessness, that's what drove people to do it. Read your history books!'

Sister Evangelina was a formidable lady. Her temper was irascible, and the fuse short. We dared not press her.

Aristocratic Sister Monica Joan, who was in her nineties and whose mind was not entirely reliable, had eaten very little. She picked at the mashed potato and onion gravy which Mrs B had lovingly prepared for her, pushed her plate aside and sat fingering her spoon, turning it this way and that as she held it between thumb and forefinger, with the other three fingers arched fan-like. She was watching the changing light in the bowl of the spoon and the reflections of those around her. She giggled.

'Now you are upside down. Now the right way up, but your face is all fat ... hee, hee, hee! Now it's thin. This is such fun. You should have a look.'

She appeared to be completely absorbed in the spoon and her own thoughts, and I doubted whether she had taken in a word of the previous conversation. How wrong one can be.

Sister Monica Joan had the instincts of an actress, and her timing was impeccable. She dropped the spoon onto the table with a clatter. Everyone jumped and looked at her. She was now the focus of attention, which she relished. She looked coolly around the table at each of us, and said unhurriedly: 'I have seen several cases of smothered babies, or perhaps I should say, where I have strongly suspected smothering, but could not prove it.'

She looked around to judge the effect of her words.

'We had a young maid at the convent – not this House, the one that was bombed out – she was a sweet girl from a respectable family. After a few months, it became clear that she was pregnant.

She was only a girl of fourteen. We were quite shocked, but kept her on, with her mother's approval, until her time. Then we delivered her baby in their little house. One of our Sisters delivered it, and everything appeared to be satisfactory, if an illegitimate baby in a respectable family can be described as satisfactory. At any rate, mother and baby were alive and well when the Sister left them. A few hours later a note was brought to the convent saying that the baby had passed away. The Sister went to the house and found the baby dead, and the child-mother deeply asleep. She could not be roused. It looked like a sleep induced by laudanum. An inquest was held, but nothing was proved.'

Sister Monica Joan picked up the spoon again and turned it in the light, gazing intently at the changing shapes.

'Everything looks so different from varying angles, doesn't it? We see things one way and assume it is correct. But then, move the light just a fraction . . .', she turned the spoon slightly, 'and you see it quite differently. Very often the death of a baby was seen as a blessing, not as a tragedy.'

'Very true,' grunted Sister Evangelina, 'if a family already had half a dozen mouths to feed, and no food and no work, it *would* be a blessing.'

'Poverty. Grinding, abject poverty with no end.' Sister Monica Joan turned the spoon again, gazing at it. 'We were the greatest empire the world had ever seen. We were the richest nation in the world. Yet turn the light just a little and you see destitution so terrible that men and women were driven to kill their own babies.'

'Surely you exaggerate, Sister?' said Sister Julienne in a shocked voice.

Sister Monica Joan turned her elegant head and raised an eyebrow. No one could have looked less like a champion of the poor!

'I do not say it happened all the time, nor that every family was guilty. But it happened. You are too young to have seen the conditions in which working people lived. A thousand people crowded into a slum street of decaying buildings with no lavatories, no furniture, no heating, no blankets, no water except the rainwater that seeped through the rotten roofs and walls and basements. And above all, never enough to eat. In this I do not exaggerate. I have *seen* it. And not just one street, but hundreds of them. An endless warren of slums, housing hundreds of thousands of people. Read General Booth or Henry Mayhew, if you don't believe me! Of course babies died all the time, and of course some were helped on their way by a desperate parent. What else would you expect?'

Trixie, Chummy and I could not speak. Her words and her appearance were so compelling that nothing further could be said. But Sister Julienne spoke.

'Let us thank God that those days are past. Such poverty will never be seen again in this country, though it exists in many parts of the world, especially since the last war, and we must pray for those people.'

At that moment Mrs B came in with pudding, which she took over to Sister Julienne. Mrs B was Queen of the Kitchen – an excellent and valued cook.

'I've made a nice junket 'ere for Sister Monica Joan. A strawberry one. I knows as 'ow she likes strawberry best.'

'Junket! Ooh yummy. And strawberry too!'

In an instant Sister Monica Joan changed into a little girl at a birthday party, contemplating the feast with gleaming eyes. She said no more about the sinister disappearance of babies, but quietly I resolved to read General Booth and Mayhew on the subject.

Cynthia was rested, but subdued and sad, when she came down for tea at four o'clock. She carried out her evening visits as usual, and over the subsequent days she continued her duties. But we could all see that the baby's death was weighing on her mind.

The post-mortem report was received a week later. The baby had died of atelectasis.

Atelectasis means a non-expansion of the lungs. It is not a disease or malfunctioning of the lungs. During foetal life the lungs are airless and collapsed (i.e. in a state of atelectasis). When the baby is born, with the first intake of breath, the lungs expand. However, small patches of atelectasis, or non-expansion could (and still can) remain for a few hours or even days, and these patches could go undetected. If the baby's general condition was good there would be no cause to suspect a collapsed or unexpanded area of lung.

Cynthia's baby was full-term and breathed vigorously at birth with perhaps only three-quarters of the lung capacity; he had a good colour and a good heartbeat and cried and kicked lustily, so there was no cause for alarm. However, a newborn baby is very delicate. As he lay still and sleeping, the effort to breathe with a reduced lung capacity may have been too much for him. Breaths would have become shallower and shallower until the lower lobes of the lungs were not expanding at all. They would then collapse, causing a larger area of atelectasis to develop. Shallow breaths drawn only into the upper lobes of the lungs cannot feed sufficient oxygen into the body to sustain life. The baby would simply have breathed more slowly and more feebly, until even the upper lobes collapsed, and the baby died.

Cynthia was completely exonerated by the post-mortem report. It confirmed that with the baby's first breaths the greater part of the lungs had expanded but had subsequently collapsed during the four hours when the baby was alone with his mother. The question of why the mother did not notice anything unusual (for example, difficulty in breathing, change of skin colour from pink to blue to pallid white, with limpness of muscle tone) and raise the alarm was left unanswered.

No blame was attached to Cynthia, and no fault was found in her delivery or her immediate postnatal care. However, the whole experience had a deeply depressing effect on a sensitive young girl who kept asking herself, 'Could I, should I have done something differently?' and the trauma did not easily go away.

LOST BABIES

How could a baby be born and then disappear? It seems impossible, but in fact it was not so very difficult. It would depend on who knew about the pregnancy in the first place, who knew about the birth, and whether the birth was registered or not.

Family births have always been recorded in parish registers, but this was not obligatory. Since 1837 parents have been required to register a birth with the General Register Office, but it took nearly a century for this law to be enforced. Scarcity of medical care, the high expense of that provision, and vast numbers of births caused thousands of babies to be born and to die unregistered. Still-born babies were not registered until 1929. This made it easy for families to describe babies who had lived for a short time and subsequently died as 'still-born'.

In the 1870s it was estimated that, out of approximately 1.25 million births annually in the UK, only 10 per cent of women had any medical attention (another survey put the figure as low as 3 per cent). Therefore each year over a million women must have given birth with no medical attention. The death rate was enormous. In the 1870s it was estimated that in some of the poorest areas, maternal deaths were around 25–30 per cent and infant deaths around 50–60 per cent. These figures were estimated and collected by the pioneers calling for the training and registration of midwives.*

The first Midwives Act was passed in 1902. Prior to that, midwifery was largely an untrained profession. Any woman could call herself a midwife and go around delivering babies

* I have drawn on several sources for this chapter. For more information a full list is given in the bibliography.

for a fee. She was also called 'the handy-woman' in many communities. She had many roles and dwelled in the shadowland of respectability and the law. She was a solo private practitioner, answerable to no one. At the turn of the nineteenth century it was estimated that around 40,000 handy-women were practising in Great Britain, many of them calling themselves 'midwives'. Some of these women had acquired a knowledge of childbirth handed down through generations, and they were good and conscientious practitioners. However, others were slatternly and often illiterate. Many women could not afford even a handy-woman, and delivered themselves, with just the help of a friend or older relative. No woman had any antenatal care, not even if she was rich, so the fact of pregnancy was not recorded.

With this lack of medical attention it would have been easy for a baby to be born and to die without anyone knowing, apart from the immediate family, who may have had any number of reasons for wanting to conceal the birth.

Illegitimacy was the main reason for hiding a birth. Young people today cannot imagine the disgrace that was once attached to a birth out of wedlock. So great was it that sometimes a young girl would commit suicide rather than reveal she was pregnant. Many a poor woman would conceal the pregnancy beneath her skirts, work until the day she went into labour, deliver the baby herself, and go straight back to work. If she did not register the birth, who would be any the wiser? If the baby died, as many did, who would know? The rich had a more subtle way of dealing with an errant daughter – she could be certified 'insane' and confined to a mental asylum for the rest of her life. The baby would then be removed and placed in a private home or orphanage, with no stain attached to the family.

Another reason for concealing a dead baby was the expense of a funeral. A burial cost money, and every respectable working-class mother spent a few pennies each week on insurance to cover family deaths. A pauper's grave was the ultimate disgrace, and to be thus shamed in front of her neighbours was every self-respecting woman's dread. But many could ill-afford burial insurance, so it would be better for women caught in this trap to pretend it had never occurred and slip the little body into the river. In the 1950s I nursed a woman who had done just that thirty years earlier.*

If the respectable poor were driven to conceal the birth and death of a baby because of the cost of registration and burial, what of the abject poor?

In 1880 nine dead babies were found in a box on the steps of an undertaker in Long Lane, Bermondsey, East London. This was reported in all the newspapers. Would a doctor or midwife have attended the birth of these babies? Would these infants have been registered by parish or state? Could the parents, or at least the mothers, be traced? Not a chance. These nine babies would have been but a few of the nameless children thrown into an unmarked grave, the offspring of the abject poor who were destitute and starving, who were outside any census and beyond enumeration, and whom Charles Booth (1844–1916), the first social statistician, numbered at 255,000 for all London and at 1.95 million for Great Britain as a whole.[†] Later surveys considered this estimate to be conservative, stating that the figure was nearer to 3 million.

Obvious mental or physical disability was another reason for concealing a birth. Fear was the catalyst – fear, amongst the poor, of having to support a sickly child who could contribute nothing to the family income. There was also fear of the stigma attached to having a disabled child. It was widely supposed that congenital defects were due to something vaguely sinister 'in the blood', which would mark the family out from its neighbours. The baby could be left to die (probably with the connivance of the mother, or the women who had helped with

---

* See *Call the Midwife*, p. 221.
[†] Charles Booth, *The Life and Labour of the People of London*, Vols. I to IX, The Journals of the Royal Statistical Society, 1887.

the birth) and then described as still-born. The father would probably have been unaware of any impairment, because men rarely had anything to do with birth in those days. 'Women's matters' were taboo, a silence enforced as much by women as by men.

The upper classes – aristocracy and royalty – were particularly fearful of the stigma of a disabled child in the family. It could lead to ostracism because of so-called 'tainted blood', and the upper classes were not above smothering their own babies at birth.

Poverty led to the abandoning of babies. How much of this really went on I don't know, but we midwives were always being told about it. The women of Poplar would say 'Gor! You don' wanna go dahn Lime'ouse [or Bow or Millwall or wherever]. Dreadful people vey are. Leaves ver babies on doorsteps, vey do.' And women of Limehouse would say exactly the same about the women of Poplar! We got the impression that babies were being left in droves on the doorsteps of every other parish. However, we never saw it, and no baby was left on the convent steps during the 1950s. I personally know a lady who comes from Manchester, and was born in 1940. She tells me that she was an abandoned baby. She was found on a doorstep one morning along with the milk bottles. The baby was very sickly, but although the couple who found her were poor, they arranged for her to go into hospital and paid for the specialist baby care. Then they fostered her for the rest of her childhood.

There are many reliable records of babies being left on workhouse steps, or at the door of one of the state-run orphanages in earlier years. These babies would be named by the workhouse and registered as 'parents unknown'.

General Booth, in his volume *In Darkest England*, records that the Salvation Army 'lasses' frequently had newborn babies thrust into their arms by desperate young mothers, with heartbreaking words such as 'You take him, dearie, he'll have a better life with you. I can't give him anything.' Then the mother would disappear into the crowd, leaving no trace of her identity or address.

Infanticide – that's an ugly word. Did deliberate infanticide go on before pregnancy and birth had to be attended by a registered midwife? It would have been a hanging matter, so the secret would have been well kept. I doubt if any mother would kill her newborn babe in cold blood, but desperate poverty could well drive a grandmother to do such a thing. History is full of grim realities. I recall reading in the national press some years ago of a Scottish woman in the remote highlands who had died at the age of ninety-three. After her death it was revealed that she had drowned seven babies born to her daughter, who was unmarried and of very limited intelligence. Forensic investigation uncovered the remains buried around the croft. What could go on undetected in the remote highlands of Scotland could well go on in the overcrowded slums of any great city, especially in centuries past. It must have happened times beyond number, and nobody knew.

Did fathers kill babies? Who knows? One of our elderly Sisters certainly thought so. I am not of the school that thinks men are the root of all evil, but it is certainly a possibility that some fathers may have been driven to it. Accident is more likely than murder, in my opinion. A newborn baby is very delicate. In overcrowded conditions someone or something falling on the baby could cause death; suffocation in the family bed could occur – there are many possibilities. It must also be remembered that domestic violence was an accepted part of life in some families. Women and children expected to be beaten up, and in such a scene a misdirected blow could easily kill a baby. If such a thing happened the mother would have done everything possible to conceal the death, and if the baby was unregistered she would probably get away with it. If her husband, the wage earner, was convicted of murder, it would be the gallows for him, or transportation if the judge was lenient. Either way, the family would be deprived of financial support.

Not all missing babies died, however. The more prosperous the family, the more reason for concealing an unwanted birth. A wealthy girl's mother could keep her confined to the house, conduct the delivery herself, perhaps with the aid of a handy-woman, dispose of the baby, and no one would know. But how? A respectable matron could not go hawking a newborn baby around the workhouses and orphanages because, firstly, the baby would be refused admission, and, secondly, the neighbours would quickly find out. So an arrangement for private fostering, or 'boarding' as it was called, had to be found. Many handy-women had an 'understanding' with women who boarded babies, acting as intermediary, and taking a fee from both parties.

I knew a woman whose daughter, then aged twenty-four, had an illegitimate baby in 1949, which is not so very long ago. The woman said to me, smugly, 'I took it away at birth, of course. My daughter was not allowed to see it. The baby went to an orphanage.' It must have been a private commercial establishment, because the baby was not an orphan. Both parents were known and living.

A decade later, I delivered the baby of a young girl in Poplar. Throughout the delivery her mother shouted repeatedly that she would 'get rid of the baby and put it in a home or institution'. At one stage she ordered me – the midwife – to 'clear off'. She could deliver the baby herself and then get rid of it. I don't know what she had in mind, but obviously she knew of some lawful way of disposing of an unwanted baby.*

The standard of care in these private 'homes' for babies would depend entirely on the person in charge. One of my friends was an illegitimate child seventy-five years ago. She was sent from one private boarding or foster parent to another, and eventually went to live with a single lady who loved and cared for her and became a lifelong guardian and friend. By way of contrast a

---

* If you want to know why the mother took that attitude, and how the story ended, you will have to read *Call the Midwife*!

woman in Clapham was prosecuted in the 1920s for having eight babies (each of which she was paid to care for) in five cots in the basement of her house. The babies ranged from newborn to three years old. The toddlers could not walk. They had never been out of their cots. They could not talk; they had not heard enough language.

Traffic in children has been going on for as long as mankind has been sinning and suffering. Josephine Butler (1828–1907) writes in her journals, pamphlets and diaries of the second half of the nineteenth century about seeing thousands (yes, *thousands*) of little girls, some as young as four or five, in the illegal brothels of London, Paris, Brussels and Geneva. It broke her heart to see them. The children had a life expectany of two years, yet the brothel owners, frequently women, seemed to have an unlimited supply of little girls for their rich clients. 'Clean' children, who were free from venereal disease, commanded a high price. All this is well documented, but strangely Mrs Butler never mentions little boys, though this branch of the trade must have been going on.★

Where did all these children come from? It could certainly not have been from the Salvation Army or the workhouses or state orphanages, nor from the established management orphanages such as Coram, Barnardo or Spurgeon. So from where, then?

A basic law of economics is that supply will meet demand. If brothel keepers wanted 'clean' children, unscrupulous women who boarded unwanted babies would supply them, for a price. No questions asked. Many children were not named or registered, and for those who were, a false birth certificate was provided. The parents or relatives probably never knew what had happened to their children. They just vanished as though they had never been born.

★ Jane Jordan, *Josephine Butler*, John Murray, 2000.

Baby selling – the last resort of a starving mother – was rife throughout the population explosion of the nineteeth century. This led to the terrible evil whereby traders, usually women, secured the custody of unwanted little ones, took out an insurance policy on their lives and then by neglect, cold and starvation ensured the death of the child and claimed the insurance. There are many recorded instances of this practice. Dr Barnardo is on record as having thwarted the murderous designs of a ruthless old harridan who had acquired three babies, insured them all, pawned their clothes, covered them in rags and left them without heat or food.

This must make terrible reading for anyone who is seriously studying family history. But life is made of happiness and tragedy in equal proportions, and we will never change that.

SOOT

Within the midwifery practice it was noticed that several babies had developed various infections: sticky eyes, pustules, aural discharge, diarrhoea, an infected umbilical stump. Not all babies were affected, but of those that were, one became quite ill. Swabs were taken for analysis, and the report came back from the pathology lab. All the infections were caused by the same strain of staphylococcus aureus. Where was it coming from?

All Sisters and nurses had to be screened, and the analysis proved that Cynthia was carrying a staphylococcus aureus infection, which she was passing on to the babies. Gentle Cynthia was horrified that she was the cause, especially as she did not look or feel ill in any way. But the report from the lab was incontrovertible. She was taken off work straight away and treated with antibiotics, and the infection cleared.

All the babies were also treated with penicillin, and they recovered. In previous decades, before the advent of antibiotics, some of the babies affected might have died. Certainly one or two would have developed chronic otitis media, or pink eye, or a lung infection, which could lead to something worse. But antibiotics, being new in those days, were more effective.

Cynthia was off work for two weeks, and returned to the district with confidence. No more infections occurred amongst the babies.

The first case Cynthia went to on returning to work was in a comfortable little house in Bow. It was a nice sort of home to be working in and everything was going well: the young mother having her fifth baby was progressing in labour; her mother was looking after the four young children downstairs; her grandmother, an experienced matriarch for whom childbirth was less alarming than a visit to the dentist, was competently helping Cynthia. She – the grandmother – was looking at the fire.

'Sulky ole fire, that. Needs a bi' of life in it afore this baby's born. We wants a nice warm room for ve new baby, eh, nurse?'

She picked up the poker, stirred the sluggish embers and opened the air vent. Flames leaped up the chimney. There was a rumbling from somewhere near the roof and a cascade of soot fell, completely dousing the fire. The grandmother screamed and rushed forward with a sheet of newspaper in an attempt to contain the soot in the grate. But there was a second rumble, louder than the first, and another fall of soot came rushing down the chimney, smothering the poor woman and flying all over the room. Cynthia's sterile delivery equipment, carefully laid out on the chest of drawers, was covered in soot; the white bed linen was black; the lovingly prepared crib with its white lace and bows was black; Cynthia, aseptically prepared for delivery in a sterile white gown, cap, mask and gloves, was black; and the woman lying on the bed was black, although she was past caring – the second stage of labour was approaching and she was suffering a massive contraction prior to full dilation of the cervix. Cynthia gazed at the scene and raised her gloved hands in horror. Her first instinct was to wash them, and she rushed over to where the washing bowl stood. But a film of soot was floating on the water, and soot clung to the sticky wet soap. She tore off her gloves and was relieved to see clean hands.

'Oh my Gawd,' moaned the grandmother, 'I never seed nuffink like it. What's you goin' 'a do, nurse?'

'There is nothing I can do. If a baby is going to be born, no power in the world will stop it. We will have to continue like this. You go downstairs for some more hot water, and take this bowl with you and get it washed. You can also ask if there is any more clean linen in the house. I don't think there will be time to get another sterile delivery pack from Nonnatus House, but you could try.'

With the last contraction the waters had broken, and viscous amniotic fluid was flowing over the absorbent mattress coverings. Falling particles of soot were rapidly sticking to it.

As Cynthia spoke particles of soot blew off her mask, so she tore the thing off. She would be better without it. The upper part of her face and eyes were black, her mouth, nose and chin were white. She looked like a comic turn.

Poor Janet, sweating profusely from the pain and pressure of advanced labour, had soot sticking to her entire body. It had even managed to penetrate beneath her nightdress. She raised her legs and vaguely rubbed her hands down her thighs, perhaps to wipe the soot away, but it only served to make thick, slimy black streaks.

'Oh Gawd, wha' a mess,' she moaned, beginning to pant. 'Vere's anuvver contraction comin', I can feel it. Aaah ...' she groaned in agony.

Cynthia did not need to make a vaginal examination. She could see the head descending.

'Don't push, Janet, whatever you do. Just pant, quickly, like a little dog. In, out, in, out – quick, shallow breaths. That's right, keep panting. I need to turn you over onto your left side in order to deliver the baby.' (We were taught, in those days, to deliver on the side.)

In the meantime the grandmother had taken the washing bowl away and returned with clean hot water. She also had some clean towels and sheets.

'We can take 'er into anuvver room, nurse.'

'That would be nice, but I doubt if it will be possible. The baby might drop out on the landing! See here, I'm holding the head back as it is. Another contraction and it will be born.'

'Oh Lor, vis is awful. Jim's gone down the road to ring ve Sisters, but he's not goin' 'a be in time, is he?'

'No. Just keep panting, Janet. Everything is all right. A bit of soot isn't going to do you or the baby any harm.'

Cynthia's warm, soft voice had a reassuring effect on the two women. The contraction was passing. Janet looked up and relaxed. She giggled, and then began to laugh uncontrollably.

'You do look funny, you two. If only you could see yourselves . . . oh no, not again . . . aaah . . .'

Another contraction came within seconds of the last.

'This is it,' she gasped, holding her breath.

'Yes it is. Now you have to turn over quickly.' Cynthia beckoned to the grandmother. 'Bring me those clean towels. Can we get this dirty maternity pad out of the way and put the towels under her, so that there is a clean surface for the baby to be born onto?'

They changed the linen, but it was not so easy to contain the soot. Their hands were filthy, and touching anything made matters worse. Cynthia turned the pillow over, so that there was a clean surface on which Janet could lay her head, but even that soon got dirty as her hair streaked across it. Her grandmother tried washing Janet's forehead in cold water, which helped a little.

The delivery was not complicated, but childbirth is sometimes a gory business and blood and amniotic fluid can get everywhere. Mixed with soot, the mess was quite indescribable. The baby, a little girl, wet and sticky, was covered in black slime, and clumps of soot. With swabs and clean water Cynthia washed it away and held the baby upside down in order to drain mucus from her throat (this procedure was thought to be helpful in those days, and we were taught to do it). The baby screamed lustily. Cynthia looked at her sterile delivery tray in despair. At this stage she would normally have cut the cord, but the scissors, clamps, swabs and sterile water were filthy.

At that moment she heard heavy footsteps on the stairs and the sound of Sister Evangelina's voice grumbling.

'What is all this about needing a new delivery bag? Calling me out to bring one! I've had to cycle half a mile to bring it. The impertinence! I suppose the nurse messed up the first one. These young midwives! Can't be trusted to do anything properly.'

The door opened. Sister Evangelina entered, stared at the scene in disbelief, and exclaimed 'What the devil have you been up to?' Then she laughed. She laughed so much it shook the house. She fell against the door frame holding her stomach, then sat down on a chair and threw her head back, knocking her wimple askew.

Sister Evangelina was a large and impressive lady. She was what is usually described as a 'rough diamond'. Born into a large family in the slums of Reading at the turn of the last century, she had grown up in desperate poverty. The First World War offered her the chance of escape from the treadmill of inherited penury. She had left school at twelve to work in a biscuit factory and at the age of fifteen had gone to work in a munitions factory. Later she had moved to a military hospital, where she trained as a nurse, and where the one romance of her life had occurred, though she never spoke of it. She joined the Sisters of St Raymund Nonnatus, becoming fully professed as a nursing nun, and had worked in Poplar for thirty years, including during the Blitz. She was a great favourite of the people of Poplar, largely because of her down-to-earth, no-nonsense approach to their ailments, her rough-and-ready ways and her crude language. Of course, she had a completely different vocabulary and use of language within the convent. In fact, with us she could be extremely dour and grumpy, and not easily given to laughter. Yet on this occasion she could not stop. Her face, which was red and mottled at the best of times, turned a deep crimson, and her nose shone like a beacon. She slapped her hand on the mantelshelf to steady herself and took out a giant-sized handkerchief with which to wipe her streaming eyes and nose. 'Ooh, I'm peeing me drawers. You don't know what you look like, you three – you've made me pee me drawers, you have.' And off she went into paroxysms of laughter again.

Sister Evangelina also enjoyed earthy vulgarity. In fact basic bodily functions were an endless source of amusement to her. This predilection for lavatorial humour was something she shared only with her Cockney patients. Within the convent she was very prim and proper, and I doubt her Sisters in God ever saw the crude side of Sister Evangelina.

She slapped her ample thighs and leaned forwards, nearly choking. In alarm Cynthia thumped her back. When she could speak, Sister gasped, 'Talk about the Black and White Minstrel Show – this is the Black and White Midwives' Show!'

Sister Evangelina did not possess a subtle wit, and her jokes were heavy, but she was delighted with her pun, and kept repeating 'Black and White Midwives – have you got it? Black and White ... Oh dear, now I'm doing it again – I'll have to have one of your sanitary towels before I can get home.'

By now, the children had come running upstairs to see what all the laughter was about. They had been alarmed when their granny had appeared, all black, demanding clean water and soap and clean sheets. They had heard rapid conversation which they did not understand, and then seen their father rushing down the road to make a telephone call. When a very large and cross-looking nun had entered the little front room, stamping and grumbling, they had hidden behind the sofa. It was all very intimidating. But then they heard guffaws of female laughter descending the stairs and brightened considerably, rushing upstairs before anyone could stop them.

The children burst in through the door, and stood stock-still for a second or two whilst they took in the scene, scarcely able to believe that grown-ups could get into such a state. Everyone was black. Everyone was laughing. The big nun, her white veil streaked with soot, was rocking backwards and forwards with her face so red she looked as though she might burst. Somewhere in the mess a baby was screaming. The children positively let rip. They jumped up and down and bounced on their mother's bed, to the alarm of Cynthia, because the baby was still attached to its mother. They rolled on the floor, getting as much soot on themselves as they could and smearing it on each other's faces. Their grandmother tried to establish order and keep control, but she didn't stand a chance.

The big red nun laughed so much she was wheezing and coughing. 'Oh dear oh dear, this is going to finish me. Pass me that towel. I can't contain myself.' She stuffed the towel up her skirts and wiped it around her legs. The children couldn't believe their luck, and crowded around, lying on the floor trying to get a look at a nun's knickers.

Meanwhile, all the laughter must have been good for labour, because the third stage was progressing rapidly. The third stage of labour can be an anxious time for a midwife, and requires a great deal of knowledge, experience and care to enable the placenta to be delivered complete. But Cynthia hardly had to do anything. Janet couldn't stop laughing and the placenta just slid out in one piece. It was a revolting sight, bloody and slimy and covered in soot, but at least it was out. Placenta and baby, of course, were still attached!

'Sister, I shall need clean scissors and clamps and swabs,' said Cynthia quietly.

Sister Evangelina was not just a comedy act for the children's entertainment. She was a professional nurse and midwife, and her mood changed instantly.

'We will have to take the baby into another room and scrub up thoroughly. We cannot cut the cord in these conditions. As it is, the soot is not going to harm the baby. But I am not sure what would happen if it got into the bloodstream.'

Disappointed children were shooed away and taken downstairs. The baby, with the placenta still attached, was carried into another bedroom, and with sterile equipment the cord was cut.

The job of cleaning up fell to the grandmother. It took her about four days, and she needed a holiday to recover.

NANCY

The harlot's curse from street to street
Shall weave old England's winding sheet.
William Blake (1757–1827)

Sister Monica Joan had fascinated me from the first time I met her on a cold November evening in Nonnatus House, when we had devoured an entire cake between us, and she had rambled on about poles diverging and saucers flying and etheric ethers converging and goodness knows what else. She has continued to fascinate me over the years, and I have never been able to resolve the enigma that was she. How could a young woman of beauty, talent, intellect and wealth reject the privileges of the Victorian upper class to work in squalor amongst the poorest of the poor at the end of the nineteenth century? How could she reject offers of love and marriage and children to become a nun? I was never able to answer these questions. A religious-minded woman who has nothing to lose by embracing the monastic life, I could understand. But Sister Monica Joan had everything to lose. Yet she gave it all up. In fact, she had given up her position in society ten years before entering the convent, by becoming a nurse – a lowly and almost despised occupation in the 1890s. She was not, however, a saint! She was wilful, haughty, sarcastic; she could be cruel and unfeeling, arrogant and demanding. All these faults I was aware of – and loved her still.

I liked nothing better than to go to her room when work permitted and listen to her talking. Sometimes her mind wandered through a muddle of various religions – Christian, pagan, oriental philosophies, occultism, theosophy, astrology; she embraced them all with uncritical enthusiasm, whilst still observing the strict monastic disciplines of her order.

★

One day I asked Sister why she had given up her life of wealth and privilege for the humble life of a nurse, a midwife and a nun.

She winked at me.

'So you think our life "humble", do you? Nonsense. Fiddle-sticks. Ours is a life of adventure, of daring, of high romance.'

'I agree with you there,' I said. 'Almost every day comes as a surprise. But I started nursing when I was eighteen, because there was no other choice. But why did you? You had plenty of choices.'

'You are wrong, my dear. The choice of which pretty dresses to wear? Pooh! The choice to spend each afternoon "visiting", and talking about nothing? Pooh! Pooh! The choice to spend hours embroidering or making lace? Oh, I couldn't stand it – when nine-tenths of the women of Britain were toiling with their half-starved, stunted broods of children. I could not leave my father's house and start nursing, or lead any sort of useful life until I was over thirty.'

She was in good form. I was on to a streak of luck, because it was always a lottery talking with Sister Monica Joan. At any moment she might say no more. I said nothing, but waited.

'When Nancy died, I had an almighty row with my father, who wanted to control me. I hated the shallow, empty life I was leading, and wanted to throw myself into the struggle. I left home to become a nurse. It was the least I could do in her memory.'

'Who was Nancy?'

'My maid. She had been surgically raped.'

'What! Surgically raped? What on earth does that mean?'

'Exactly what it says. Josephine Butler had rescued the child and she asked me if I could take her on as my lady's maid. I was eighteen at the time, and my mother permitted me to have a lady's maid of my choice. Nancy was thirteen.'

'Who was Josephine Butler?'

'An unknown saint. You are ignorant, child! I cannot waste

my time with such ignorance. Go, fetch my tea, if your mind cannot rise to higher thoughts.'

Sister Monica Joan closed her fine, hooded eyes, and haughtily turned her head on her long neck, to signify that she was offended, and that the conversation was over.

Humiliated by her cruel tongue and furious with her (not for the first or last time), I retreated to the kitchen. But that same evening I asked Sister Julienne about Josephine Butler.

Josephine Butler, born in 1828, was the daughter of a wealthy landowner in Northumberland.* The whole family of seven children were highly educated and brought up to think deeply about class inequality and the conditions of the poor. In those days, this was considered to be radical, unconventional and dangerous. Her grandfather had worked with Wilberforce for the abolition of the slave trade, and Josephine had listened to adult discussions about slavery, child labour, factory work and related subjects throughout her childhood. In later life she said, 'From an early age I mourned about the condition of the oppressed.' She was particularly drawn to the condition of women whose abject poverty drove them into prostitution, through which they would frequently become pregnant, and then both the woman and child would be destitute.

In 1852, at the age of twenty-four, Josephine married George Butler, an academic and professor at Oxford University. He was ten years older than her and was a reformer and radical thinker, just as her father had been. It proved to be a perfect meeting of minds. After the marriage Josephine moved with her husband to Liverpool. It was not difficult to find poverty in Liverpool in the 1850s. The workhouse alone housed 5,000 souls. She visited and worked in the oakum sheds: 'vast underground cellars, unfurnished, with damp

---

* For this account of the life of Josephine Butler, I have referred to several sources, all of which are detailed in the Bibliography.

floors and oozing walls, where women sat on the floor all day picking their allotted portion of oakum. Yet they came voluntarily, driven by hunger and destitution, begging for a few nights' shelter and a piece of bread.'

In 1864 their little daughter Eva, aged five, fell downstairs and was killed. Josephine was paralysed with grief. She had always been deeply religious, but now she turned in on herself, rejecting all comfort, all consolation.

Unknown to Josephine, and indeed to most people in Britain, 1864 was the year in which the Contagious Diseases (Women) Act was passed in Parliament. When she did learn about it two years later it came as a shock and was the catharsis needed to rouse her from deepening depression.

The Contagious Diseases (Women) Act of 1864, intended 'for the prevention of contagious diseases at certain naval and military stations', was profoundly immoral. Venereal disease was spreading rapidly among the armed forces and was thought likely to undermine military strength. It was widely assumed in those days that women spread the diseases, and that to curtail the spread of infection prostitution must be controlled. So far, so good – in theory. But there were not, and never had been, legalised brothels in England. Women touted for their customers in the streets, and so the Act empowered the police to find their victims in the streets.

The Contagious Diseases Act was administered by a special unit of volunteers from the Metropolitan Police who were known as 'the Spy Police'. These men had the power to arrest *on suspicion only* any woman found alone in the streets whom they thought might be soliciting, confine her in a cell and call a doctor to examine her vaginally for evidence of venereal disease (Josephine Butler called this 'surgical rape'). There were no female police officers or doctors in those days so the women were handled entirely by men *who had volunteered for the job in the first place*, and no witnesses were required. If evidence of venereal disease was found the woman would be confined to a lock hospital★ for treatment. If no evidence was found, she would be given a certificate saying that she was 'clean', but her name would be kept on a special police register and she could be arrested and re-examined at any time. In theory the woman had to give written consent for the first examination, but this was a cynical farce because the Act stated that a woman who refused to sign should be confined indefinitely until she did consent to be examined.

Any woman of any age could be subjected to this horrifying treatment. At the time the age of consent was thirteen, so a child of that age could legally be regarded as a woman. The Contagious Diseases Act affected only working-class women, because upper-class women never walked in the streets alone, but would be accompanied or in a carriage. Men of any age or class were exempt from arrest and examination, even if caught in the act of soliciting, because the Act of 1864 was specifically designed for the control of women.

Josephine was stirred to the depths of her soul by the injustice and the immorality of the Act. She saw at once that the floodgate had been opened for the police to abuse women with impunity, and she vowed to God, and to her husband, that she would devote all her strength to getting it repealed. George was the perfect husband for her. In those days men controlled their wives absolutely. A respectable woman was not supposed to know about things like prostitution and syphilis, still less to talk about them publicly. George could have forbidden Josephine to take any action; instead he supported her.

Josephine addressed meetings all over the country, she wrote articles and pamphlets, she lobbied Parliament. She shocked and scandalised Victorian Society with her outspoken language at public meetings, describing 'the surgical violation of women'. She not only insisted that the medical examination

---

★ A lock hospital was the official term for a hospital treating venereal disease. The infected patients could not leave and were locked in. It was effectively a prison.

of women by the speculum was a form of rape, but also made public accusations against the police, doctors, magistrates and Members of Parliament, saying, in the strongest language, 'There is such a thing as the medical lust of indecently handling women, as well as the legislative desire to rule women with an iron hand for the purpose of gratifying vicious propensities in men.'

Such speeches from the lips of an educated middle-class lady were deeply shocking, but they were enough to stir the conscience of the nation, and in 1883 the Contagious Diseases (Women) Act was removed from the statute books of Great Britain.

Nancy's misfortune was that she was the daughter of a poor woman who lived in Southampton, a naval dock town. She was the eldest of five children whose father had died. Their mother took in washing from the garrison, and Nancy carried it back and forth. She was thirteen at the time of her arrest.

One of the volunteer police had observed her coming and going and lusted after her. He had unlimited power. One evening he accosted her.

'What do you go to the Docks for?'

'Please, sir, I take the washing.'

'And what else?'

'I collect the money, if you please, sir.'

'What money?'

'For the washing, sir.'

'Is that all?'

'Yes, sir.' Nancy was beginning to feel frightened.

'You're a bad girl. You're telling me lies.'

'I'm not, sir. I'm a good girl,' she whispered.

'You're a wicked girl. Come with me.'

He grabbed her arm and hustled her along the dark street. She was sobbing now.

'My mum's expecting me. I must go home.'

'If your mum knew what you'd been up to, she wouldn't want you home, ever.'

'I'm a good girl. I haven't been up to anything. And I've got threepence in my pocket for the washing, and my mum needs it.'

'Your mum would be ashamed to touch the money you've been earning if she knew how you'd earned it, you wicked girl.'

They reached the police station, and he pushed the terrified child into a cell.

'Wait there,' he ordered, going out and locking the door.

The Act required that a doctor should carry out the examination, so the police officer sent a message boy to call the doctor, who came quickly. They were hand in glove: two men, lustful and eager to discharge their duties to the letter of the law, and well beyond it, if they were sufficiently aroused. There were no witnesses, and none were required.

The doctor barked at Nancy, 'Can you write your name?' She nodded, too terrified to speak. 'Then write it here.' He thrust a piece of paper and a pen at her. She signed. Unknowingly, she had consented to be examined.

Swiftly the policeman picked her up and laid her on the half-length couch, pulling her skirts above her head and tying the ends under the table, effectively blinding and gagging her. The doctor grabbed her legs, pushed her knees towards her chest, and fixed her heels in the leather straps that were attached to metal stirrups. Her thighs were forced wide apart, and her bloomers were ripped off. Nancy thrashed around in terror, and, even though her legs were secured, she succeeded in throwing the upper half of her body off the table.

As she fell backwards, hanging by her legs, one of her lower vertebrae was crushed against the metal edge of the couch. It was an injury from which she never recovered. The policeman swore and yanked her back on the couch, securing her arms and body with a leather strap, so that she was unable to move at all.

Then the examination began. The Act required that the examining surgeon should first assess if a gonorrhoeal discharge or warts, or a syphilitic chancre was present on the external labia. If necessary, he could explore the vagina with his fingers, to feel for a chancre or other signs of venereal disease. If he was in any doubt he could use a vaginal speculum and forceps with which to examine the cervix. The doctor and the police officer took full advantage of all their legal rights. It took them forty-five minutes to conduct an examination that should only have taken two or three minutes.

Today a clear plastic vaginal speculum is still used for clinical examination. Then it was a heavy metal instrument about five or six inches long made of two halves. When closed, it is roughly circular, about one and a half inches in diameter. This is inserted into the vagina. The jaws then open to about three or four inches, and a central ratchet holds it open so the cervix is visible. In the nineteenth century, the speculum would have been made of rough, unpolished metal, and I doubt if anyone would have taken the trouble to lubricate it.

The surgeon and policeman thrust the speculum repeatedly into Nancy, twisting and turning it. They thrust their hands into her young body. Then they introduced other instruments, including long-handled forceps, with which they were able to grab hold of the cervix, pulling and turning it, ostensibly to examine for signs of venereal disease. Can you imagine the pain for a thirteen-year-old virgin? Whether they raped her phallically as well is not known. When they were satisfied they untied her. 'She is clean. No sign of venereal disease. We can give her the certificate. Get up, girl, you can have your certificate to say that you are clean. Your mother will be pleased.'

The distraught mother was powerless. There was no one to complain to. If she had been so bold as to complain to the police, she would probably have been victimised herself. In any case the men had acted within the requirements of the law. If they had raped the girl it was of no consequence because the speculum had opened up the vagina. Josephine Butler coined the phrase 'surgical rape', and thousands of innocent women were subjected to it.

Nancy's mother wrote to the Association for Repeal of the Contagious Diseases (Women) Act and received a visit from Mrs Butler herself, who advised her that Nancy must leave Southampton at once, because she could be seized again at any time and re-examined. Mrs Butler promised to find a position for the child, and that is how Nancy came to be the lady's maid to young Monica Joan, the rebel daughter of a baronet.

Sister said, 'Her back was badly injured, she could hardly walk. She was cringing and terrified. She was with me for eleven years, and then she died of tuberculosis of the spine.'

She said no more about Nancy. Perhaps it would have been too poignant, too troubling, after all those years, for Sister Monica Joan to recall.

MEGAN'MAVE

Megan'mave were identical twins and masters in the art of grumbling. They must have spent their time in the womb grumbling to each other about cramped living conditions, a damp environment, too dark, smelly, and wet. And when they emerged into the world kicking and screaming they would have started to complain about too much light, noise, fuss and bustle. Their cot would have been too hard or too soft; their clothes too tight or too loose; their milk too hot or too cold; and the breast (if they ever had suckled a breast) would have been grabbed by relentless baby hands as they each sucked a nipple voraciously, each fixing black unblinking eyes on the mirror image of herself across the soft and yielding body of the mother. After feeding they would have grumbled to each other about excesses of wind and gripe; they would surely have grumbled about the paucity of the milk, or the lack of proper nourishment to which they were daily subjected, and which would be the cause of untold suffering as they grew up. Over the years they honed their chosen art to an unprecedented level, finding fault with everything and everyone.

Megan'mave kept a fruit and vegetable stall in Chrisp Street market. From Wednesday to Saturday each week they could be heard shouting more loudly and more aggressively than any other coster. They had an intimidating way of glaring at a potential customer and demanding, 'Well?' If the unwary buyer, perhaps through nervousness, were to hesitate, they would lean forward menacingly, black gypsy eyes gleaming, and repeat, 'Well? What do you want?' even more loudly. Should the innocent buyer have supposed that the customer was always right, that error would soon be rectified. Megan'mave were always right, and the customer was always wrong.

It was surprising that they sold anything at all, but, strange to say, they were very successful, and their stall was easily the most popular. Women in curlers, wearing headscarves and carpet slippers, with Woodbines and babies appended, crowded forward with their shopping bags to be bullied and insulted as they acquired their bargains. Perhaps that was the secret of Megan'mave's success – everything was a penny or a halfpenny cheaper than it was on other stalls. But I have watched them at work, and wonder if the bargains were not more apparent than real. The two women moved about with lightning speed and ferocious energy. They could weigh a pound of carrots or turnips, throw them in a bag, twist the corners, add the cost to the last item, glare at the customer, and demand 'that will be three shillings and sevenpence halfpenny' before the average person could draw breath. Mental arithmetic was their genius – and their prodigious memory. They would rattle off, with machine-gun precision, a list of about fifteen different items, together with the prices, adding it all up in complicated shillings and pence (there were twelve pence to a shilling, not ten), and no one dared to question them. Once I saw a bold woman look at her change and say, 'I gave you a ten shilling note. I should have three and fourpence change, not two and elevenpence!' The two women behind the stall drew together. They grabbed the shopping basket, tipped everything out, weighed it again, shouted out the prices, tossed figures back and forward to each other, and came up with the magic total of seven and a penny. They pushed the bag at the woman: 'There you are, and there's yer change, two and eleven. An' don' come back 'ere. We don' wan' your sort. Next?' The poor woman wandered off, bewildered, counting her pennies.

Perhaps most of their customers were too mesmerized by the speed of delivery and the confidence of their joint attack. No one could be as quick as they were. Singly, each was as sharp as a razor, but together they resembled a double-edged sword. To

Megan'mave all customers were there to be manipulated, to be squeezed of a couple of pence here and there, to be bullied into buying more than they wanted, and to be hypnotized into thinking they had got a bargain.

The physical appearance of Megan'mave was singular, to say the very least. They looked like something out of another century, and another country. They had fine features, high cheek bones and clear but slightly swarthy skin. I have mentioned their black, flashing eyes, which undoubtedly had an unnerving effect on their customers. They were both very thin, almost skeletal, but strong and muscular; their hands were large and bony, and their fingers long. Their clothes – how on earth can one describe their clothes? To begin with, they were identical, like their wearers, and excessively plain, yet would have stood out in any crowd. Megan'mave always wore garments of dark brown or fusty black, long in the skirt and shapeless in the body, pulled tightly into their waists by heavy leather belts, from which hung two or three rings of keys. Their stockings were thick lisle, and their shoes were old, shapeless, and unpolished. Their headgear, without which they were never seen, was distinctive. Each wore a headscarf, an ordinary headscarf that any woman could buy, but it was the way they wore them that arrested attention. The scarves were pulled down low over their foreheads, so that barely the eyebrows were visible, and tied very tightly at the nape of the neck, so that not a wisp of hair could be seen. So tight were the knots that the scarves were strained almost to splitting. I sometimes wondered if the two women were bald, as the result of some rare disease, but this proved not to be the case. What with their clothes and their headscarves they looked rather like Buddhist nuns, but without the smile. I was reminded of a Hogarth etching of very poor women from the back streets of eighteenth-century London transported to the life and vitality of Chrisp Street market, Poplar.

Megan'mave were married. It was said that the banns had been read out on three successive Sundays for Margaret, spinster of this parish, but that Mavis had signed the register, or perhaps it was the other way round – hearsay can be notoriously unreliable. To be sure, both of them answered to the title of Mrs M. Carter. Which of them had stood at the altar and vowed to love, honour and obey, no one was quite sure, least of all Sid, the man of their choice. If he had ever had any illusions about the reality of these ancient marriage vows, Megan'mave soon relieved him of such fantasies. Megan'mave were the boss, and Sid had to honour and obey! In his romantic younger days Sid may have thought that he was getting a bargain – two women for the price of one – but life taught him that Megan'mave were the ones who got all the bargains, while everyone else paid the price. He was a little wisp of a Cockney, about five and a half feet tall and seven stone in weight, who was always seen in the market carrying boxes of apples and pears, cabbages and turnips, to the stall where his wives were doing their strident stuff. Unlike other Cockneys he never laughed and joked, never went for a drink with the other costers, never joined in when dirty yarns were being spun, could never see the funny side of life. He never even smiled. He just doggedly carried on, humping the boxes and crates, his thin frame sometimes trembling under the weight, his cap pulled well down over his eyes and his lips fixed in a tight, straight line. He spoke to no one, and invited no one to speak to him. When the market was over, he vanished. If he had a favourite pub, or a favoured walk or haunt by the river edge, no one knew what or where it was.

When Mave became pregnant it was a shock to the three of them. They had been married for several years with no issue, to use the old biblical term, and life without children was comfortable enough. They were thirty-eight, and Mavis assumed a saintly, martyred expression. Poor Sid got the rough end. The wives grumbled and nagged at him mercilessly, until he lost another stone in weight and looked as if he might disappear altogether.

Mave's pregnancy brought out the warrior in Meg. Mave

became rather docile and quiet, whilst Meg doubled her energy
and aggression. She had found a new meaning to life. It would
be no exaggeration to say that her whole life had hitherto been
leading up to this point. She suddenly discovered that Mavis had
been suffering for years from numerous diseases and infirmities
caused by neglect, hardship, ignorance (other people's) but most
seriously by medical error. The catalogue of ailments could
easily be traced to babyhood, when Mave, the second twin, had
had her arm pulled by a stupid and ignorant midwife, who
ought to have been strung up, Meg reckoned. Everyone could
see that there was nothing wrong with Mave's arm; she had
been heaving fruit and veg around the markets for twenty years,
but Meg was unimpressed by the evidence. 'An' look at her
constitooshun! It's 'er constitooshun, see! No proper nourishment when she was a baby – ooh, terrible it was, I tells yer.
Dad – he drank, an' Mum – no good she was, couldn't stand
up to 'im. No proper nourishment – vat's what started it – an'
look at 'er now – can't expect 'er to go through wiv bein'
pregnant. She ain't got no constitooshun, see?'

Long-standing complaints and grudges against the medical
profession were remembered, dragged up and exploited for all
they were worth. 'Medical blunders' became her pet phrase.

'Welliclose weins. She 'ad welliclose weins, see? Right mess
they made of 'em. Stripped 'em, they did. Well, they shouldn't
'ave done it. I've been readin' up about it, an' it was done all
wrong. Medical blunder! Made 'er 'alf lame. Look at 'er. It
wasn't done right. Them weins is all swellin' up. Show 'em yer
legs, Mave.'

Mave pulled down her stockings. 'Well, vat's not right. If
them weins 'ad been done proper in ve first place, they wouldn't
be swellin' up now. Doctors! I could teach 'em a thing or two.
Don't know nuffink, vey don't.'

Another day it was 'golf stones'.

'Look at 'er. Gone yeller she 'as. I tells ve doctor, I sez, look
'ere, she's gone yeller – it's golf stones, see? You wan's 'a do

somefink about it, or I'll call the Medical Council. But 'e wouldn't do nuffink. Too busy playin' golf, if you ask me.'

Meg became a voracious reader. She plundered all the second-hand bookstalls and book fairs from Portobello Road to Poplar, searching for ancient medical text-books. Most of the stall holders were glad to get rid of the old rubbish, out of date medically by a century or two, but Meg was delighted with her purchases and bore them home triumphantly. 'Ancient wisdom,' she called it. Megan'mave devoured the faded print and agreed that everything the doctors said about Mave's pregnancy was based on error, ignorance, stupidity, or downright malevolence, and was not to be trusted.

Because of her age – thirty-eight years – Mavis was told by her doctor that she must have a hospital confinement for the delivery of her first baby. Meg immediately came in, all guns firing. ''ospital! Don't make me laugh. Charnel 'ouse, you mean. I know vese infirmaries, I do. You can't pull the wool over my eyes, you can't. Women die like flies in them infirmaries!'

In vain the doctor protested that modern hospitals were not like the old infirmaries, but Megan'mave were adamant. With cold and crafty eye, Meg produced from her bag a book, yellow with age and disfigured with damp marks, and gave him a knowing look.

'What do you say to this, ven? "Pregnancy is a natural process, requiring little mechanical assistance. No man should act as accoucheur, but women should be instructed to do all that is required." What do you say to that, Dr Clever Dick? It's 'ere, in ve book.' Triumphantly Meg pushed the book towards him. 'Read it.'

'But this is Dr A. I. Coffin, *Treatise on Midwifery*, published in 1866. Medical and midwifery practice have moved on since then.'

'Don't come vat one on me. You doctors is all the same. I know your sort. Medical neglect, vat's what you get in 'ospitals. She needs special treatment. Look at 'er. Weak constitooshun, she's got.' Mave put on her martyred expression. 'An' all from medical blunders years ago.'

Mave pursed her lips. 'Terrible, it was.'

Meg did the same, and echoed, 'Terrible.'

They both rolled their eyes and sucked in their breath: 'Shocking!'

The doctor could hardly refrain from laughing.

'What do you want, then, if you don't want to go into hospital?'

'Special treatment, that's what, the best.'

'I'll speak to Sister Julienne, the Sister-in-Charge of the Midwives of St Raymund Nonnatus. They are a very old established order of midwives who have been practising in the area since the time when Dr Coffin wrote his book. Sister Julienne might agree to accept Mavis.'

Sister Julienne accepted Mavis for antenatal care and for delivery at home, but she would require a doctor present at the birth because of the age of the mother having her first baby.

Meg rapidly became an expert in pregnancy, antenatal care and childbirth. She studied Nicholas Culpeper, a seventeenth-century apothecary famous for his herbal remedies, and his *A Guide to Having Lusty Children*, published in 1651. She applied all his remedies to Mavis. She found on a stall a copy of Culpeper's *Directory for Midwives*, published in 1656, which greatly impressed her, because the burden of the text was the castigation of all other manuals on midwifery – an easy approach that suited Meg's turn of mind precisely. However, she failed to notice the confession made by Culpeper that the book contained no practical advice as he, the author, knew nothing about midwifery.

Then she discovered Jane Sharp's *The Whole Art of Midwifery* of 1671 and started talking about lily, hyacinth, columbine, jasmine and cyclamen, to hasten delivery and ease the pains of childbirth; cinnamon and aniseed to nourish the child in the womb; poultices of fennel and parsley to lay over the abdomen; caraway and cumin seeds to increase the breast milk. 'Ancient wisdom,' Meg said, with a knowing air.

In the 1950s the rules of the Central Midwives Board required women to be seen at antenatal clinic once a month for the first six months; once a fortnight from six to eight months pregnancy; and each week during the final month. This was not good enough for Megan'mave. They came in to clinic every week, and sometimes twice a week, because we held two clinics, one in Poplar and the other in Millwall. Each visit they reported another serious illness which must be examined at once, and every new complaint was accompanied by a new book, or a new chapter in an old book that had suddenly revealed there was something wrong with Mavis, which the ignorant and neglectful doctors and midwives had failed to notice. The consequences would have been calamitous had it not been for the untiring vigilance of Meg.

It had been an exhausting Tuesday afternoon clinic in the converted church hall next to Nonnatus House – hot, sticky, smelly, sweaty. I was just about at the end of my tether, having examined dozens of women, some of them none too clean, and boiled up dozens of urine samples to test for albumen, nearly being sick at the stench every time, when Megan'mave entered the clinic door. Four midwives were on duty, and one of the nuns. We all looked sideways at each other and groaned inwardly. My table was nearest to the door, and unfortunately no one was with me. Megan'mave sat down, and without a word of introduction Meg barked, 'Well, what 'ave you got to say to vis?' She pushed a book towards me.

Wearily I looked up at the four black eyes staring at me accusingly. The headscarves were pulled down low, identical features wore the same expression of mistrust, four hands rested on the table, four solid feet were planted firmly on the floor. They had come to do battle.

'But Megan, I don't know ...'

'Me name's not Megan!'

'Oh, I'm sorry.' I fumbled with my notes to gain time.

'My name is Meg, short for Margaret, see, an' I'll thank you to get it right, young lady.'

'Oh, I see. Certainly. Now what is the trouble?'

'The fillipin toobs is crossed.'

'The what?'

'Fillipin toobs. Don't you listen?'

'Yes, I heard you. But what are fillipin toobs?'

'Call yerself a midwife, an' you don't know?'

'I'm sorry, but I've never heard of them.'

Both women drew in their breath and rolled their eyes backwards and sideways in an exaggerated expression of disbelief. 'Shocking!' 'Sheer ignorance!' 'Never 'eard of 'em?' 'Medical incompetence!' They shook their heads, groaned, rolled their eyes and tut-tutted to each other. One of them behaving in such a way would have raised a smile, but the two of them with identical body language doing it was indescribably funny. This is going to be rich, I thought to myself and perked up no end.

'You will have to enlighten me,' I said sweetly.

'We've got to teach ve midwives, 'ave we?'

'I'm only a student,' I murmured humbly.

'Shockin. An' vey call this the National 'ealth Service.'

They showed the whites of their eyes again and sucked in their breath, and I had to dig my fingernails into my skin to prevent myself from laughing.

'Well, young lady, since you don't know, I'll 'ave to tell you. The fillipin toobs is 'ere in vis book.' She opened a grimy old book at what seemed to be a very primitive sketch of the female genital tract. Meg pointed with a dirty fingernail.

'Vat's the toobs, an' Mave's, they're crossed, see?'

Mave put on her martyred look, and groaned again. Meg took her hand.

'Vat's what's doin' it. Makin' 'er feel bad.'

'I'm not sure that I understand you.'

'No, you don't know nuffink, you don't. I'm tellin' yer, the fillipin toobs is crossed, an' it's makin' her bad. Now d'you understand?'

'I understand the Fallopian tubes. But they can't be crossed. It's not possible.'

'Course it's possible. Don't try no cover-ups. You can't fool me, you can't. They've tried that afore, but I'm too smart for 'em. Medical blunders, an' medical cover-ups. Mave, she 'ad 'er 'pendix out when she was fourteen – show 'em yer scar, Mave.' Mave obligingly lifted her skirts. 'an' vey sewed 'er up wrong an' got the toobs crossed, an' she's bin sufferin' ever since, see? Oooh, I could write a book on the sufferin' she's 'ad. Write a book, I could.'

Both women started rolling their eyes again, and I had to stand up to control myself. Trixie had finished her afternoon's work, and she sauntered over, sensing a bit of fun. 'What's up?' she enquired.

Meg described for her the whole saga of the 'pendix and the fillipin toobs, and the medical blunders that Mavis had suffered, starting with the withered arm caused by a midwife who should have known better, and welliclose weins stripped by a surgeon as didn't know what 'e was doin', and golf stones the doctor wouldn't do nuffink abaht, and the fact that now Mave was pregnant she was sufferin' because the toobs was all crossed.

Trixie was an outspoken girl, short on tact.

'Don't be daft,' she said bluntly.

Meg leaped to her feet and clenched her fists. She would possibly have struck Trixie full in the face, had not the gentle Novice Ruth come up at that moment.

'Ladies, ladies, please, what is the matter?'

'Matter? She called me daft, vat's what's the matter.'

Novice Ruth looked disapprovingly at Trixie, who shrugged. 'You haven't heard the story yet.'

The nun turned to Megan'mave.

'I apologise if one of our nurses has been rude to you. I assure you it will not happen again. Now, please tell me your troubles. I'm sure we can help.'

The opportunity was too good to miss, and the two women jointly, with mirrored body language, moans and groans, rolling eyes and hissing breath, recalled every misfortune that Mavis had suffered at the hands of an incompetent and hostile medical profession.

Novice Ruth was very sympathetic, but she looked a bit vague.

'What can we do to help?' she enquired.

'It's the fillipin toobs what's crossed. They wants uncrossin,' said Meg emphatically.

Novice Ruth looked as though she was losing the plot.

'Fallopian tubes,' I whispered.

'Oh, I see. But how can they be crossed?' she enquired innocently.

'I'm tellin' yer. Ve surgeon, 'e sewed 'er up wrong wiv her 'pendix an' got ve toobs crossed. Vat's why she's sufferin'. Bin sufferin' for years, she 'as.'

Novice Ruth looked down at her crucifix, and I saw a flicker of a smile play at the corners of her mouth.

'I will examine Mavis,' she said quietly. 'Please follow me to the examination room.'

Meg gave me a triumphant glance and shot a look of pure venom at Trixie. Mave undressed as requested and lay down on the couch. Novice Ruth, an expert and experienced midwife, examined Mavis, asked several questions which Meg answered, and when she had finished the examination said, 'Both you and your baby seem to be in perfect condition for thirty-two weeks of pregnancy. The baby is developing normally, and the heart-beat is good. You, Mavis, are perfectly fit. I have examined everything possible – heart, blood pressure, urine. I can find nothing wrong with you. If you are suffering discomfort, I think it is probably heartburn, or wind, which afflicts a lot of pregnant women.'

'Heartburn? Wind? What about ve toobs?' shouted Meg.

'I was coming to the toobs,' lied the saintly Novice Ruth convincingly. 'I have examined them carefully, and can assure you that although they may have been crossed at the time of the unfortunate appendicitis operation, they have now uncrossed themselves. Nature is a wonderful healer. You have nothing more to fear from the Fallopian tubes.'

MEG THE GYPSY

The practice was extremely busy. Every midwife will tell you the same story. You can tick over comfortably for weeks, and then suddenly there are more women in labour than midwives to cope with them. Some say it is the phases of the moon, others say it is the local beer.

Trixie had been working all night. A delivery at 10 p.m. and another at 4 a.m. had left her exhausted, and she still had a day's work to get through. An hour of sleep after lunch had helped, though the evening visits were heavy. At nine, a long luxuriant bath with her favourite salts had eased her mind, and she was looking forward to the bliss of sleep.

The telephone rang. Not me, thought Trixie. Someone else is on first call, and she sank deeper into the water, turning on the hot tap with her toes.

A moment later there was a bang on the door.

'Trixie, old sport. You in there?' Chummy's voice sounded through the door.

'Yes.'

'I've got to go out. You're on first call now.'

'What! You're joking. I can't be.'

'Sorry and all that. But Cynthia is already out on a delivery, and Jennifer has a day off. It's up to you.'

'I just don't believe it.' Trixie groaned and felt sleep enveloping her.

'What did you say? Never mind, I can't hang around.'

Chummy's footsteps retreated down the corridor.

Trixie's tired mind refused to take in the reality of the situation. She felt she might doze off in the bath, but forced herself to get out, dried and into bed, where she immediately fell into a deep and dreamless sleep.

At 11.30 the phone rang. Usually a midwife on first call will hear it instantly, be out of bed and alert within seconds. The subconscious will keep the mind half-awake, ready for action. But Trixie slept on. Eventually the persistent ringing penetrated her ears, and she awoke confused – someone had better answer that damned phone, she thought. Then she remembered Chummy's bang on the bathroom door.

Horrified, she struggled out of bed and picked up the phone.

'Yes. Nonnatus House here. Who is it?'

'And about time, too! What d'you fink yer playing at? She coulda died afore you answered the telephone,' a harsh female voice barked.

Trixie shook her head vigorously, trying to focus her thoughts.

'Who is dying? What is the trouble?'

'Trouble? The trouble is you. You lazy good-for-nothing.'

Trixie groaned and sank onto the wooden bench beside the telephone, but her training came to the rescue. Mechanically she heard herself say, 'Please give me your name and address and tell me, as clearly as you can, what is the matter.'

'It's Meg, from Mile End, and it's Mave, see. Mave's in labour, and you gotta come quick.'

The clouds were lifting from Trixie's tired brain.

'But Mave is not due yet. Not for another month.'

'Don't you come vat one over me. You just get 'ere at the double, or I'll report yer to the authorities for negligence, refusin' to come to a woman in labour.'

Trixie was wide awake now. Mave was thirty-six weeks pregnant. A premature labour would be a serious matter, and dangerous for the baby.

'I'll come straight away,' she said and put down the phone.

Trixie hastened into her uniform. But before going to the clinical room for her bag, she went to the Sisters' corridor and knocked on Sister Bernadette's door to tell her that, according to Meg, Mavis was in premature labour.

'Go and assess the situation and inform me. If premature labour is established, she must be transferred immediately to hospital,' were the instructions.

Trixie collected her bag and attached it to her bicycle. She had a three-mile ride, and a fine drizzle was falling, the sort that gets you damp all over. Her legs were heavy, and turning the pedals seemed like one of the twelve labours of Hercules.

She reached the Mile End Road, which is broad and straight, and cycled along it looking for the turning, but missed it, and had to go back. This can't be happening to me, she thought. Once in the narrow street of identical terraced houses, the only light in a window led her to the correct address. She was met at the door by Meg.

'Call vis straight away, do yer? More like a snail's pace, I call it. You bin twenty minutes gettin' 'ere.'

If Meg thought she could intimidate Trixie, she was in for a shock.

'If you can get here any quicker on a bicycle, you are welcome to try. Now, cut the criticism and take me to your sister.'

In the bedroom it was hot and stuffy. A big fire was burning, and the windows were closed tight. Mave was lying on the bed moaning pathetically, clutching her stomach with both hands.

'See, she's sufferin' somefink wicked. Bin like vis for a couple of hours, she 'as. Somefink wicked.'

Mave moaned and whimpered. 'When's ve baby comin? I can't stand much more of vis. They'll 'ave to take it away. Cut me open.'

Meg echoed, 'She can't stand no more. It's 'orrible. Too much for 'er, with 'er weak constitooshun.'

Trixie took off her coat and sat down beside the bed.

'Ainchoo goin' a do nuffink?' demanded Meg.

'I am doing something,' said Trixie, 'I'm assessing the progress of labour.'

''Sessin'? Wha'choo mean, 'sessin'? She needs treatment. Dr Smellie in 'is book, 'e says the midwife should put ve woman on a birfin' stool.'

'Birthing stool! Where do you get that rubbish from?'

'It's 'ere in 'is book. You read it. You're supposed to know about vese fings.'

Trixie glanced at the aged book.

'That is two hundred years out of date. Don't cram your head with a lot of stuff you don't understand. No one uses birthing stools any more.'

Meg stared hard at Trixie, and recognition dawned.

'Ain't you ve one what called me daft?'

'Perhaps I did, and I wouldn't have been far wrong. Now be quiet with all your mumbo-jumbo, and let me get on with my job.'

'Look 'ere, I'm not 'avin' you. You can send for someone what knows what to do.'

'There's no one else on call. I should be delighted to go back to bed, but there is no one else who could come. You're stuck with me, and if you don't like it you can lump it. Now be quiet. I want to examine Mave.'

Trixie pulled back the bedclothes and palpated the uterus. The head was above the symphysis pubis, but she could not feel anything else definitive. There seemed to be lumps all over the place. She stood still, thinking, head on one side.

'Well, Miss Stoopid, what you goin' a do now?'

'I'm going to listen to the baby's heartbeat,' replied Trixie coldly, trying hard to ignore the woman's insults. She took out her Pinards and applied it to the abdomen.

'You better get on wiv this and stop messin' abaht. My sister's in labour, I tells yer.'

'Be quiet, will you? I can't hear a thing with you making all that noise.'

Meg rolled her eyes to the ceiling and sucked in her breath, indicating her total lack of confidence in the procedure.

Trixie listened carefully and counted a steady 120 beats per minute. She stood up, satisfied.

'Well, the baby is quite healthy. Now I must ask you some questions. When did you first feel contractions, Mave?'

Meg answered, 'About ten o'clock. Came on sudden. Terrible it was.'

'Will you be quiet. I'm asking Mave. Not you.'

Trixie was too tired to be patient. She turned to Mave.

'And how frequent are the contractions?'

Meg answered regardless: 'All ve time. Can'choo see? She's sufferin'.'

Trixie's slender reserves of patience snapped.

'Will you shut up and get out of here? Either you go or I will go. I'm not prepared to carry on like this.'

Trixie was taking a risk and she knew it. If she deserted a woman in labour the consequences would be severe. But the gamble paid off. Meg left.

Trixie could now devote her attention to Mave. She was puzzled because, although she had been observing Mave for at least twenty minutes, and although Mave looked and sounded as if she were in advanced labour, there appeared to be no contractions.

'When did this start?'

'About ten o'clock,' Mave groaned.

'And how frequent were the contractions? Did you time them?'

Mave looked pained.

'They was all ve time. Never stoppin'. Meg says Dr Smellie says . . '

'Never mind what Dr Smellie says. Contractions don't just start and never stop. It's not possible.'

Mave assumed her martyr's expression.

'You don't understand. I'm dyin'. You don't care.'

She hung onto her belly and rolled onto her side.

'Stop all this fuss,' barked Trixie. 'You are no more dying

than I am. I haven't seen a contraction since I came into this house.'

'That's 'cause you don't know nuffink. Meg, she says . . .'

'I won't hear any more about Meg. Now tell me, when did you last open your bowels?'

'What?' Mave jerked round to face Trixie.

'You heard. When?'

'I'm not sure. Couple of weeks ago, p'raps.'

'You are constipated. And what did you have for supper?'

'Gooseberry pie and custard.'

'Green gooseberries?'

'Yes. Two 'elpin's.'

'Well, that's the trouble, then. You've got gut ache. You're not in labour at all, you old fraud. Getting me out of bed for a stomach ache!' Trixie was furious. 'Do you realise I have been working for forty hours with no sleep, and you wake me up for nothing. I will give you some castor oil and an enema, and then I am going back to my bed and leaving you to get on with it.'

That was the first of many false labours. During the next four weeks, twice a week, Meg called us out. Several times she sent Sid, their husband, with a message of impending disaster. Poor man! He stood cap in hand, his sheep eyes watering with embarrassment, muttering something quite unintelligible. Wearily we had to attend the call to assess the situation, but we knew that we were being led up the garden path. Meg was never grateful, nor even polite. She continued to tell us that we didn't know our job, and we should read some of the books she had been readin', an' Mave should be confined in a darkened room, with a binding on her belly, an' 'ad we got ve muvver's caudle an' ve birfin' stool, an' smellin' salts an' salt candle, an' she 'ad jest got a book by Dr Jacob Rueff which was written in Latin in 1554, but she'd got an English translation, called *The Expert Midwife*, which says that ve baby's cord must be cut with a special knife which was blessed by the Bishop an' if it's a baby boy ve cord must be cut long, because as 'e grew up it would make 'is penis long, see, an' did we know all vis, wha' she knewed? It was difficult to answer without giggling, and what with Doctors Smellie, Rueff and Coffin, the whole saga became an on-going joke around the big dining table each lunchtime, when we were all assembled together.

However, quite inadvertently, Meg did us a service, and I, for one, learned a great deal about the horrifying conditions in which women had given birth in previous centuries.

Sid stood at the convent door again. The market had just closed, and he was in his workman's clothes. He was too conscious of his appearance to step into the hallway. Meekly he handed Trixie a note and muttered, 'Meg, she says . . .' He shook his head sorrowfully, raised his eyes appealingly and left.

It was just after lunch, morning visits were done, the practice was reasonably quiet, and we had settled down in our sitting room for a nice, peaceful afternoon. Trixie burst in, note in hand.

'I won't go. It's that infernal woman again.'

Cynthia looked up from her book.

'Try telling that to Sister Julienne.'

'But it will be another false labour.'

'Very probably. But you are on first call, and you can't refuse to go.'

Trixie sighed noisily, defeated by the facts.

'Well, I won't stay long, that's all.'

Grimly she cycled the well-worn path to Mile End. Meg was at the door.

'Oh, it's you, is it?'

'Yes. I'm sorry to say it is.'

'Well, I 'ope as 'ow you knows what yer doin' vis time, because Mave's in labour an' we don't want no bunglers.'

'Speak for yourself,' said Trixie drily.

She went upstairs to the bedroom. It was pitch dark inside,

so she went straight to the curtains and drew them back. Daylight flooded in.

'Don't do that,' shouted Meg.

'I must see what I am doing.'

'It's dangerous.'

'Yes, it will be dangerous if I can't see.'

'I mean, a woman in labour must be confined in a dark room.'

'Rubbish.'

'Don't you rubbish me.'

'I will if you talk rubbish. Now I've come to look at Mave, not to talk to you.'

She went over to the bed. Mave was sitting up, looking quite comfortable.

'Meg gets worried. I 'ad a few pains an hour ago, but they've gone, an' I reckons as 'ow you can go home now.'

Trixie ground her teeth crossly.

'You'll cry wolf once too often.'

'Wha'choo mean?'

'I mean if you carry on like this, you'll call when you really need us, we won't believe you, and we won't come.'

'That's negligence,' shouted Meg.

'It'll be your own fault.'

Both women sucked in their breath – 'shockin', a disgrace, I tells yer. Vey don't care, vey don't. Can't trust no one.'

Trixie ignored them and sat down beside Mave.

'I must examine you, and then I shall go. Lie flat, please.'

She palpated the uterus, and could feel a head low down, which satisfied her that the woman was close to full term, but not necessarily in labour. The foetal heart was very vigorous and could be heard in several places. Just then, the uterus tightened, and Mave gave a slight moan. Trixie sat still with her hand on the uterus, and took out her watch, counting about fifty seconds before the tightening relaxed.

Meg opened her mouth to speak, but Trixie silenced her.

'Would you go and make a cup of tea, please? Mave looks thirsty and needs a drink.'

Meg, grumbling about not being anyone's servant, left the room.

Trixie sat quietly. Ten minutes later she felt another contraction, slightly stronger than the first.

'You are in labour, Mave. And this time it is not a false alarm. Your baby will be born today.'

Meg came in with the tea.

'I'm in labour, Meg. Our baby'll be born soon.'

Mave looked unusually cheerful, but Meg turned white, and the teacups rattled in the saucers so much that they nearly fell out of her shaking hands.

'I must go to the telephone on the corner to ring Sister Bernadette,' said Trixie.

'You're not leavin' 'er. That's negligence, that is,' shouted Meg.

'It would be negligence if I didn't go. I'll be back before the next contraction comes. You two have your tea, and you can discuss my negligence while I'm gone.'

Sister Bernadette said she would come straight away. A primi-gravida of thirty eight years requires careful treatment. Mave had been told quite categorically that she should have her baby delivered in hospital, but she had refused. The fear of hospitalisation was so entrenched in working-class women of limited education in those days that nothing could shift it. They associated hospitals with the old infirmaries that were converted workhouses. Very likely if she had been taken into hospital, Mave would have been so tense and terrified that the psychological strain would have had a damaging effect on labour. So a home delivery, with an experienced midwife and if possible a doctor present, was the best compromise.

Trixie returned to the bedroom, which was in darkness again. She went over to the curtains to draw them back, but Meg stopped her.

'She's gotta be in a dark room.'

'She has not.'

'She must. Ve book, it says . . .'

'I don't care what your old book says. I'm in charge here, not you.'

Quite a tussle ensued, but the curtains were finally drawn back, filling the room with daylight. Mave was sitting up in bed looking quite fit and cheerful, but Meg was hovering around, grumbling under her breath and throwing nasty looks at Trixie.

'If you two have finished your tea,' said Trixie, 'you can take the cups away. I want to prepare my equipment for a delivery.'

Meg took the cup and saucer from Mave and stared into it. She gasped, and stared harder, then went deathly pale and trembled all over. The cup fell from her hand and shattered into pieces on the floor. She moaned, 'Oh no, no, no,' and fell against the wardrobe, half fainting. Trixie grabbed her arm.

'Hold on! Steady. What's the matter with you?'

Meg seemed unable to speak.

'You had better get out of here.'

Trixie led her to the door. The woman looked stricken and clung to her arm for support.

Finally Meg found her voice. 'It's an omen, an evil omen.'

'What is?'

'Ve tea leaves. An' then ve cup breakin'. It's bad. Bad. I ain't seen worse.'

'What are you talking about?'

'Vey never lie. Never.'

'Who don't?'

'It's an omen. Bad, I tells yer. Ve tea leaves never lie.'

Sister Bernadette arrived, required to see Mave at once, and said that the doctor would come as soon as he had finished his surgery. She examined Mave vaginally and assessed an os two fingers dilated with a foetal head low down, anterior presentation. The foetal heart was strong, the mother relaxed and cheerful. Mave looked happier than she had been throughout pregnancy.

By contrast, Meg was going to pieces. She hovered in the doorway, whimpering and moaning. Her face was the colour of one of her old books. Whenever Mave had a contraction, Meg groaned and rolled her eyes and many times looked near to collapsing. She moaned 'Vis is goin' to kill 'er, vis is. She can't stand it. She's got a weak constitooshun. You gotta do somefink – it can't go on like vis. The omens are bad.'

Quietly but firmly Sister Bernadette ordered her to leave the delivery room. Meg wailed and whined, but just for once Mave did not agree with her. She looked at Sister Bernadette and nodded. Then she said, 'You go, Meg. I'll be all right without you.'

Labour was progressing normally. Sister Bernadette and Trixie settled down to waiting and watching. Sister took out her breviary and said her evening office. Time ticked by. The doctor came, saw that things were going well and said that he had a few evening visits to make, but would return after they were completed. Trixie showed him to the door.

Returning through the living room, she heard strange sounds coming from the kitchen, so she looked round the door. The kitchen was filled with a weird greenish-yellow light. Smoke was coming from a burner and she spied Meg dressed from head to foot in a long green robe. A green scarf covered her head, pulled down low over her brow. Her face was white, and dark circles surrounded black, black eyes. She did not see Trixie, so engrossed was she in her activity.

Meg the gypsy was dealing out cards. She was cutting the pack methodically, laying down four cards face upwards, slowly and deliberately, then cutting the pack again. She was muttering, 'Death! I see it. Mortuary. Coffin. Grave.' Then she would shuffle the cards and cut again. 'Ve same. Always ve same. Them cards never lie.' She shuffled again, and laid down four different cards, and lastly, slowly, fearfully, cut the pack once more. Her skin shone with a ghastly greenish light. 'Ve same. First, ve teacup, now ve cards, vey cannot lie. Death. Death.' Her head fell forwards onto her arms, and the cards slithered across the floor.

MAVE THE MOTHER

The atmosphere in the delivery room was quiet and cheerful. Sister Bernadette had a presence. She was a young woman of about thirty to thirty-five, deeply religious, and her monastic vocation filled her with happiness. She was also a highly professional nurse and midwife. She radiated control, confidence and calm, which had a soothing effect on any woman with whom she was working. Mave looked quite different. Her martyred air had gone, her eyes were bright, and she seemed excited. Contractions were regular, every ten minutes. Sister had given Mavis a dose of castor oil, and Trixie had shaved her and given her an enema (the required practice in those days).

The doctor returned at 9 p.m. and agreed that he would stay. General practitioners, although they were not trained obstetricians, were the first point of call for a midwife. In fact, a medical student's training involved 50 per cent clinical experience in hospital under an obstetrician and 50 per cent district midwifery under a midwife. Consequently the general practitioner, unless he had a great deal of experience, frequently knew less about childbirth than the midwife. This could sometimes lead to a strained situation, particularly if the midwife did not trust the doctor's judgement. But we were fortunate. The Sisters of St Raymund Nonnatus had been practising for so long in the East End of London, with such a good record, that all the local doctors respected their judgement.

Mave was sleeping lightly between contractions, having had a dose of chloral hydrate. At 11 p.m. the waters broke. Sister prepared to do a vaginal examination, but with the next contraction the head was visible. She told Trixie to scrub up and to take the delivery.

The second stage of labour was surprisingly quick. Mave was nearly forty, and this was her first pregnancy, but she was relaxed and comfortable, the uterine muscles were strong, and her perineum stretched without difficulty. Only two more contractions were necessary and the head crowned. Sister Bernadette smiled at Mave, who looked up at her trustingly.

'Now, with the next contraction I don't want you to push. Just pant and concentrate on your breathing, because we want the baby's head to be born slowly.'

Mave was wonderful. We had all expected her to create a terrible fuss during labour and refuse to cooperate, but not at all. With the next contraction the head was born. Trixie waited for restitution of the head, and after only a few moments the shoulder slid under the pubic arch and the baby was born.

'She's a little girl.'

'Oh, thank God. I don't like boys,' said Mave.

The baby gave a lusty scream, and Meg put her head round the door. She was still wearing her strange green outfit, and her black eyes devoured us all, her gloomy features contrasting with Mave's radiant smile.

'We wan'ed a li'le girl, Meg, and we got one.'

'She'll die. I seed it all.'

'Don't talk like that.' Sister Bernadette was angry.

'Worms an' coffins. It's in ve cards.'

'Will you go away. I won't have you in here,' the nun said.

'Vey never lie.'

'I never heard such nonsense. Now go away this minute.'

Meg rolled her eyes, making herself look weirder than ever.

'It's all worms an' coffins,' she muttered as she left, shaking her head mournfully.

If Mavis heard these words of doom she did not seem to take any notice, as she cuddled her baby in a state of exhausted euphoria.

The cord was clamped and cut, and Sister took the baby to examine and weigh her. She was a very small baby, weighing only 4 lb 12 oz, but was not premature and appeared to be normal and healthy in every way. Trixie left the baby to Sister, and concentrated on the management of the third stage of labour. There were no contractions, so Trixie waited. After ten minutes she decided to massage the fundus to stimulate another contraction. The uterus felt bulky, and then she saw a movement, like a kick, as the wall of the uterus rose and fell briefly. She put her hand over the place, and it happened again.

'Sister, I think there is another baby in here,' she said.

Midwife and doctor were at the bedside in an instant.

'That would account for a small first baby,' Sister said as she palpated the uterus. 'You are quite right, nurse, and I think it is a transverse lie. Pass me the Pinards, please.'

She listened carefully. The heartbeat could be heard low down, just over the pubic bone. It was rapid but regular. Sister counted 140 beats per minute. She asked the doctor to confirm the lie of the baby. He said that he could not tell and would rely on Sister's judgement, but whatever the lie of the baby he advised we call the Flying Squad, and immediately transfer Mavis to hospital.

Until that moment Mavis had appeared unconcerned and relaxed, but at the word 'hospital' she wailed in anguish. Meg rushed into the room.

'Wha'choo doin' to 'er?' Her voice was harsh and aggressive.

'Vey're goin' 'a put me away. In an infirmary.'

'Over my dead body.'

'It's not an infirmary,' said the doctor, 'it's a modern hospital, where Mavis will get the best treatment.'

'She'll never come out alive. Or never come out a' all. I know wha' goes on in them places. Vey keeps the likes of Mave an' me, an' never lets 'em out. Uses 'em for speriments, that's wha' vey do.'

Mavis became almost hysterical, shrieking and sobbing, 'I won't go,' and Meg threw her arms protectively around her. Sister felt Mave's pulse, which had been normal until that moment, but had now risen to an alarming 110 beats per minute.

'If this goes on, the baby will be in serious distress,' remarked Sister. 'We must prepare for a twin birth at home. You will not be sent to hospital, Mavis. But Meg, you must go. I am not prepared to deliver the second baby with you in the room.'

Meg rolled her eyes. 'I told yer, didn't I? It was an evil omen wiv the tea leaves. An' ve cards. Vey'll die. You mark my words.'

Sister pushed her out of the room. Then she scrubbed up. She was calm and controlled.

'There have been no contractions since the birth of the first baby. If the foetus is lying transversely this will help me. First I must make quite sure of the lie of the baby, and secondly ascertain whether or not the waters have broken. If the uterus is inert, and the membranes intact, it is usually possible to turn the baby to the correct position for delivery. I want you to monitor the foetal heart every few minutes, nurse.'

Trixie listened and said the heartbeat remained at 140. Sister carried out a vaginal examination.

'Yes. I can feel the amniotic sac bulging through the dilated os — splendid — but I cannot identify the presenting part. It is certainly not a head. It might be a breech, I suppose, but I cannot be sure. I'm not going to do too much ... remember, that, nurse. Never try poking around too much in a twin birth. You might rupture the membranes, and if an arm or a shoulder is presenting and descends into the birth canal, you will then have an impacted foetus which cannot be delivered vaginally.'

Sister withdrew her hand and removed her gloves.

'I am going to attempt an external version — unless you want to do it, doctor?'

The doctor shook his head.

'It would be better if you did it, Sister.'

Sister nodded.

'What is the foetal heartbeat, nurse?'

'One hundred and fifty; a little raised, Sister.'

'Yes. Now Mavis, lie quite still and relax. You are not in any pain, are you?'

'Nope.'

'I have to turn your baby. I am going to exert a lot of pressure. I want you to breathe deeply all the time and concentrate on relaxing.'

Mavis nodded and smiled. Since the threat of hospitalisation had been removed, she had been quite relaxed, and her pulse had dropped to a steady seventy-two beats per minute.

'I want you to watch me carefully, nurse, so that you will know how to do it another time.' Trixie fervently hoped that would never happen.

'Here in the right iliac fossa is the head ... feel it, nurse ... I'm correct, am I not?' Trixie nodded, though she could feel no identifiable head. 'And over here is the breech ... can you feel that?'

Trixie nodded vaguely. 'I think so, Sister.'

'Good. Now what I cannot tell is whether the foetus is lying dorso-anterior or dorso-posterior. You said that you saw and felt a kick. Where? Point to the spot.'

Trixie did so.

'Hmmm – not much help. Now what I want to do is to flex the foetus into a ball as much as I can, which will enable me to turn it more readily.'

Sister grasped what she had identified as the head and the breech and slowly closed her hands together.

'Yes ... it is moving ... the foetus is definitely flexing. The head is closing towards the breech, and the back is curved under the fundus. Splendid! Feel it now, nurse. Can you feel the difference?'

Trixie felt but could not truthfully say she noticed anything different. The doctor felt also and nodded approvingly.

'You must have X-ray hands, Sister,' he murmured.

'I must turn the foetus now, and I want to turn it so that it follows its nose. About a quarter circle will be sufficient, and the head will be presenting. This is going to hurt, Mave, but only for a minute. I want you to relax as much as you can.'

Sister Bernadette, the expert midwife, with the ball of her right thumb behind the head, and with the fingers of the left hand beneath the breech, firmly and slowly, her two hands working together, feeling her way, successfully achieved external cephalic version of the foetus. She turned the baby.

'The head is now lying just above the pubic arch ... can you feel it, nurse?'

To her surprise, Trixie could and she nodded enthusiastically.

'To ensure that it remains in that position I am going to ask you to hold it there ... grasp it firmly ... and hold the breech with the other hand. After version a foetus can slip back into its former position. I am going to puncture the membranes to permit the head to engage. This can usually be done quite easily with blunt forceps.'

Sister scrubbed up again and punctured the membranes. Amniotic fluid flowed over the bed.

'While I am here I will want to feel the foetal skull to find the position of the fontanelle, which will tell me if it is an anterior or a posterior presentation ... ah, marvellous! The head is well down in the pelvis. Couldn't be better. Now all we need are some good contractions and your other baby will be born.' She smiled at Mavis, who responded warmly.

They waited, but still a contraction did not come. Trixie listened to the foetal heart again. It was 160. Sister and doctor looked at each other without speaking.

Minutes ticked by. Sister looked at her watch.

'Twenty-five minutes have passed since the birth of the first baby, and no contraction. The foetal heartbeat is going up. We cannot allow this to go on beyond thirty minutes. Why do I say that, nurse?'

Trixie was startled by the sudden question. She hadn't a clue! She mumbled something about 'The mother needs to rest'.

'Nonsense!' snapped Sister Bernadette. 'Didn't they teach

you anything in the classroom? You'd better pay attention, because there is no teacher like experience. One day you may find yourself in a similar situation, with no one to help you.'

Trixie was terrified at the thought, but muttered, 'Yes, Sister.'

'We cannot allow the uterus to rest for too long because of the risk to the mother and baby. We do not know the condition of the placenta, which is the life blood of the foetus. If the twins are uniovular . . . and what does that mean, nurse?'

'It means that they have developed from one ovum.'

'Correct. That would mean that, after the birth of the first baby, there is the possibility of the placenta separating from the uterine wall while the second twin is still in utero. I need not continue.'

Sister indicated that Mavis was listening to the viva voce, but her unfinished sentence protected Mavis from hearing that if the placenta of uniovular twins separated after the birth of the first baby and before the second was born, the second twin would be robbed of its blood supply and would die in utero. If that were not bad enough, the risk of haemorrhage might kill the mother also, because contraction and retraction of the uterine muscle controls bleeding during the third stage of labour. If a second foetus is still in the uterus, its presence will interfere with the third stage, and the raw placental site will bleed freely.

Sister asked Trixie to record the foetal heart again. It was still 160.

'Satisfactory. Now I want to stimulate the uterus. There are three simple ways in which we can do this. What are they, nurse?'

Trixie's mind went blank.

'Really! I sometimes wonder what they taught you in the classroom. You did have lectures on twin births?'

'Yes. I think so, Sister.'

'You only think so! I trust you were not asleep during the lectures, nurse.'

'Oh no, Sister. Never,' said Trixie untruthfully.

'I hope not! Well, we can stimulate uterine contractions by puncturing the amniotic sac. This I have already done, and I did it to make the head engage after cephalic version. However, it has not stimulated uterine contractions. Secondly, we can massage the fundus, just as we do to stimulate the third stage of labour.'

Sister massaged the fundus vigorously, but it did not have the desired effect.

'If these two methods fail, we can put the first baby to the breast. And how will this help, nurse?'

Trixie was dreading another question, and this was the worst. She swallowed, and shook her head.

'As you will doubtless be aware, nurse, the posterior lobe of the pituitary gland produces a hormone we call pituitrin.'

Trixie nodded her head, and tried to look as if she already knew what Sister was talking about.

'Pituitrin, as you will know, plays a part in lactation.'

'Oh yes, of course, Sister.'

'Can you describe to me, please, the role of pituitrin in lactation?'

Me and my big mouth, thought Trixie, ruefully.

'Well, as you do not seem to know, I will tell you. The stimulation of the nipple by the infant activates the posterior lobe of the pituitary gland to secrete pituitrin, which acts on the unstriped muscle surrounding the breast lobules and ducts, producing a flow of milk. But also – and this is the important point – pituitrin stimulates contraction of the muscles of the uterus.'

Sister Bernadette put the baby to the breast, but she was too sleepy and would not suck.

'It is now thirty minutes since the birth of the first baby. Uterine inertia can go on for hours, and all the time the risk to mother and baby increases. This is where medical assistance is needed.'

The doctor was unpacking his case, laying out several drugs, syringes and instruments, including Haig Ferguson's obstetric forceps.

'What will be the first line of medical intervention, nurse?'

Trixie was on the spot again so she glanced at the doctor's equipment.

'Well, forceps, I suppose.'

'Nonsense. Forceps will be the *last* thing we use. First we must get the uterus to contract. In the past I have known quinine to be used, but it is not advisable. As you may remember, a synthetic preparation of pituitrin is now available, called Pitocin, which is much more reliable and safe, and which I am sure Doctor is planning to use.'

She looked towards the doctor.

'Quite right, Sister. I am preparing a small dose – 0.25 ml – to be injected intramuscularly. If the uterine muscles do not respond, the procedure can be repeated every half hour for two hours. But hopefully after the first injection we will see some action.'

'Pitocin is usually effective,' continued Sister, 'but there are certain specific contra-indications to its use. What are they, nurse?'

Again Trixie was under interrogation. She tried desperately to think back to her lectures, but was tired and couldn't remember a thing.

'Come now, nurse. This won't do at all. Pitocin should not be given if there is any risk to the mother or baby by stimulating the uterus. Firstly, disproportion; if it is apparent that a foetus cannot descend into a narrow or misshapen pelvis, as we see with a rachitic pelvis, giving Pitocin would be disastrous. Secondly, malpresentation: this baby was lying transverse or obliquely. If Pitocin had been given too early, before I carried out an external version, an impacted foetus would have been the result. Lastly, the condition of the foetus. What should be a contra-indication for the use of Pitocin, nurse?'

Finally something stirred at the back of Trixie's mind. 'The foetal heart.'

'Excellent. Foetal distress can be determined from the heart-beat. And I shall want another recording, please, before the injection is given.'

Trixie listened again. 'One hundred and seventy, Sister, and quite regular.'

'That is satisfactory because it is regular. It is when the heartbeat is swinging wildly that we should worry about foetal distress. I think we are ready, doctor.'

The doctor injected 0.25 ml, and they all waited in silence. Mavis, warm and comfortable, had fallen asleep. Her three attendants were tense and anxious. Sister sat with her hand resting on the fundus, but no contractions came. She listened to the foetal heart a couple of times. It was 170 and rising. Half an hour had passed. She looked at the doctor, who said, 'I think I will inject 0.30 ml this time, Sister.' She nodded in agreement.

More waiting. The foetal heart remained rapid, far too rapid, and Sister was biting her lip with anxiety. Another twenty minutes, and still no contractions came. Sister Bernadette and the doctor exchanged glances every so often, and Trixie could feel the mounting tension in the room.

It all happened at once, Trixie said later. A powerful move-ment of the uterus, and immediately a violent rush of blood from the vagina, a pint or more.

'The placenta has separated. Quick. Give me the foetal stetho-scope,' cried Sister in alarm. Mavis was awake and the foetal heart was racing so fast that Sister could not count it.

'We have to get this baby out immediately. Mavis – you must come to the bottom of the bed – never mind about the blood, just slither down – now raise your legs to your chest. Nurse, hold the legs steady in the lithotomy position.'

There was no anaesthetic available. It was far too late even to give a Pethidine injection. Mavis had to bear the pain. The gas and air machine might have helped her a little, but no one would claim that it was a full anaesthetic.

Sister reached again for the Pinards. The heartbeat had dropped to a dangerously low eighty beats per minute. 'We haven't a moment to lose,' she whispered.

The doctor placed two fingers into the vagina and hooked them behind the perineum, pulling it as taut as possible. With sharp episiotomy scissors he then cut the perineum diagonally. Mavis let out a piercing scream, and Meg rushed into the room. Seeing Mavis in a lithotomy position surrounded by blood she yelled, 'Murder!' and rushed over to the bed. She attempted to fight the doctor, but Sister pulled her back by the shoulders. Meg turned on her like a tigress and slapped her face so hard that the poor Sister fell against the wall. But she stood up again quickly, her face burning.

'If you interfere, Mavis will die. There *is* no alternative. You may not believe it, but we know what we are doing. And we are doing it to save the life of mother and baby.' She repeated more emphatically: 'If you interfere, your sister will die.'

Meg stared at her blankly. The shock of Sister's words reduced her to silence.

'Now, if you want to help, and I am sure you do, you will hold this gas and air mask over your sister's face . . . keep it firm over her nose and mouth . . . turn the knob up to maximum and talk to Mavis quietly, try to keep her calm. This is going to hurt, but you can help a great deal if you do as I say. Mavis needs you. Her life depends on it.'

Meg calmed down. She administered the gas and air. Giving her something to do was the best thing that Sister could have suggested.

Sister Bernadette listened to the foetal heartbeat. It had dropped to sixty beats per minute, and was weak and irregular. The doctor inserted the first blade of the forceps into the vagina, muttering to Trixie, 'Whatever you do keep her legs in that position. Don't let her move.' Trixie, who was trembling and felt sick, put all her weight on the two legs.

'Sister, the os is still fully dilated, thank God, but the head is above the rim. Can you apply steady pressure on the fundus to try to force the baby down an inch or two? There's not a moment to lose.'

Sister grasped the fundus with both hands and pressed down as hard as she could. There was a massive spurt of blood and meconium from the vagina, splattering the doctor all over. He hardly noticed it.

'Quickly. The head is down a little. But more.'

Sister applied more pressure, and a contraction developed.

'That's better. It's coming. Now I can get hold of it.'

The doctor inserted the second blade of the forceps around the head of the baby. Muffled screams were heard from Mavis, behind the gas and air mask, and Meg was looking grim, but held the mask in place.

Slowly, steadily, the doctor pulled the forceps, with Sister applying pressure from above.

'Keep those legs still,' muttered Sister to Trixie. 'She must not move at this stage.' It took all of Trixie's strength to prevent Mavis from throwing herself off the bed.

Within half a minute the head was born. The baby's face had no colour. Sister immediately left the bedside, took a couple of swabs and a fine catheter, and tried to clean the airways, but the baby did not move or attempt to breathe.

The doctor hooked a finger under the presenting shoulder and with one swift movement pulled the baby upwards towards the mother's abdomen. It was another little girl, completely white and limp. She looked dead.

A mere ninety seconds had elapsed between the first haemorrhage and the birth of the baby, yet Trixie told us later that it had seemed like ninety minutes. Time had stretched unnaturally. Even the steady tick, tick, tick of the clock seemed to slow down, as if time itself were suspended.

The baby was separated from the mother. She was like a rag doll and seemed to be quite dead. Sister carried her near to the fire. The doctor stretched out his hand and touched a tiny arm that swung lifelessly. He looked at Sister.

'Do what you can,' he said sadly, 'we might have to ...'

But there was no time to speculate. There was another spurt of fresh blood, and the cord, which was protruding from the vagina, lengthened.

'The placenta is coming. Quick, nurse, fetch a kidney dish,' he said.

Trixie tried to get one, but her legs were shaking and she could not move. The placenta slid out onto the floor.

'We will examine it later,' said the doctor, pushing it aside with his foot. 'First, I must control the haemorrhage.'

Blood continued to seep out, then another spurt of fresh blood. The prognosis for Mavis was not looking good. She was no longer in pain, but was extremely weak and sweating from shock. Meg's know-all arrogance had burst like a bubble. The speed and drama of events had shaken her. She sat quietly at Mave's head, stroking her hair, whispering words of love and comfort.

The doctor massaged the uterus vigorously and squeezed out clots by further kneading and fundal pressure. Mavis groaned and weakly moved a leg.

'I think that is all the residual blood clots. I need to administer intravenous Ergometrine, but I want you, nurse, to exert external bi-manual compression of the uterus while I am preparing the injection. Have you ever done it before?'

Trixie shook her head.

'This is what you do, then. It will be only for a minute or two, but we cannot allow the uterus to relax. If it does we might get another haemorrhage.'

'Right, then, stand here ... press the left hand into the abdomen just above the umbilicus, like this. Now, clench your right hand into a fist and press down as far as possible behind the symphysis pubis ... that's it ... now push the ball of the uterus upwards and compress it between the two hands as hard as you can ... harder ... that's it. Keep it there.'

The doctor went over to his medical kit to draw up the injection. He returned to the bedside and bound the upper arm tightly in order to inject into a vein at the bend of the elbow. But he could not find a vein. Mavis had lost so much blood that her veins were flat and slippery. He made several attempts with no success. He swore under his breath.

'Keep that compression going, nurse. Another haemorrhage could be fatal. I must get an intramuscular injection. They take longer to work, but if I can't get a vein it will have to be an IM.'

Trixie continued exerting bi-manual compression of the uterus. She was feeling sick and faint, but the sight of Mavis looking so ill and the thought of another haemorrhage and its consequences kept her strength up.

The doctor returned and swiftly plunged the needle into Mavis's thigh. 'That'll do the trick.' Then, to Trixie: 'I'll take over now. I want you to go and ring the hospital.'

Meg interrupted. 'No. I won' let 'em take 'er.'

The doctor turned on her savagely.

'Will you be quiet, woman, and stop interfering. If Mavis had gone into hospital, as I advised in the first place six months ago, all this might never have happened.'

Meg held her peace.

Sister Bernadette had carried the baby closer to the fire and had wrapped a roll of soft cotton wool around her. She cleared the airways with a fine mucus catheter. Blood, mucus and meconium were sucked out of the nose, mouth and throat. She held the tongue forwards with fine baby forceps, because if the tongue is without muscle tone and flaccid, it can fall backwards into the throat, blocking the airways. She held the baby completely upside down for a few seconds, and then sucked out the airways again. She turned the baby face downwards and massaged the back from base of spine upwards, then cleared the airways once more. Next she undertook a procedure known as Eve's Rocking – that is, alternately raising the head and feet of the baby by about forty-five degrees. The baby did not respond. Sister administered mouth to mouth resuscitation by filling her cheeks with air and puffing three puffs into the tiny white lips, then twenty seconds of Eve's Rocking again, then three more puffs. After about two minutes of this procedure she listened to the baby's heartbeat.

Her face became radiant. 'I can hear a faint heartbeat – around eighty per minute. Praise the Lord.' And she continued her efforts. Suddenly the baby gave a short, convulsive gasp, sucking air into its lungs and then lay quite still again, making no further attempt to breathe. But a baby can take shallow breaths that are almost imperceptible to the observer. Sister could still hear a faint heartbeat, so she continued. A couple of minutes later the baby gave another convulsive gasp, repeated thirty seconds later, and this pattern continued for nearly half an hour, during which time the heartbeat increased to a healthy 120 per minute.

Sister Bernadette had no drugs, no oxygen, no incubator or modern equipment for resuscitating an infant with asphyxia pallida. She had only the methods described above, and the baby did not die.

The intramuscular injection of Ergometrine given to Mave by the doctor worked within five minutes. The uterus contracted into a firm hard ball, and all fears of further haemorrhage were removed. Mavis looked terribly ill, however. Her skin was white, cold and clammy, caused by pain and blood loss. She was in a state of obstetric shock, but her condition was stable. Sleep would benefit her, so the doctor gave an injection of morphine, which he could not have done while the baby was in utero. She dozed off in Meg's arms.

The doctor prepared for suturing. There was now no hurry, so he gave Mavis a local anaesthetic around the perineum and the vaginal wall, and sat back, waiting for it to take effect. Once the local anaesthetic had numbed the perineum, the doctor was able to repair the episiotomy. He was relieved to find that the cervix was not torn.

Meanwhile Trixie was down the road ringing the Flying Squad. She had taken off her gown and cap but had forgotten to take off her mask. There was blood on her hands and arms, and smeared down her uniform and legs. As she ran down the road she did not notice that people were looking at her rather strangely. It was not until she was inside the telephone box that she realised she did not have the three pennies on her with which to make a telephone call, so she stopped a passer-by. 'Can you let me have threepence for an urgent telephone call?' Only then did she notice the mask, so she pulled it off. Her hand was trembling, and she noticed the blood on it for the first time.

'I must have threepence. I forgot to bring it. I must ring the hospital.' Trixie's voice was shrill. Dubiously the man dug into his pocket and produced three pennies. 'Thanks.' She dived into the box, but her hand was shaking so much that she could not dial the number or put the pennies in the slot, so she called the man back.

'You're in a bad way, nurse,' he said.

Trixie felt too weak to answer, so she merely handed him a bit of paper.

'Ring that number for me, please.'

The phone rang, and a voice answered immediately. Briefly Trixie explained the situation and gave the address. 'We will send the Flying Squad immediately,' the voice said.

'Do you need any help getting back to the house?' asked the man kindly.

'I'll be all right. Thanks for your help.'

When Trixie returned to the house, Meg was shouting at the doctor and Sister.

'You murderers! Look wha' you done. You've hurt 'er. I'll

report you to ve authorities, I will. Look at ve blood. You nearly killed 'er, you did.'

The doctor tried to defend himself

'The placenta separated prematurely. That was the cause of the blood loss. I did not cause it.'

'Liar! Tell vat to the judge. Medical blunderers.'

She turned on Sister. 'An' you, yer no better. You'll kill vat baby afore you're finished. An' it'll be your fault if she dies. I'll not forget vis, I'll not.'

Bewildered, the doctor looked at Sister.

'Can you explain?' he asked plaintively.

'I doubt it,' said Sister wearily. Her eye was swelling up, from the blow she had received from Meg. 'We've been trying for six months with no success. I doubt if any explanation will get through.'

'I'll not forget vis. You jest wait. You'll pay fer vis an' all, the pair of you.' Meg rolled her eyes and spat on the floor.

The Obstetric Flying Squad arrived. This was an emergency service held in readiness by all big hospitals for the support of domiciliary midwives. It was their proud boast that they could get to any emergency in twenty minutes, and they seldom failed to do so. An obstetrician, a paediatrician, and a nurse came, armed with an incubator, oxygen, drip, drugs, anaesthetics and all the other equipment used for obstetric surgery and infant resuscitation. They entered a small, hot and stuffy room that looked like a battle scene. Blood was literally everywhere. The doctor, covered in blood, was suturing the patient. The placenta still lay on the floor. Sister Bernadette, who was tending the baby, looked as though she had been in the front line. The skin around her eye was now blue, her face red and swollen, and her veil streaked with blood. A weird-looking woman in green glared at the hospital team with accusing eyes. 'More murderers. I'll see you don't get 'er,' she hissed venomously.

The doctor and the obstetrician consulted. Mavis was sleeping peacefully because of the morphine given half an hour earlier by the doctor. But she had lost a lot of blood, and the shock was severe. An intravenous infusion of blood plasma by drip was installed.

The placenta was scooped up off the floor, and the two doctors examined it. It was large, but appeared to be complete. The consultant palpated the woman's abdomen. The uterus was firm and hard, about the size of a grapefruit, as it should be. He looked around the small, stuffy room that contained not a vestige of clinical apparatus; at the woman in a state of primary obstetric shock; at the volume of blood loss; at the first baby sleeping peacefully in the crib; at Sister Bernadette tending the asphyxiated twin.

'In circumstances like these, undiagnosed twins, a transverse lie, premature separation of the placenta and haemorrhage could spell certain death. You have done really well, old chap.'

'Thanks,' said the doctor wearily. He seemed to be in a state of exhaustion. 'We do our best.'

'You done yer best!' shouted Meg. 'You wants lockin' up, I say. If you'd done like what I said an' put 'er on a birfin' stool in ve first place, vis would never 'ave 'appened.'

The consultant looked at Meg in astonishment.

'Take no notice, we've had this the whole time,' whispered the doctor. 'Nothing will convince her.'

The nurse took the baby from Sister Bernadette and placed the child in the incubator, warmed to 95 degrees F, and humidified to avoid drying of the respiratory mucous membranes. The baby was breathing, but her breaths were shallow. Her muscle tone was flaccid, and her skin tone bluish. Her heartbeat was regular, but faint. The paediatrician, after examining the baby, injected 1 cc of Lobeline into the umbilical vein in the cord and milked it towards the abdomen. Oxygen was attached to the incubator, and the oxygen input adjusted to 30 per cent.

The paediatrician advised immediate transfer to Great Ormond Street Hospital. Paradoxically, Meg, who had so violently opposed hospital for Mavis, did not object. The baby was kept in Great Ormond Street for six weeks until her weight was over five pounds, and then she returned home. Both babies thrived. They grew up to be strong, healthy girls, brought up entirely by their mother and aunt. They were a regular sight in Chrisp Street market, helping on the fruit and veg stall, and they became great favourites with the locals.

Thirty years later I was visiting Trixie, who had recently moved to Basildon in Essex. We went shopping, and she insisted we call at the market. It was a large and lively market, with open stalls and old-fashioned costers crying out their wares. I heard the strident voice of a woman calling out, 'Best apples, only thirty pence a pound. You won't find cheaper anywhere. Best bananas. Melons. Grapefruits.'

We approached the stall.

'Well? Wha'choo want?' demanded the female.

I gasped, staring at two identical women in drab brown dresses, leather belts at the waist, men's boots, and tight head-scarves pulled down low over the forehead. I could not speak.

'If you don't know wha'choo want, I can't hang about. Next.'

The years rolled back. 'Megan'mave,' I exclaimed.

'What?' The two women drew together. Black eyes flashed a challenge.

'Megan'mave! But you can't be – it's not possible!'

'Mave's our mum, an' Meg's our aunt. D'you wanna make somefink of it?'

No, I didn't. Trixie grinned at me, and we slipped quietly away, chuckling.

MADONNA OF THE PAVEMENT

I saw them in High Holborn. They stood out from the tense, jostling crowd because they seemed to have no object in life, nowhere to go, nothing to do; they were aimless, lost. They stood out also because they were so poor. Poverty is such a relative thing; but no man is really poor till life becomes a desert island that gives him neither food nor shelter nor hope. They were such obvious failures at this game of getting and keeping called success. If they had suddenly shouted in pain above the thunder of the passing wheels they could hardly have been more spectacular in their misery, this man, this woman, this child.

He slouched along a few yards in advance of the woman. He looked as though Life had been knocking him down for a long time, then waiting for him to get up so that it might knock him down again. His bent body was clothed in greenish rags and his naked feet were exposed in gashed boots. He was not entirely pathetic. He was the kind of man to whom you would gladly give half a crown to salve your conscience; but you would never allow him out of sight with your suit-case!

She carried her baby against her breast in a ragged old brown cloth knotted round her shoulders. Perhaps she was twenty-five, but she looked fifty because no one had ever taken care of her, or had given her that pride in herself which is necessary to a woman's existence. She had not even the happiness of being wanted or necessary – a condition in which the altruistic soul of woman thrives. This man of hers would obviously be better off without her. She had once been pretty.

The shame of it! To parade her woman's body draped in rags through streets full of other women in their neat clothes, to meet the pitying eyes of other wives and mothers, and to drag on, tied like a slave, behind this shambling, shifty man. Is there a crucifixion for a woman worse than this?

He walked ahead so that she had plenty of time to wonder why she married him. Now and then he would turn and jerk his head, trying to make her quicken her pace. She took no notice, just plodded on in who knows what merciful dullness?

Then the sleeping child in her old brown shawl awakened and moved with the curious boneless writhing of a young baby. The mother's arms tightened on it and held its small body closer to hers. She stopped, went over to a shop window, and lent her knee on a ledge of stone. She placed one finger so gently in the fold of cloth and looked down into it . . .

I tell you that for one second you ceased to pity and you reverenced. Over that tired face of chiselled alabaster, smoothed and softened in a smile, came the only spiritual thing left in these two lives: the beatitude of a Madonna. This same unchanging smile has melted men's hearts for countless generations. The first time a man sees a woman look at his child in exactly that way something trembles inside him. Men have seen it from piled pillows in rooms smelling faintly of perfume, in night nurseries, in many a comfortable nest which they have fought to build to shield their own. No different! The same smile in all its rich, swift beauty was here in the mud and the bleakness of a London street.

They went on into the crowd and were forgotten. I went on with the knowledge that out of rags and misery had come, full and splendid, the spirit that, for good or ill, holds the world to its course.

Two beggars in a London crowd, but at the breast of one – the Future. Poor, beautiful Madonna of the Pavement . . .

H. V. Morton, first published in the Daily Express, 1923.

Human memory is the strangest thing. Apparently we have millions, perhaps billions of interconnecting fibres in our brains, triggered by electrical impulses, which can record our experiences. But sometimes these stores lie dormant for years, and the memories seem to be completely lost. But they are still there, waiting for some spark to ignite them.

A book of essays by H. V. Morton was the spark for me. I took them with me on holiday and after a strenuous day of swimming and cycling I was sitting in the last long rays of the evening sun, reading. As I read this beautiful and tragic story of a bully of a man and a downtrodden woman, it all came back to me. I had completely forgotten the Laceys. I read the first page of the essay – the description of the shiftless couple in the streets of London – without much thought, but then came the heart-rending but uplifting paragraphs about the baby and the woman's love. The spark of memory had been ignited and the memory of the Laceys was there, in a flash, as they say. It only remained to be written down.

John Lacey was the landlord of the Holly Bush, just off Poplar High Street. As I came to know him better, I found it incredible that Trueman's (the brewers) had ever granted him a licence and continued to pay his wages, but stranger things have happened in the world of employment, and he enjoyed the role that fate had generously offered him.

John Lacey had been diagnosed as having late-onset diabetes. It was not very severe at the time of diagnosis, and the doctor had advised that it could be controlled by a diet of reduced sugar and carbohydrate. But John Lacey refused to cooperate, and his blood-sugar level rose higher. Insulin injections were prescribed, and the doctor – judging that if the patient would not control his diet, he would not inject himself regularly and accurately – asked the Sisters to give the injections twice daily. This was very time-consuming. Soluble insulin was used in those days, and each injection only lasted twelve hours in the body. We received a lot of requests to attend diabetics because back then it was very difficult to assess and maintain the correct dose of insulin and to inject it hypodermically.

Sister Evangelina and I went to assess Mr Lacey. The pub was in a side street and was in no way attractive. The street was narrow and dingy, several houses had been bombed, and many walls were held up with scaffolding. The pub itself was hardly noticeable, the frontage resembling any of the houses around it: dark brown paint flaking off, windows caked with dirt, a narrow front door, always shut. The only thing that might at one time have distinguished the pub from its neighbours was its sign; but it was so old that it hung from only one hinge, and most of the paint had worn off.

Sister Evangelina and I entered by the pub door, which was the only entry to the landlord's living accommodation upstairs. The public bar was about twenty feet square, high-ceilinged with a wooden floor. A few cheap wooden tables and chairs stood around the place, with the bar itself to one side. An unshaded electric light bulb, around which flies buzzed continuously, hung from the centre of the ceiling. The walls and ceiling were a dirty yellowish brown and were spotted all over with fly-stains. A single picture hung on a wall, but it was so dingy and faded that one would have been hard pressed to say whether it was a seascape or a hunting scene.

It was 12.30 p.m. when we arrived – opening time – and the pub, which at that time of day should have been humming with life, had only one customer: a solitary man of indeterminate age staring at the wall and sieving a pint of beer through his moustaches. The silence was oppressive.

A woman stood behind the bar, half-heartedly wiping a few glasses with a grimy cloth. She was old, far too old to be a barmaid. Her grey hair was scooped into an untidy bun at the back of her head, and wisps hung across her face, which was lined and grey. Her eyes seemed dull and lifeless, and her lips lacked any colour. She was small and thin and had no teeth. She looked up as we entered.

'You wants 'a see Mr Lacey, I s'pose? I'll take you to 'im.'

She turned towards the man with the moustaches.

'Look to ve bar a bit, will yer, Mr 'arris? If anyone comes in, call me, will yer?'

She had an apologetic, deferential air about her, and her voice echoed bleakly in the bare room. The man grunted and continued sieving his beer, as he watched us over the rim of his glass.

We followed the woman up a dark, uncarpeted stairway. 'Vere's no light,' she said. 'Watch yer step.'

We entered the rooms above the bar, and she led us to the bedroom. A large, fat, pink man lay on a bed in a fair-sized room also swarming with flies. A bar-table covered in fag-ends and a rough wooden cupboard were the only other furniture. It was summer time, and a thin army blanket was thrown over the man's stomach, apart from which he was naked. The light was dim, because the sunlight struggled to penetrate the dirt on the windows.

'Is that my beer, Annie?'

'No, John, it's ve Sister's.'

'You idle, useless, woman, I told you 'a get me a beer. I don't want no bloody Sisters.'

Sister Evangelina strode across the room.

'Don't you call me a "bloody Sister", and I'll thank you to keep a civil tongue in your head. What are you doing in bed at this time of day? Sit up.'

'Who the hell are you?'

'I'm the "bloody Sister", now sit up. Go on.'

The man looked at her in astonishment and struggled to a sitting position, keeping the grey blanket carefully over his middle. The woman crept into a corner and stood there, meekly fingering her apron.

'That's better. Now what's wrong with you that a good dose of salts wouldn't clear?'

'I'm ill.' He groaned and raised his eyes to Heaven.

'Rubbish. You're fat. That's what's wrong with you. When did you last open your bowels? What you need is a good clear-out.'

'No, I'm ill. I'm in agony.' He groaned again and rubbed his hands over his chest and stomach. 'It's no use. You're too late. I'm dying.' He leaned back on the pillows and sighed weakly.

'Good riddance, if you ask me.'

The man jerked his eyes open. 'What?'

'You old fraud. You're no more dying than this young nurse here. Now what's wrong with you?'

'I got die-betes.'

'Is that all? Millions of people have cancer.'

'I'm dying, I tells ya.'

'Rubbish. Now get up. I want some of your pee to test for sugar.'

'I can't get up. I tells ya, I got DIE-betes. I'm dying yer see?'

'You'll do as you're told, and no arguments. Is there a lavatory in the flat? Right, go and fill a pot of pee. I don't want the stinking stuff, but I have to test it for sugar. Now off you go, quick. I haven't got all day.'

More from astonishment than compliance the man struggled to his feet, pulled the blanket across his middle and shuffled out of the room, his bare buttocks wobbling with every step. When he had gone Sister turned to the woman.

'Is he always like this?'

'Not never no different.'

'Never gets up?'

'No.'

'Humph. A good dose of salts and an enema up the arse is what he needs.'

''e wont like vat, 'e wont.'

'Clear his system, it would. He's all clogged up, that's the trouble with him. I don't hold with all this new-fangled medical clap-trap. Staphluses and coccuses and viruses and what have you. A good strong dose of salts and a good hot soap and water enema is all he needs to clear his system. Then there wouldn't be any more of this nonsense about being ill and dying.'

The man shuffled back into the room, groaning and rolling his eyes in a touching affectation of exhaustion. He put the chamber pot on the table and flopped into the bed.

Sister took the blood-sugar-testing equipment from her bag. With a pipette she counted ten drops of water and five drops of urine into a test tube and dropped a tablet into it. The tablet fizzed and bubbled, and the liquid turned bright orange.

'It's high in sugar, not surprising. You'll have to stop the beer and have an injection every day, twice a day.'

The man gave a howl of anguish.

'Not ve needle, oh no! I couldn't stand no needle. Never could stomach needles. I shall faint. Faint, I tells yer.'

'Well, you faint, then. Every day if you like.'

'You're 'ard,' he murmured, weakly.

Sister drew up a syringe and came towards him. The man screamed, leaped out of bed with the agility of a mountain goat and stood stark naked in the corner, whimpering. Sister advanced on him, and as he could not retreat any further, she plunged the needle into his leg and the injection was over in a second.

I heard a stifled sound from the other corner and turned. For the first time the woman's features relaxed and she giggled. I caught her eye and winked.

The man was whingeing and rubbing his leg.

'You're 'ard, I tells yer, 'ard. No pity on a man wha's never done you no 'arm.'

Sister Evangelina was unmoved.

'Cover up your balls and bits, get dressed and get on with your work in the pub.'

'I can't. I'm ill. Annie, get me a beer. I've 'ad a nasty shock.'

'Oh no, you don't. You've got to cut out the beer.'

He gave her a sly, shifty look:

'If I cuts out ve beer, will you cut out ve needle?'

'Perhaps, in time, when your blood sugar is lower.'

'Then p'raps, in time, I'll cut out ve beer.'

'You old weasle. You may be lazy, but you're not daft. Have it your own way. Kill yourself, if you want to, but don't expect any pity from me.'

With that, Sister stomped out of the room. At the door, she said, 'Expect the nurse, every morning and evening, for the needle.'

★

Bullies are always cowards. Sister Evangelina had, as usual, struck exactly the right note with her patient on the first visit. I had the thankless task of injecting Mr Lacey twice daily with insulin, and although he whined and whinged every time, he did not resist. In fact, after a few days, he assumed a heroic stance, telling me that not many men could bear such pain, and he ought to be in the medical books. With each injection, he screwed up his face into an expression of noble endurance, and when it was done he sank back on the pillows, a heap of exhausted suffering. He took himself absolutely seriously. He was both comic and contemptible.

Daily visits to the pub enabled me to get to know Mrs Lacey. Whatever time of day I called, she was always working. She did everything necessary to keep the pub running. She received the barrels of beer on delivery days, when they were rolled down the hatch into the cellar, then single-handed she rolled them across the floor and fixed them to the pumps going up to the bar. She carried crates of bottles up and down the narrow stone stairs from cellar to bar, and the crates of empties into the street for collection. She cleaned the bar room, scrubbed the tables, washed the glasses. She emptied the spitoons and cleaned the outside lavatory. She served behind the bar during opening hours when a few men sat sullenly, drinking beer. She did it all with a slow, methodical dullness as though she expected nothing else. She always looked tired, she always looked spiritless, she seldom spoke. She just carried on working, eighteen hours a day, seven days a week, 365 days a year.

The only time Mrs Lacey left the pub was to go shopping. Then she would cook a meal and take it up to her husband in bed. I had seen her cooking and told her that he must have no sweet things.

'I daren't cross 'im,' she whimpered. ''e must 'ave 'is puddings. Won't do wivout 'em.'

It was pointless trying to reason with her. The poor woman clearly lived in fear of her husband.

The same applied to his beer consumption. Visiting twice a day enabled me to see just what went on. He would thump on the floor and scream out, 'Fetch us a beer and look lively,' and she would run upstairs with a pint. The doctor, Sister Evangelina and I all told him it was making him worse, but he sneered. 'If I gets worse it's all your fault. You're supposed to get me better.' I tested his urine twice daily and kept a careful chart of his blood–sugar levels, but they were always high, and sometimes dangerously high.

Mrs Lacey looked at least twenty years older than she was. She had a cringing, apologetic way of talking, quite unlike so many Poplar women who were full of breezy self-confidence. She called me 'madam' and 'lady nurse' and asked if she could carry my bag upstairs. When I refused she said, 'But it's too heavy for a lady like you. I'll take it.' And she did. When I thanked her she looked surprised and said, 'It's good of you, madam, real kind. I don't expect no thanks. Real kind, I says. I 'preciate it, I do.' Up in the bedroom her husband shouted to her 'Put ve bag on ve table, you lazy slut, an' ge' out. I'm the one who's got to suffer ve needle to keep me from dying. Now ge' ou'.' If I had been carrying a 4-inch intramuscular needle with me that day, I would have rammed it deep into his fat buttocks and been glad to do so!

Down in the bar I said to her: 'You shouldn't let him talk to you like that.'

'Like wha', madam?'

'Calling you lazy. Telling you to get out.'

'I don' notice nuffink.'

Poor woman. She did not notice all the insults, but she had noticed a word of thanks.

The next time I called she was in the cellar, struggling to get a great barrel of beer across the floor to the pump taps. I went down to give her a hand. She was deeply troubled.

'Oh, no, no. A lady like you can't be movin' barrels o' beer. It's not righ', not fittin' like. I can do it by meself.'

I ignored her.

'You take one side, I'll take the other. We'll have the job done in no time.'

And we did. She sat down on the barrel sweating.

'It takes me twen'y minutes 'a get a barrel fixed up by meself. An' we done it in two. Oh, madam, I'm vat grateful, I am. I wish I 'ad a daughter. Every woman needs a daugh'er as she gets on.'

'Have you any children?'

'I got a boy. A lovely boy, 'e is. Bob. 'e's in Americky. 'e's doin' well, doin' nicely. I'm proud on 'im. Loves 'is ol' mum, 'e do.' She gave me a bleak smile.

We climbed the treacherous stone steps from cellar to bar and immediately heard continuous banging on the ceiling. Upstairs in the bedroom Mr Lacey was in a frenzy of rage.

'You idle, useless woman,' he shouted. 'What 'ave you been doin' all vis time, eh? Sitting around, drinkin' tea an' gossipin', that's wha'! When me, your lawful 'usband, wha's sufferin' an' dyin', wants yer. Now listen 'ere, you stupid wench, them letters you brought up. Well one of 'em is from Bob. 'e's comin' 'ome. In three weeks. Sailin' from New York, 'e is. Says 'e's got a surprise for us.'

Mrs Lacey gave a faint moan and clung to the table.

'Bob? My Bobby? Comin' 'ome? An' got a su-prise for us?'

'Yes. Three weeks. Now I shall want a new shirt an' a new pair o' trousies, an' some new socks, if you're not too idle to ge' yerself round shops an' buy me some. Now ge' on with it. I gotta suffer ve needle, an' I'm goin' 'a need all me strength to bear ve pain.'

After the injection Mr Lacey moaned, 'Bob's goin' to see wha' 'is poor old dad 'as to suffer. His poor ole dad wha' was good to 'im and sacrificed everyfing to bring 'im up proper an' give 'im a good ejication, wha's dyin' now with no one to care for 'im.' Tears of self-pity rolled down his fat cheeks.

Each time I called that week and the next, Mrs Lacey was in a flurry of excitement. Her usual slow, listless behaviour was replaced by smiling activity. She was decorating his bedroom. Paints and brushes, wallpaper, new curtains, a light shade – everything had to be perfect for her Bob. I couldn't imagine how she found the time to do it, as well as all the work of running the pub, but she did, and gladly.

One morning when I entered the private bar she was emerging from the cellar, carrying a crate of bottles. The weight was obviously as much as her strength could bear, and she let the crate down with an exhausted sigh. I was indignant.

'You shouldn't have to work so hard,' I said.

'It's better'n no work.'

She was panting and perspiring, so she wiped her face with the dirty glass cloth. She sat down on the bar stool for a moment.

'It's better'n draggin' yerself through ve streets wiv nowhere 'a go, no place to rest yer 'ead, nowhere to rest ve baby.'

I looked at her silently, wondering what she had suffered during the great depression, when there was no work for men, even those who were eager to work – and I doubted Lacey had ever been eager. She looked up, and a rare smile lit her tired features.

'An' Bobby was my baby. Bob wha's comin' 'ome next week. Comin' 'ome to 'is mum. He's a lovely boy, 'e is. Doin' well, vey say. Doin' nicely. His letter's a treat, 'e's got a good 'and. Writes real nice, 'e do. I'm vat proud, I can tell yer.'

By the beginning of the third week the room was decorated, and she wanted to show it to me. She was doubtful about the choice of curtains. Did I think he would like them? Did they match the room?

In contrast to the rest of the dreary pub, the room was bright and cheerful, and I gasped with genuine admiration when I entered and saw all that she had achieved in a fortnight. She saw my face and giggled with pleasure.

'An' ve curtains. Will 'e like 'em?'

'The curtains are lovely. I'm sure he'll be thrilled.'

'I bin sewing 'em every day sittin' behind ve bar.'

Two days later she said shyly, 'I got meself a new blouse. I mus' look me best when 'e comes. Bu' now I got it 'ome, I'm not sure. If I puts it on, will you tell me if it suits me?'

When I came down after seeing Mr Lacey, his wife was in the bar, wearing a pink blouse. It was not what is described as 'shocking pink', but any colour in that dingy brown and puce room would have been a shock. She stood nervously, biting her lip with her toothless gums.

'Is it too bright?'

I couldn't say 'yes', could I?

'It is lovely. Bob will be proud of you. You look really pretty.'

She glowed with pleasure. Had anyone ever paid her a compliment before?

'We 'ad a letter vis morning from Southampton. Ve boat come in yesterday. 'e's comin' tomorrow or ve next day, an' he'll be 'ere for three weeks. Three weeks! My Bob.'

Her voice trailed away in emotion.

'I'll 'ave to ge' vis blouse off, keep it clean. Can' 'ave it grubby afore 'e comes. An' you really like it?' She looked up wistfully. 'Really?'

For two days Mrs Lacey stood in the bar in her pink blouse, wiping the tables, serving her customers. Mr Lacey came downstairs, dressed in his new shirt and trousers, and sat at a table drinking beer and smoking Woodbines. Both of them were on edge. Many times she went out into the street and ran to the corner just to have a look. But no Bob. 'Somefink musta delayed 'im, he'll be 'ere by an' by,' she kept saying.

At eleven o'clock on the second evening, she wearily called, 'Time. Finish yer glasses. Time please,' and shut the bar. Mr

Lacey shouted, 'Fine son you got,' and went to bed. She sat at a table, her head on her arms, and wept bitterly.

On the evening of the third day the door of the bar opened, and a young man entered. He was good-looking and well dressed in a style not common in Poplar. The bar was empty.

'Hello. Anyone there?' he shouted. He was well spoken, with a slight American accent.

'Fine sort of homecoming this is – anyone there? Jeepers, what a hole! Sorry about this,' he said to his companion, a tall shapely girl with blonde hair, cut in the pageboy style. Her clothes were tight-fitting and well cut. The neckline of her jacket plunged low enough to reveal an enticing cleavage. Her shoes were high and pointed, and fine nylon stockings covered her shapely legs. Her lips were vivid red, her eyes deeply blackened, and her perfume was subtle and exotic. She was smoking, and she used a long cigarette holder.

She looked around the grimy, desolate beer-den. She looked at the flies buzzing round the light bulb. She looked at the yellowing ceiling, and at the filthy windows, and said, 'Jeez, what a dump! Is this where you were brought up?'

Bob coloured.

'Oh no, no. They've only been here eight years. They moved here after I left home. They've come down in the world, I'm sorry to say. I was brought up in a fine house in the country. We had a maid and a gardener in those days. But look, we don't have to stay if you don't want to. We could easily slip away. No one knows we're here.'

The American girl was about to speak when the door leading from the cellar was kicked open. Mrs Lacey entered the room, struggling to carry a great crate of bottles. Her attention was entirely focused on getting the crate to the bar without dropping it. She loosed her hold, and stood trembling, leaning on the bar. She was dishevelled and the dirt on her face was streaked with tears. The girl stared at her in amazement and whispered, 'Who's that?' He whispered, 'Ssshhh. Let's get out,' and made a move towards the door. But the girl's high heels made a sharp clicking sound on the floor, and the woman turned. She gave a strangled cry.

'Bob, my Bob. You've come, then. I knowed as 'ow you would. Come 'ome to yer ole muvver. My boy.'

She ran across the room and laid her dirty grey head on his clean white shirt.

'Steady on, ol' girl. Don't make a show of yourself. I said I'd come, didn't I?'

He untangled her arms from around him, and took a couple of steps backwards. She sat down on one of the chairs, leaning her arms on the table. Tears were streaming down her face, and she wiped them away with a hand covered in dust from the cellar.

'My Bobby. It's my Bob. My lad. Come 'ome.' She had not noticed the girl.

'Yes, it's me. Now pull yourself together, Mum. I said in my letter I had a surprise for you. I want to introduce you to Trudie. We are going to get married and she wanted to meet you.'

The two women stared at each other as though they were from different planets. It would be hard to say which received the greater shock. Neither spoke.

Bob said, 'Where's Dad?'

Mrs Lacey roused herself. 'Of course. Yer dad. I'll get 'im,' and she ran off upstairs.

'Is she really your mother, Bob?' enquired the girl.

''fraid so.'

He kicked the leg of a table.

'We shouldn't have come. It was a mistake.'

Footsteps were heard on the stairs, and Mr Lacey lurched into the bar. He had not shaved for two days, and his new shirt and trousers were covered in cigarette ash and beer stains. He staggered towards them and held out a hand.

'Great ter see yer, son. Welcome 'ome.'

Bob winced and took another step backwards.

'Good to see you, Dad. This is Trudie, my fiancée. I wanted you to meet her.'

The older man ogled the girl, then reeled towards her.

'Cor, not 'alf. Nice bi' of crumpet.'

He attempted to kiss her, but she jumped aside. He did not notice the expression on her face, but Bob did.

'Take a seat. Take a seat.'

Mr Lacey waved his arm, the jovial, expansive landlord.

'We'll 'ave beer'n whisky. We'll 'ave a chat, catch up on yer news, son. Sit down. This is a celebration.'

He sat down himself.

'Annie' he yelled, thumping the table. 'Annie! Where is tha' idle, stupid woman. Never there when she's wanted. Come 'ere, can'cher. We wants a drink.'

Mrs Lacey re-entered the bar. She was wearing her pink blouse, and had washed her face. She was trembling with excitement.

'Do somefink useful for a change, you lazy slu', an' ge' us some drinks, an' a packet o' crisps.'

He turned towards the girl.

'I got die-betes. I aint goin'ter live long. 'as to have a needle every day. Agony, it is. Dyin', vat's me.'

He leaned over the table and looked down her cleavage. She drew back. Bob nearly hit his father.

Mrs Lacey brought some beer and some whisky to the table.

'We don' 'ave much call fer anyfink else 'ere. Bu' I can get some rum if you prefer.'

She sat down next to Bob and shyly touched his jacket.

'My boy. My dear boy,' she whispered, gazing at him with adoring eyes.

'Well, wha' 'ave you been up to, Bob? Apart from touchin' up ve girls?'

The father leered at Trudie suggestively.

'I'm in insurance,' said Bob coldly, 'doing well. Lots of room for promotion.'

His mother stroked his arm and echoed, 'Insurance. My boy. Jes' fancy. Insurance. Yer doin' nicely, ven. I'm vat proud on yer, I am.'

Her face glowed with happiness.

The door opened, and a couple of down-at-heel men entered. Both were dirty, and a powerful smell of unwashed body odour entered with them. They stared at the four people round the table and went to sit at the far end of the room. Mrs Lacey jumped up to serve them and then came back and sat down beside Bob. She took his hand and with her forefinger traced little circles on his wrist.

'It's bin a long time. Eight years you bin in Amcricky. An' yer doin' nicely. Insurance. Cor, my boy in insurance. Wha'choo fink o' va', eh, Dad?'

'Oh, give over, Muvver. Yer daft. Bob don't wan'cher maulin' 'im. Do you, son?'

Bob couldn't answer, but he moved his hand away and looked at Trudie.

'Well, we'd better be on our way. I'm showing Trudie the old country, and we've got a tight schedule.'

'I'll cook a meal for us all. Yer room's ready. I done it special for yer,' said his mother eagerly.

'Oh no. We're not stopping. We've booked into an hotel up West, and I have dinner reservations for us tonight.'

'Not stoppin'?' Her face was blank with sorrow.

'No. There's a lot I want to show Trudie. She's never been to England before and she wants to see so much.'

'Of course. I understand.' Mrs Lacey's voice was barcly audible. She spoke to Trudie. 'You're a lucky girl. You got a good man. He's my Bob, an' he'll be a good husband. There's somefink I wanna give you, if you can wait a moment.'

She slipped upstairs.

The three round the table looked uncomfortable. The young

people looked at each other and squeezed hands under the table. The father leaned forward.

'Did I tell you I got die-betees? Killin' me, it is. Injections every day. Agony, real agony, an' I can't get no 'elp from 'er.' He jerked his thumb towards the door whence his wife had departed. He made a scornful hissing sound. 'Useless, I tells yer straight. Useless.' He coughed and retched in his throat, leaned across, pulled the spittoon towards him and spat messily into it. Trudie looked as though she was going to be sick.

Mrs Lacey returned to the table. In her hand she held a folded envelope of tissue paper. She sat down beside Trudie and opened it for the girl to see inside.

'It's for you, dear. It were Bob's, when he was a baby. I kep' it all vese years, an treasured it. Bu' now it's for you.'

She opened the paper and revealed a baby's bonnet, yellow with age, cheap lace half torn off and ribbons frayed and crumbling.

'Take it, dear. It's yourn now.'

The girl looked bewildered and muttered a quick 'Thank you'.

The young people stood up.

'Well, we must be on our way,' said Bob with forced cheerfulness. 'Nice seeing you both. Don't forget you'll always be welcome in America. It's a big country. Lots of space. There will always be a welcome for you.' And they left.

An hour or so later, Mrs Lacey was putting some crates in the street. There, in the gutter, lay the precious bonnet. She went upstairs and took off the pink blouse. She never wore it again.

THE FIGHT

A district midwife in Poplar, East London, in the 1950s could find herself in many strange and unexpected situations. It was about 7 o'clock when I reached the tenements on a cold, wet night, and a menacing sound greeted me. Two women were fighting. I had never seen such a thing before and crept closer to listen to the comments of bystanders.

The fight, apparently, was over a man. Well of course, I thought, what else would two women fight about?

It was dark, but light from some of the windows illuminated the scene sufficiently to show that both women's blouses had been torn off, and they were clawing, hitting, punching, biting and kicking each other. One had long hair, which was a great disadvantage to her, as it gave her adversary something to grab hold of. Literally hundreds of people were in the courtyard – men, women and children – shouting, jeering, cheering, egging them on. The woman with the long hair had now been forced to the ground, and the other was on top of her, banging her head against the cobblestones.

Just as I was thinking, Dear God, someone's got to stop this, I heard the piercing sound of police whistles, and two policemen rushed into the yard, wielding their truncheons to show that they meant business. Had they not come when they did, the woman on her back might have been seriously concussed, if not killed. The police were everywhere in the East End in those days, always on the beat – on foot, of course, as there were very few police cars. Within minutes at least another ten policemen had arrived, summoned by the shrill and distinctive sound of the whistle – there were no short-wave radios to connect members of the force, and the whistle was the only means of summoning help. If they heard it, police would run from every direction towards the source of the sound. Now, at the sight of the Law, the crowd disappeared.

Within less than two minutes I was alone in the courtyard with the police and the two women, who had by now been separated. The injured one was shivering and moaning in pain. The other was standing over her, held back by a young policeman; but that didn't stop her snarling and swearing and spitting at the woman on the ground.

'You'll be charged for this,' warned the officer.

'Fuck you, see if I care,' she screamed and attempted to kick him. Another prevented her, saying, 'If you attack a policeman it will be the worse for you. And if this woman dies it will be a hanging matter.'

That brought her to her senses. It had not been many years before that Ruth Ellis had been hanged for murdering her lover. The episode had shaken the nation, and memories were still very much alive. Even in the dark and rain, with filth streaked over her face, the woman seemed to turn pale.

I kneeled down on the wet cobbles to examine the other female, who lay quite still. She was soaking wet, and her long, sodden hair hung down over her face and shoulders. I examined her as best I could in the dark and said, 'The first thing we have to do is get some blankets. She is in a state of shock, and the cold will do her as much harm as the head injury. Then we must get her to hospital for an X-ray.'

She moaned, 'Nah, nah, I don' wan' no 'ospital. I'll be all right.'

It seemed terribly quiet after all the noise. There was not a soul in sight. A policeman shouted out into the night air, 'Anyone who can hear me, bring a couple of blankets.' His voice echoed around the four walls of the tenement courtyard.

A few minutes later several doors opened, and women came out carrying blankets. They gave them to us and retreated silently back to their flats, shutting the doors behind them. All the lights were off by this time, and faces that we could feel but not see were pressed against every window.

I rubbed the prostrate woman's limbs with a blanket to try to warm her, and we wrapped another one around her. Finally she sat up.

Her assailant perked up no end.

'Garn, she's all righ', the cow, she deserves more'n she got, more's the pi'y. I'd like to see 'er in 'ell.'

'We're taking you to the station,' said the young policeman.

'She started it, the fuckin' bitch.'

Then suddenly she changed her tune. Perhaps in the heat of the moment she hadn't realised that she was half-naked and surrounded by men – or maybe, in her state of undress, the idea of a police station seemed an attractive one. She sidled up to the young officer and rubbed her bare breast against his arm, giving him a lewd wink. Her shrill voice dropped about an octave and a half, and she said huskily, 'Is tha' an invitation, dearie?'

I, and most of the policemen, laughed. This dirty, rain-soaked woman trying to play Delilah looked so ridiculous. But the funniest part of all was the young policeman's reaction. He could not have been a day over nineteen, young enough to be her son. He looked pink and clean and high-minded. He glanced down at the substantial breast rubbing his arm and jumped like a scalded cat. We roared with laughter. All the faces watching at the windows must have been laughing too. The young man was covered with confusion and turned scarlet.

'Where are your clothes?' he spluttered in a prim Scottish accent. I don't suppose he meant to sound pompous and priggish, but he did.

It was a fair question, too. Where indeed were her clothes? They were scattered around the place, trodden by the crowd into the puddles. She advanced on the confused young man and with each hand lifted a huge, pendulous breast, waving her nipples in his face.

'Your guess is as good as mine, dearie.'

With a cry of alarm the young policeman leaped away. None of his colleagues was going to help him out; the scene was too good to miss. He knew he was beaten, so he grabbed a spare blanket that was lying on the ground and gave it to his tormentor.

'In the name of Heaven, woman, cover your nakedness,' he appealed to her in desperation. The other men fell about laughing. But things were getting out of hand, and the dignity of the Law had to be preserved. An older officer stepped forward.

'We are not going to charge you,' he said. 'Go to your flat, but I want your name and flat number.'

She turned sullen again. Her moment of exhibitionism over, she reluctantly gave her details.

'Now off you go, and don't let's have any more of this, or you'll be in real trouble. This is a caution.'

Then he turned to his men.

'Now all of you, back to your duties. You two stay here with the nurse and the injured woman. Report back if you need help.'

They left, suppressing their mirth and as they walked away I could hear voices saying, 'Coverr yourr nakedness, woman!' The young Scot bit his lip and looked to be on the verge of tears. He wouldn't live this moment down and he knew it.

The injured woman was sitting on the wet ground throughout this scene. As the other left, she screamed out, 'Look at 'er, the filthy slut. She's always like that, throwin 'erself around. She's no be'er than a whore. Trollop! Filth! Garbage!'

She screamed the words at the retreating figure, who made to come back and attack her again, but the second policeman barred the way.

'Now get off!' he said. 'If there's any more trouble you will be charged.'

Finally she left. The injured woman had obviously got her verbal energy back, but I was concerned about her head, having seen and heard several terrible blows as it was banged against the stones. She could easily have sustained a fracture and needed medical treatment.

I said, 'We've got to get her to hospital for an X-ray.'

'Nah! Nah!' she cried; 'I won' go to no 'ospital. Yer can't make me. I'll be all right. Jes leave me alone.'

We couldn't possibly just leave her there in the rain, so we agreed that we would take her back to her flat and then depart. She was still shaky and weak. She pulled the blanket around her, shivering. The young Scot was very kind.

'You can lean on me,' he said. 'Just show us the way, and we'll get you home.'

There were four flights of stairs to climb, and she could scarcely walk, but she managed it, grim determination forcing her on. She kept muttering 'no 'ospital, no 'ospital.' I think it was the dread of hospitals, and the fear that if she stumbled and fell she would be forcibly carried to one, that kept her going.

The long walk around the balconies seemed interminable. I could see faces pressed against the windows which vanished as we drew close. One little boy's face remained as we passed, and a hand shot out and snatched him back. I heard a curse, a heavy slap and a yelp of pain. I winced for the child. He was only being curious.

When we got to her door, the woman refused to let us come in with her.

'Nah, get orf,' she said, 'bleed orf. I'll be all right.'

We left, and I never saw her again. Women were tough in those days, really tough. Perhaps this woman was so used to violence that it had become part of life. Perhaps some kind neighbour took care of her for a few days. If she did have a hairline fracture of the skull, it mended in its own time and with no assistance from the doctors.

A charge was not brought against either woman. For one thing the injured woman made no official complaint, and for another personal fights in those days were common. Police just separated the adversaries and, unless some other crime was involved, charges were seldom made.

Such scenes were no surprise to the Sisters, I discovered, when, full of the importance of my story, I related it at luncheon the following day. The nuns had seen it all before, and sometimes a great deal worse. It was a violent area. However – and we all agreed on this – overall we saw far more goodness and kindness and open-handed generosity than the opposite.

On reflection it was surprising there was not more violence in the tenements, because people lived so close to each other. There was no privacy, no chance of solitude, seldom even quiet. Nerves must frequently have been stretched to breaking point within the family and between neighbours. Domestic violence was regarded as a fact of life. Even in the 1950s it was accepted that men beat their wives. We often saw women with bruises or black eyes, or limping. They never complained to the police: 'keep out o' the way o' coppers' was the rule. They may have talked about it among themselves, but in an attitude of resignation, rather than complaint. Times were changing, however, and the younger women, those of the post-war generation, were certainly developing more independence. But the older women accepted it all. The saying was 'If 'e don't beat yer, 'e don't love yer.' Twisted logic if ever there was some, but it was a belief widely held on to.

Life was not easy for the men either. They worked desperately hard and were accustomed to harsh treatment from their employers – it was just accepted as an aspect of their employment. The majority of Poplar men were dockers, and traditionally dockers were treated as beasts of burden, and expendable at that. Such treatment would brutalise any man. Yet the vast majority were not brutes; they were decent hardworking blokes who brought home most of their money to their wives and tried to live as good husbands and fathers. But, for all their hard work, they did not seem to get much peace or comfort in their homes, because of the overcrowding and too many children. What man, after ten or twelve hours of hard manual labour, would look forward to returning home to two or three small rooms with half a dozen kids running around? It was a matriarchal society, and 'home' was for women and children. The men were often made to feel like outsiders in their own homes.

Consequently the men spent most of their time in each other's company – all day at work and in the evenings meeting their mates at the Working Men's Clubs, the numerous Seamen's Clubs, the dog races, football, speedway and pubs. Pub life was convivial and provided the welcome and good cheer that home so frequently did not. Pubs also provided alcohol, which relaxed tired muscles, soothed frayed tempers and consoled the yearning for hopes and dreams long since abandoned.

THE MASTER'S ARMS

Oh what can ail thee, knight-at-arms,
Alone and palely loitering?
The sedge has withered from the lake,
And no birds sing.

I see a lily on thy brow,
With anguish moist and fever-dew,
And on thy cheek a fading rose
Fast withereth too.
'La Belle Dame Sans Merci', by John Keats

The Master's Arms in Poplar had seen much history in its hundred years. It was a freehold, started by old Ben Masterton in 1850, and passed from father to son over four generations. Many of the big breweries had tried to buy the family out, but they were a stubborn lot, the Mastertons, and in spite of the difficulties of running a freehold, not to mention the financial insecurity, they had always refused to sell, preferring shaky independence to safe wage earning. It was said that old Ben, with his one sound leg and one wooden one, had fallen off a trading vessel when drunk, and the ship had sailed away without him. He had nothing else to do but indulge his favourite activity, so he started a drinking house, which became a firm favourite among the seamen. He married a local girl who enjoyed the bawdy life, and she bore fourteen children, six of whom survived childhood. Old Ben ultimately expired in an alcoholic stupor, as everyone had said he would, and two of his sons took over the business, at the time of the economic depression in the 1880s, when it was nearly impossible to get work in the docks, and thousands starved as a result. In times of hardship pubs always flourish, and people will always drink, whatever the suffering of their families.

When the Jack the Ripper furore broke out in 1888, and the area became the centre for ghoulish visitors, the two brothers decided to expand their cramped premises, smarten up the dingy interior and put a few macabre pictures and posters on the walls proclaiming: 'This is where it all happened.' The visitors flocked in, and one of the two brothers led a guided tour of all the murder spots, with grisly details of how the killings were done, embellished for the shivering delight of the crowd, who then returned to the pub for suitable refreshment. Business was looking good.

The pub took on a life of its own after that and became well known for its landlords, its warmth and hospitality and its easy-going atmosphere. Every pub was easy-going in those days, but there were limits to how easy the going should be, and the brothers set the tone. There was to be no fighting, no child prostitution, no illegal gambling, or money handling and no opium smoking. Again the Masterton brothers were successful, and the pub flourished.

In the year that Queen Victoria died, one of the brothers died also. His funeral was less spectacular than the Queen's but lavish enough by Poplar standards, and was enjoyed by all. There's nothing like a good East End funeral to raise the spirits, and the Master's Arms opened its generous doors to patrons after the church solemnities. The surviving brother decided to hang up his boots and pass the freehold on to his son, who ran the pub efficiently for twenty-five years throughout the Edwardian period, the disaster of the 1914-18 War and the chaos of the years that followed. It was he who bought a piano, found a piano-player and introduced the communal sing-songs. He did so because of the misery of the times, with the hope that it would cheer people up to have a good sing – or a good cry if need be. The sing-songs and dancing became a feature of the Master's Arms, and, try as they might, no other pub in the area could rival the Arms for their Saturday night entertainment.

In 1926, the year of the great General Strike, when most

industry in Britain was forced to close, Bill Masterton's father died, and he, fourth generation, took over the Master's Arms. He was a thick-set man, a little above average height, with great strength and phenomenal energy. He could work any other man into the ground without breaking sweat. He had a good, practical intelligence, ideal for running a small business, and was known by all as the Master. He was married to an Essex girl, who had not expected a pub life when she married a self-employed carter, and she never really settled down in Poplar or took to the life. Bill once persuaded her to act as barmaid, but she hated it so much that he said she would drive the customers away with her miserable face. Relieved, she devoted her time to her children.

Oliver, her eldest, was the joy of her heart, resembling his good-looking father in appearance, but with a more loving nature. Julia, her second, was a bit of a mystery; she was a solemn little girl who never said much, and children who don't talk always make grown-ups feel uneasy. But Mrs Masterton had plenty to do with the three younger boys, who tumbled and romped all over the place. Then she found herself pregnant again, and a little girl was born, as pretty a baby as you could wish for. They called her Gillian. Her husband seemed to like the last baby, which was a surprise to the newly delivered mother. He had not taken much notice of the others, always saying, 'The children are your concern. You look after them – I'll look after the money. Can't say fairer than that.'

And indeed he couldn't. He worked hard, and the pub was profitable. Mrs Masterton was never short of money, unlike so many Poplar women. She did not want to see her children growing up like the Cockney kids and with a Cockney accent, so, when the time came, they all went to a small private school outside the borough. Her husband grumbled, but paid the term's fees for each child, saying, 'You know best when it comes to the kids. Let's hope it's worth the money.' Husband and wife rubbed along together, each with their own role, but with little communication or understanding. 'You're more interested in your pub than your children,' grumbled Mrs Masterton sometimes. 'Don't be daft,' her husband remarked, 'what do you expect me to do – change nappies? Ha, ha, I should think! Anyway they're all right, aren't they? Doing nicely. What more do you want?'

Julia was nine when her older brother started coughing. 'It's a winter cold,' said his mother and rubbed his chest with Vick. But the cough continued. 'It will go in the spring,' said the mother and applied a flannel jerkin under his school clothes. But the cough did not go away.

Oliver wanted to be chosen for the school football team. He practised his kicking and passing skills resolutely; the cough was a nuisance. He didn't really feel ill, and he didn't see why it should interfere with his soccer career. When he started coughing up thick, yellowish phlegm, he spat into a bit of paper and put it in the dustbin. He didn't tell his mother. Mothers fussed so, and he wasn't going to be fussed. Not him. He was going to be captain of the team.

When his mother found blood on his pillow one morning, she was very alarmed. She questioned him about his health, but he said he felt all right. Nonetheless she called the doctor, who on examining the child suspected tuberculosis and advised an X-ray and a pathology lab analysis of his sputum. Both results confirmed the presence of tuberculosis. As a precaution, the doctor arranged for all other members of the family to be X-rayed, but they were all pronounced clear. He also arranged for Oliver to be removed immediately from school because, he told the parents, the boy would probably infect other children. He would be sent to a special school attached to Colindale Sanatorium in North London. He would have to reside there, and he would have the latest and best medical treatment available.

Oliver was deeply distressed. What about his football, and the athletics team he had joined? The doctor tried to explain that sports were played at the new school, but nothing would console the child. His mother was distressed for other reasons. Her adored eldest son, her pride and joy, was being sent away, and although she could visit him, it was small consolation.

Oliver stayed for about six months at Colindale. He settled down and began to enjoy himself. The country air suited him, and all summer he played games and appeared to improve greatly. His mother was delighted, and was given permission by the doctors to take him away for a summer holiday by the sea. 'It will do him good,' they all said. Hope is so important during illness. But he never got as far as the sea. He never left Colindale. 'Le Belle Dame Sans Merci' had him in thrall.

Oliver died, and the family was thrown into a state of shock. The poor mother nearly went demented with grief, and it seemed as though she would never raise herself again. The father became very quiet and withdrawn, but opened the pub as usual.

Whenever Julia thought of that first death – her big brother, whom she had idolised – she was filled with anger and disgust. The family rooms were over the pub, and the child was lying in an open coffin for family and neighbours to come in and pay their respects. The children, aged from two to nine, were subdued and sad, their mother was weeping all the time, while their father said nothing. Women, some known to the children, some strangers, came in with flowers and small gifts. They laid their posies on the young body and sniffed. 'You'll have to bear up, Amy. Think of the others,' they said. Her mother wept and could not answer. The women crept downstairs, leaving the family with their loss. And all the time the noise from the pub was rending the quiet. The piano was pounding out popular songs, raucous voices were singing 'Pack up yer troubles in yer old kit bag and smile, smile, smile'. The stamp of feet shook the table on which the coffin was laid. The shrieks and screams of half-drunken voices continued until late evening, after which there came peace, which the poor mother yearned for. One night Julia went into the room and sat with her mother in the blessed quiet. They fell asleep together in the armchair. 'You are my comfort,' said her mother and stroked her hair.

The day of the funeral was a nightmare. It took place on Whitsun Bank Holiday. Julia's mother had begged her father not to open the pub that day, but he refused. There was a terrible row, and the children cowered in the attic, terrified. Their mother and grandmother and aunts all went at him, telling him to show some respect, but still he would not change his mind. 'Business must go on,' he shouted, as he ran downstairs to open up. On bank holidays, pubs could be open from 10 a.m. until the small hours of the morning and always did good business.

The hearse drew up at the back of the pub while crowds of excited holiday-makers were pouring in the front. The mother had wanted a horse-drawn funeral cortège for her eldest son, but it turned out to be a fiasco. The coffin was reverently carried downstairs and placed in the carriage, but at that moment a group of excited youths emerged from the pub and staggered round the corner, closely chased by four shrieking girls. The high-pitched voices frightened the horses, one of them reared, and this was the signal for panic among the other three. They bucked and lunged in all directions. The funeral directors lost their solemn demeanour and started shouting and pulling on reins and bridles in a desperate effort to prevent the carriage overturning. The coffin could be heard crashing against the wooden panels of the carriage. The group of mourners wearing black, the women veiled and the children carrying flowers, were distressed and terrified.

The horses eventually calmed down and the funeral was conducted calmly, but with frozen silence between Julia's mother and father. Neither tried to comfort the other for the loss of their first-born. Immediately after the ceremony, her father said, 'I must get back to the Arms; it's going to be a busy day. Are you coming, Amy?' She shook her head, 'I can't go back to that noise, not feeling as I do.' 'Please yourself,' he replied and walked off. The family stayed out all day, and most of the evening, but finally they had to return because the little children were tired and crying. The noise from the pub was deafening as they drew near, and a crowd of half-drunk holiday-makers grabbed Mrs Masterton and tried to get her to join in the dancing. With difficulty she tore herself away and shepherded her children upstairs, then slammed and bolted the door. The singing reached a crescendo at about eleven o'clock with 'Hands, knees and boompsey-daisy, let's make the party a wow, wow-wow'. Men and women clapped, slapped their knees and then banged their bottoms together to shrieks of laughter and cat-calls and lewd whistles. As it was a Bank Holiday, the grieving family had to endure several hours more of the high jinks.

That was just the first death. Even though they had been screened and pronounced clear, one after another the three younger boys contracted the disease. The distraught mother nursed them. Two went to Colindale Sanatorium, but came home to die when the doctors said that there was nothing more that could be done. Julia could never forget the years spent with the hush of death upstairs and the din of drunkenness downstairs. Her mother seemed to be numb with grief, and her father increasingly morose and silent, but each time he said, 'Business as usual,' and opened the pub. This caused tension between husband and wife, giving rise to terrible quarrels as each vented their anger and frustration on the other.

The last remaining boy was nine when he first showed signs of weight loss, fainting and sweating. He did not cough, but the doctor advised Mrs Masterton to take him away to the country to get more fresh air. They went to Skegness, where the sea air is bracing, so they say.

Mrs Masterton took Gillian with them also. 'Just to be on the safe side,' she told her family and friends. She did not consult her husband. By then, husband and wife were barely on speaking terms. Gillian was the youngest, and her father's favourite. She was a pretty, affectionate child, and she adored her father, who spoiled her shamefully. He had paid six months' advance rental on a cottage by the sea and had assumed that just his wife and youngest son were going. They left during pub hours whilst Mr Masterton was working, and it was not until later in the day, when Gillian did not return from school, that he realized with a shock that she had gone.

The impact was terrible. He had not reckoned that women could be so devious. He was filled with rage and his first instinct was to take the next train to Skegness and bring the girl back. But he was an intelligent man. After closing the pub that night he sat in his office to brood, head in hands. He felt hot tears coming, so he locked the door – he didn't want anyone to see signs of weakness. Perhaps she was right. They had lost three boys, and now the fourth was showing signs of illness. He slumped over his desk and bit his lip until he tasted blood. If his Gillian, his pretty little girl, died, he felt he would die also. She was better off by the sea, away from the foul London air. She would be back in six months, and her chatter and laughter would fill his heart again.

Julia stayed at home with her father. She was sixteen and doing well at school, coming up to her School Certificate, which her teachers were confident she would pass with Matriculation. Father and daughter were left alone together.

The relationship was tricky. Julia had never liked her father and felt that he did not like her. In reality they had both suffered from the fact that they were too similar in temperament. In particular, neither of them could talk much, which was a great disadvantage. Both of them imagined that the other was looking at them with some sort of malign thought, whereas each one was actually trying desperately to think of something meaningful to say. So long periods of silence existed between them, each wanting to break the ice, but not knowing how to do so.

They were both intelligent, but the gulf widened because they each had a different type of mind. His was entirely practical and instinctive, whilst hers was becoming increasingly academic. She would be doing her homework, and he would pick up a book and say 'What's this?'

'Algebra.'

'What's that?'

'A branch of mathematics.'

'You mean arithmetic?'

'Yes, if you like.'

'Looks like a load of rubbish.'

'Well it's not. It's beautiful.'

'Beautiful! What do you mean?'

And so it went on. The publican spent just about all his time immersed in his business, and Julia spent all her time at school, in the public library, or doing her homework. Each of them, father and daughter, were locked into their own worlds of loneliness and unhappiness.

But the young can be perceptive beyond their years. Although she said little, or perhaps *because* she spoke little, Julia observed, absorbed and interpreted everything. She began to think that her father was not as indifferent as he appeared to be. She and her mother wrote to each other every week. Mrs Masterton never wrote to her husband, but every time a letter arrived from Skegness her father was eager to know the news.

'How are the children, are they doin' all right?' and he grunted with satisfaction at the weekly good news. Once he shyly handed to Julia some pretty hair ribbons and a child's bolero. 'It's Gillian's birthday. Send this to her, will you? I hope it's the right size.' He kept on repeating, 'I hope I got the size right. The woman in the shop said it would fit. It's pretty, don't you think? Do you think she'll like it?' Nervously he repeated the doubts and questions several times. When a picture done with coloured crayons and a letter in childish print arrived for him he seemed happier than Julia had ever seen him. She was surprised and saw her father with new eyes, but still she could not speak openly to him. Neither of them had ever shown any affection towards the other, and it was impossible now that he was so completely turned in on himself and his business, and she was verging on adulthood, expanding her mind and emotions to the world beyond the Master's Arms.

Six months passed, and the boy seemed to be completely better after the summer at the seaside. The family returned home, and Mr Masterton had his little girl again.

Julia watched them together and was amazed at the liberties he allowed. Gillian would sit on his knee at breakfast and dip bread-and-butter soldiers into his boiled egg – something it would have been unthinkable for any of the other children to do. He brushed her hair and tied a ribbon in it. He seemed to notice the little boy more too, and was kind to him. 'You did right,' he said to his wife with grudging respect. 'They are glowing with health.'

But tuberculosis is cruel. A person can contract the disease, and the bacillus will lie dormant for years, sometimes for a whole lifetime, and the host will not even know it is there. At other times it can strike and kill within months or even weeks – that sort used to be called galloping consumption. The little boy came home from school with a temperature. His mother put him straight to bed and called the doctor. He was transferred to the sanatorium and given all the treatment known at the time. But, three months later, the doctors advised that there was nothing more that could be done for him, and he would be happier if he came home to die.

Grief again gripped the family with cold, grey hands. The boy was laid out in the parlour, like his brothers before him, and family and friends came to pay their respects. 'You've got your girls to comfort you,' they said to the weeping mother. 'It always strikes the boys first. It's their constitution, see.' Mrs Masterton did not ask her husband to close the pub; she knew it would be useless. 'I'll come to the funeral,' he said, 'In the meantime, business as usual.' Daytimes were quiet enough, but each evening the racket started. 'I hate the pub,' said Mrs Masterton, who looked more like sixty than forty. 'So do I,' said Julia. 'With all my heart, I hate it.'

Julia passed her School Certificate with Matriculation. She had but one longing – to leave home. But it was not easy for young girls in the 1930s. Britain was in the grip of the Great Depression, opportunities for girls were few, and wages were very low. She wanted to continue her studies, but could not do so without money. It should have been possible; the pub was profitable and her father was not hard up, but she did not feel she could ask him to finance a college course. She discussed it with her mother, who said, 'You must ask your father,' but so wide was the gulf between father and daughter that she could not bring herself to say a word. So, in the end, she applied to the Post Office for telegrapher's training. She went to Leytonstone, which was more genteel than Poplar but less interesting, and lived in a hostel for girls.

She was lonely, very lonely. She never felt herself to be one of the girls. She always felt apart from them, separated by something inside her that she could not understand. She developed the habits of an observer, sitting on the outside of a group of giggling girls, watching, but quite unable to join in their light-hearted chatter. This was not popular. At different times several girls demanded, 'What are you looking at us for?' to which she had no answer. They proclaimed her stuck-up. She was friendly, in a superficial way, with several of the girls, but had no real friends. Once she did venture out with a crowd of girls, and afterwards vowed never again! The greatest part of her time, when she was not working, she spent in the public library, and she read everything available – history, novels, theology, travel, science fiction, poetry – literally anything she could lay her hands on. The world of books extended her mind and compensated for the dull routine of the telephone exchange. She dared not leave her job because in the depression of the 1930s she was lucky to have a job at all.

She did not really enjoy the work, either. She applied herself, but knew in her heart that, intellectually, it was beneath her. The superintendent was a bitch, and seemed to pick on Julia, perhaps because she was different, and tried to make her life a misery. It was not a happy time, but at least she was away from the foul atmosphere at home between her mother and father, away from the riotous revelry of the pub, and away from the figure of death that seemed to stalk every room. She would put up with anything rather than go back.

Each week mother and daughter corresponded. Neither of them had much to say in their letters, but it kept them in touch. The best news was always that Gillian was well, doing nicely at school, was friends with the vicar's daughter, was going on a Sunday School outing, and so on. The mother said little about herself, and nothing about her husband.

Then came the terrible news that Gillian was unwell. The vicar was praying for her. The doctor had been called. A sanatorium was advised. The mother went with the child, and the husband rented a small cottage for his wife so that she could be near. The sanatorium came highly recommended, but then they heard that the air in Switzerland would be better. Santa Limogue in the Alps achieved a very good cure rate, it was said. So a place was booked, and Gillian and her mother crossed the Channel in the middle of winter by sea, then were conducted by train to the haven of miracle cures for tuberculosis. But the journey, lasting two days and nights, was too much for the child, and she died shortly after arrival.

Julia wept. Her family was cursed. She hid her tears under the bedclothes in the dormitory where she slept with twenty other girls, and during the day she was more silent than ever. She wrote a long, grieving letter to her mother, for the first time opening her heart to her, which to her surprise she found liberating. She wrote a brief letter to her father but could not think what to say. She remembered him with little Gillian on his knee, as she dipped soldiers into his boiled egg; she remembered the present of hair ribbons and a bolero. But still she could not think of what to say to him. So in the end she sent a few words on half a sheet of notepaper, to which he sent no reply.

The funeral took place in Switzerland. The mother returned home, but after a few months she left her husband to live with a sister in Essex. Correspondence continued between mother and daughter, and they met every so often and had a day out together. The father continued to run the pub, but they never corresponded, and Julia never visited. In spite of loneliness, which had become a way of life for Julia, she did not regret leaving home. The memories of drunken revelry repelled her, and thoughts of death haunted her.

No, she would never, she vowed, never go back to the Master's Arms.

TUBERCULOSIS

Youth grows pale, and sceptre-thin, and dies.
'Ode to a Nightingale', by John Keats

Tuberculosis is as old as mankind. Evidence of the disease has been found in a Neolithic burial ground near Heidelberg, Germany and in mummies from Egyptian tombs 1000 years BC; and Hindu writings refer to 'a consumption'. Hippocrates used the word *phthisis* to describe the cough, wasting, and ultimate destruction of the lungs. The disease is universal, and bears no relation to climate. It has been found in native tribes of North America, in primitive African tribes and amongst the Inuits of Alaska; China, Japan, Australia, Russia, Corsica, Malaya, Persia have all known it. There is probably no tribe or nation on earth that has been free from tuberculosis.

The disease has waxed and waned throughout recorded history, usually starting unnoticed, then reaching epidemic proportions, then waning as the population acquires collective immunity to the tubercle bacillus, over approximately a 200-year cycle. In Europe and North America it reached epidemic proportions between around 1650 to 1850 (varying somewhat from nation to nation), and it has been confidently concluded by medical scientists and historians that at the height of an epidemic 90 per cent of any population would have been infected. Of this number 10 per cent would have died. The lungs are the main focus of the bacillus, but they are not the only target; the meninges, bones, kidneys, liver, spine, skin, intestines, eyes – practically all human tissue and organs can be and have been destroyed by tuberculosis. It was called 'the Great White Plague of Europe'.

Historically, the highest morbidity from tuberculosis occurred between the ages of fifteen and thirty. Throughout European literature of the eighteenth and nineteenth centuries the tremendous creative outburst of the 'Sturm and Drang' writers and poets of the Romantic movement dominated the public imagination. Today we look back on their sickly characters, amazed at apparently healthy young women fainting and going into a terminal decline, or languorous youths too weak to do anything much except sit around looking pale and interesting and writing poetry. But this was no morbid fantasy. Lassitude, weakness, weariness, loss of weight and colour were common amongst the young, and they were early signs of infection, unrecognised by most people. By the time coughing, fever and lung haemorrhage occurred the condition was called consumption, and it was too late for effective treatment. The flower of youth was gathered in its prime.

From ancient times there has been a belief that some relationship exists between tuberculosis and genius. The intellectually gifted are the more likely to contract the disease, and the fire which consumes the body makes the mind burn more brightly. Throughout Europe in the eighteenth and nineteenth centuries, the idea was fostered in the public imagination that consumption was the product of a sensitive nature and a creative imagination. Did not famous musicians, poets, painters and authors die from consumption? The tenuous connection was widely accepted with gratitude by those grieving the death of an only son or a beloved daughter. Grief needs an outward expression, and if a mother can interpret a few morbid poems written by her dying son as evidence of a genius snatched too soon from the world, she is somewhat comforted.

Indeed the immense creativity of this period of European history might have been an indirect product of tuberculosis. Opium was widely prescribed for the control of coughing, and it has been said that many consumptives who could afford it were addicted to opium. Many drugs are hallucinogenic, but not all arouse creativity as opium does.

★

Dwellers in the cold North assumed that grey skies, foggy winters and biting winds caused tuberculosis. Therefore the consumptive rich flocked in droves to Southern climates, trying to escape the cold North, but to little avail. They carried the seed of death with them and spread it amongst their hosts. In the South of France, Nice, once a pretty fishing village, suddenly became fashionable. Hotels were built, and filled with cadaverous consumptives, ghostly pale, with sunken features and haunted eyes. It was said that performances at the Opera House could not be heard above the sound of coughing and spitting! Rich Americans fled south to Florida and New Mexico to beg of the sun a last ray of hope. But the sun had no healing powers to cure advanced galloping consumption; in fact, exposure to the sun could have a negative effect.

Medical advice changed. Mountain air was prescribed – desert air, sea air, tropical air, moist air, dry air, gentle winds, fierce winds, no wind. Consumptives who could afford to do so journeyed hither and thither in vain. By the end of the eighteenth century it was obvious to everyone that tuberculosis did not respond to any climatic conditions, and respected no geographical boundaries.

Medical science was in its infancy, and treatments were rudimentary. The unpredictability of the course and outcome of tuberculosis had always baffled doctors – some consumptives died within months of contracting the disease, others recovered spontaneously with no treatment, whilst some lived a long and active life with intermittent bouts of debility. The sick begged for treatment; anything that might offer a glimmer of hope was clutched with shaking hands. But the outcome of the treatment was as unpredictable as the disease itself, and probably had little effect upon the course of the illness anyway. Despite that, one fashionable treatment followed another. Bleeding and blistering were common, as were leeches, plasters and poultices, cuppings and inhalations. Lifestyle was tackled, and various courses advised: vigorous exercise, such as skiing, riding, walking, or sea bathing sometimes helped. Deep breathing was advocated, also flute playing and singing. Other physicians insisted that rest was essential – total bed rest for months or years on end, often in an enclosed, heated room in which it was forbidden to open a window. Elizabeth Barrett lay in bed for years until Robert Browning romantically carried her off to Italy, where she spontaneously recovered!

Diet is important in any illness, and dietary fads followed each other with bewildering speed. Some physicians advised extreme abstention – a starvation diet we would call it today – and the Brontë sisters almost certainly suffered from malnutrition, imposed by their father and his medical advisers. Others went for diets rich in meat, offal, warm animal blood, fat, cream, fish, eggs and milk – asses' milk, goat's milk, camel milk, sheep's milk and human milk (still favoured in the United States in 1900). All have had their day.

Drug therapy was almost non-existent. Ancient herbal remedies existed in every culture or tribe from time immemorial, some of which would ease symptoms, but none of which could destroy the tubercle bacillus. In the eighteenth and nineteenth centuries digitalis, quinine and mercury were used, although the universal balm and comforter was opium.

The great flaw in all treatments was the fact that the highly contagious nature of tuberculosis was not recognised. No special precautions in the care of a dying consumptive were advised by physicians. Quite the contrary, a hot stuffy room, with windows never opened, was favoured. Many are the testimonies of a loving parent or sibling who spent whole days and nights in the same room, and often in the same bed, as the sufferer. Millions of people who showed no signs of disease were carriers.

If all the money in the world could not protect the rich from the ravages of tuberculosis, what became of the labouring poor? Not for them the luxury of hotels in southern France or Alpine Switzerland, or even the cost of a doctor. They could barely afford an aspirin, or a day off work. Loss of work could spell destitution, so they laboured on until they died.

In industrial cities, firstly in England and later throughout Europe and America, crowded into factories and workshops, cold, half-starved men, women and children laboured for twelve or more hours a day in enclosed, foetid conditions and returned at night to tenement dwellings the sanitary conditions of which were beyond our imaginings. Infection would have passed with rampant speed from one sad individual to another, made more livid and virulent by the physical debility of the victim, caused by overwork and malnutrition.

In previous centuries all over Europe, child labour was the norm. From 1750 onwards, in industrial Europe, children were confined in closed, ill-ventilated rooms, working up to twelve hours a day. The Royal Commission on Child Labour in Manufacture of 1843 described children of seven and eight years as ... 'stunted in growth, pale and sickly; the diseases most prevalent are disorders of the nutritive system, curvature of the spine, deformity of the limbs, and diseases of the lungs, ending in consumption'. The number of deaths from tuberculosis amongst these children may not even have been recorded. They were child paupers, frequently gleaned from workhouses, unwanted, unprotected, endlessly expendable.

In the enclosed workhouses of Britain, where inmates were confined and not allowed out, contagion would have been a continuous fact of life. The only record I have been able to find of the incidence of tuberculosis in a workhouse was from one in Kent, where in 1884 it was recorded that *all* of the seventy-eight boy inmates suffered from tuberculosis, and that amongst ninety-four girls only three could be found who were not infected. It has not been recorded how many of these workhouse children died, but many would have. Undoubtedly the worse the living conditions, the worse the effects of the tuberculosis bacillus. In the Jewish ghetto of Vienna, at the height of the epidemic, it was recorded that 100 per cent of the dwellers were affected, of whom 20 per cent died. The rich Viennese were terrified to go anywhere near the area.

For the poor, consumption was not the romantic image of pale, wasting youth. It was not the occasion to lie in bed for months on end, writing long, sad poems. It did not lead to extended travel abroad. No, indeed; for the labouring poor consumption was the great killer, the breeder of destitution, the father of orphaned children.

While the highest mortality from tuberculosis occurred in young adults, children also died. In the graveyard of Burton on the Welsh Borders, where my father and grandparents are buried, can be found the tragic memorial to ten children from one family who died between the ages of six months and twelve years from 'wasting consumption'. The composer Gustav Mahler was one of fourteen children, seven of whom died of tuberculosis. The Masterton family, whose tragic story I tell, were not the only ones with such a history. In the tenements of Poplar lived the parents of six children, all of whom, I was told, had died of consumption. The prevalent sadness of the parents is, to this day, alive in my memory.

Contagion – the possibility of the spread of disease from one person to another by some unseen agent, but especially by breath – was not part of medical thinking at the time. Consumption was considered to be an hereditary malformation of the lungs, and the fact that so many families were consumptive lent weight to this theory. Strangely, the equally observable fact that, inside closed religious orders, where monks and nuns were not related, up to 100 per cent could be found to be infected, did not prompt physicians to pursue another line of thought.

However, in 1722 an English physician, Benjamin Marten, published a paper postulating that 'a species of animalculae, or wonderfully minute living creatures, capable of subsisting in our bodies, may be fretting and gnawing at the vessels of the lungs'. The idea was considered so preposterous that the medical thinkers of the time refused to believe it. Had Marten's hypothesis been accepted, and proper isolation and decontamination procedures been adopted, the Great White Plague of Europe might never have occurred.

In 1882, the German scientist Robert Koch, in a home-made laboratory, isolated the tuberculous bacillus for the first time and demonstrated by animal experiments that the bacillus was responsible for the disease that had baffled generations of researchers and medical thinkers. He also demonstrated that the bacillus could cross from man to animals and vice versa, thus proving that milk from tuberculous cows could infect human beings, especially children.

From that time onwards, massive public health programmes were ordered in all European countries and in America. The public were instructed in the facts of infection and contagion, which were completely new concepts for them to grasp. The strange and novel process of sterilisation had to be taught. Limiting the spread of infection was the order of the day, and this continued for nearly eighty years.

Pasteurisation of milk was started in the 1920s. This was nearly forty years after Koch had demonstrated the cross-infection from animals to humans, but even then a great many people would not believe it and refused to buy pasteurised milk. TB testing of cattle was at first voluntary for farmers, but became obligatory in the 1930s. In the 1920s large notices saying 'SPITTING PROHIBITED' were displayed in all public buildings, meeting places, and on public transport – and these notices were still displayed in the 1950s and '60s. All pubs and private bars, such as those in golf and tennis clubs, had a spittoon in the bar.

Consumptives were removed from the workplace; even the idle rich were no longer free to wander around the South of France infecting others; they had to be treated in isolated sanatoria. Medical and nursing staff were specialists. Strict barrier nursing of TB patients was undertaken, and TB nurses did not enter general hospitals. A consumptive parent was removed from his or her children. A consumptive child was removed from school. Due to these measures tuberculosis, which had terrorised Europe, began to lose its grip.

The possibility of vaccination was considered. Vaccination against infectious disease was first developed in 1796 by Edward Jenner, who had observed the link between cow-pox and human smallpox. In the 1880s, when Robert Koch discovered the tuberculous bacillus, he held out great hopes that a vaccine could be prepared from dead tuberculous bacilli. This should have gone well, but, in the early use of the treatment, tragedy struck. A batch of the vaccine had been improperly prepared, and living bacilli were injected into a large group of children, all of whom contracted tuberculosis, and many of whom died. This disaster halted the use of a vaccine for over sixty years, and a safe and effective treatment had to wait until the 1950s, when the BCG (Bacillus-Calmette-Guerin) strain became available for the prevention of tuberculosis.

But a vaccine is preventative, not curative for those already infected. In the first half of the twentieth century many curative drugs were developed and used. In the 1930s sulphanilamide was tried; in the 1940s para-animo-salicylic acid; in the 1950s streptomycin was the first of the antibiotics to be introduced, and this one saved millions of lives.

X-rays were invented as long ago as 1895, and could determine the extent of the disease. Surgery was attempted, and by the 1930s was relatively well advanced, from removal of a whole lung to removal of one or more diseased lobes of the lungs. Thoracoplasty and artificial pneumo-thorax, aimed at resting the lungs, was attempted in the 1890s and developed throughout the early part of the twentieth century.

But it was the public health programmes carried out over eighty years that were chiefly responsible for success, and by the end of the 1960s tuberculosis was no longer a major cause of death in European countries and America.

★

We, the favoured few of the twenty-first century, do not, cannot know the dreadful impact that tuberculosis had in days gone by. Let us be thankful for the advance in medical knowledge, and let us strive to extend it worldwide.*

---

* This essay is not intended as a medical analysis of tuberculosis. I am not a doctor and did not train as a tuberculin nurse. It is merely intended to provide an historical background to the story of the Masterton family, for those who may be interested. My main source of information has been the book *The White Plague* by René and Jean Dubois, published in 1953 by Victor Gollancz Ltd.

THE MASTER

And there she lulled me asleep
And there I dreamed – Ah! Woe betide! –
The latest dream I ever dreamt
On the cold hill side.
'La Belle Dame Sans Merci', by John Keats

They were having tea in Lyon's Corner House in The Strand. They usually met there. Mrs Masterton liked the atmosphere. Refined, she called it. It was their usual afternoon out, once a month. Mrs Masterton poured the tea.

'They tell me your father's ill,' she said abruptly.

'Dad? Ill? I didn't know.'

'I heard it from our milkman, whose brother is a cab driver. Cabbies get to know everything. He said the Master of the Master's Arms in Poplar is ill. That's all I know.'

'What's wrong?'

'I don't know.'

'Have you seen him?'

'No. That's why I wanted to talk to you, Julia. When did you last see him?'

'Some years ago. I'm not sure.'

'There was no rift, or anything, between you? No harsh words, nothing like that?'

'No. We never quarrelled. We just barely spoke. I never knew what he was thinking. I always thought he was giving me funny looks. I don't know why. Perhaps he wasn't. I don't know. He loved Gillian, but he never loved me, I'm sure of that. Did he love the boys?'

'I think he did, in his way.' The bereaved mother sighed. 'He's a funny man. Never could show his feelings, but I think he loved the boys. And yes, he loved Gillian. She was the apple of his eye.'

Mrs Masterton screwed up her table napkin and forced back her tears.

'Life can be so hard. All gone, and only you, my comfort, left.'

Mother and daughter squeezed hands across the table, as the afternoon pianist enjoyed his runs and trills. Both women were lost in memories. Julia broke the silence.

'I ought to go and see him.'

'I was hoping you would say that, dear.'

'I'll go on my day off.'

'That's my girl.'

Mrs Masterton paused, fumbling for her lipstick, then said hesitantly, 'Ask him if he wants to see me, will you, dear? I won't push myself on him, but if he wants, I'll come. Poor old Dad. I don't like to think of him alone and ill. He wasn't a bad husband. I'm sure he meant well. But we never got on, and the pub always came first.'

Julia went to Poplar early in the morning. She wanted to get there before the Master's Arms opened. The tram rattled on its rails to an area she had not visited for more than six years. She couldn't get away fast enough when she was seventeen. Now at the age of twenty-three it filled her with interest, and she eagerly watched for landmarks she had known since childhood. She felt strangely excited, almost exhilarated, which was the opposite of what she had expected after so long an absence.

She got off a stop before the Master's Arms, in order to walk the last quarter mile, and she noted all the shops she had known: the general store on the corner which sold sweets – she and her brothers had haunted it; the baker's that always gave off lovely smells; the pawnbrokers, with their three brass balls and ever-open door; the Jewish tailor. She knew them all and felt comforted by the familiarity.

A man was sweeping the pavement outside the Master's Arms. She accosted him, and asked if Mr Masterton was at home. He was, but he was ill, and not receiving visitors, the man informed her. Julia said 'He will see me. Can you let me in, please? I'm his daughter.'

The man stopped sweeping, leaned on his broom and stared at her.

'His daughter! I never knew 'e 'ad a daughter. Said 'is family was all dead.'

The daughter that never was, thought Julia sadly. He doesn't even mention me. But then, to be fair, she had never mentioned her father to the girls at the telephone exchange; so why would he, who was equally reserved, be likely to talk about her to his employees?

'I am his only living daughter. Can you let me in?'

The man was immediately respectful.

'No, ma'am, but Terry 'as a key. 'e was 'ead barman, but 'e's been manager since ve boss got ill. I'll take yer to him.'

Terry was equally surprised at the news of a daughter and muttered something about 'Me mum looks after ve old boy.' Julia did not like the familiarity.

'If you mean my father, then please refer to him as Mr Masterton,' she said coldly. 'Now please, let me in to the family quarters.'

She ascended the wooden stairs that she knew so well. All was quiet, save for her footsteps. She entered the big rooms where the family had lived together in happier days, where the children had laughed and played before Death spread its dark shadow over them. She saw the door of the room where her brothers had been laid out before burial, but she did not open it. Instead she went into the kitchen – it was clean but cold and appeared to be unused. Was no one there at all? She called out, 'Dad, are you here?' A voice answered 'Who's there? Is that Mrs Weston?' She went towards the sound of the voice. 'No, it's not Mrs Weston. It's me, Julia.'

She went into a bedroom. In a single bed by the window lay a man she did not recognise. His face was thin and shrunken, his eyes sunk deep into the eye-sockets. His breathing was fast, difficult and noisy and his neck was so thin it looked as though it might snap. His skin was grey, but two patches of bright red colouring under the eyes made him look as if he had been painted like a clown. Thin hands rested on the sheets, and bony fingers with long nails were plucking at the bedclothes. 'Is that you, Mrs Weston?' he croaked. He turned his head, and his dull eyes grew wider as he recognised her.

'Julia! What are you doing here?' His voice was husky.

'I heard you were ill, Dad.'

'It's nothing much. Just a passing fancy. The doctor's been. He says I'm getting along nicely. I'll be up and doing in a few days. Nice to see you, girl. Sit down.'

She took a chair and sat next to the bed.

'Why didn't you let me know you were ill?'

'No need to bother anyone. You've got your own life to lead. I do all right here. Mrs Weston comes in and does for me. I thought you were her just now when you called. I didn't think for a moment it would be you.'

Julia felt herself choking with emotion.

'I'm sorry, Dad. I should have come earlier, long ago.'

'No, no, girl. 'course not. You've got your own life. And you're doing all right, I dare say. Is it still the Telephone Exchange?' She nodded. 'A good job, good prospects. You'll be doing all right – your own life, your own friends – you can't be looking backwards over your shoulder all the time.'

Julia compared the imaginary contentment his words implied with the bleak reality of her life. She did not know what to say.

'Do you get enough food?'

'Mrs Weston comes in and cooks for me, but I don't want much. Can't seem to get it down.'

'Oh, Dad. What can I do?' Julia felt close to tears.

'Nothing, girl, nothing. You get on and enjoy your own life. You're only young once; make the most of it.'

'But Dad, I must do something.'

'Don't take on, girl. I want for nothing. Mrs Weston gets me all I need, and I've appointed her son Terry as manager. He'll keep the pub going until I'm up and doing myself.'

He sank back on the pillows. The effort of speaking had exhausted him. Julia sat quietly, engulfed in remorse, regret and self-reproach. Her own father, whom she had not seen for six years, and he looked to be on the point of death. His eyes were closed, but he stretched out a limp hand towards her and whispered rather than spoke.

'It's nice to see you, lass. Good of you to come. I appreciate it.'

'Would you like Mum to come?'

'Your mother? I don't know as she would want to.'

'She says she will if you would like her to. She won't push herself on you she says.' He did not reply, but sighed deeply, closed his eyes and appeared to drift off to sleep. Julia sat beside him looking at the tragic waste of the man she had always called Dad but had never really known. A man who had always been so alive and vital, who commanded instant respect and obedience from his staff, who excelled them all in strength and energy, who ran the Master's Arms with a Master's efficiency.

She knew what she must do. She would leave the telephone exchange without notice and quit her room. She need not leave her father even to collect things – her landlady could send them on, there was little enough to send. She pondered all that she would have to do – see the doctor, arrange for a day nurse, get advice on diet, exercise and how best to keep her father comfortable. She felt nervous of her own inexperience and longed for her mother to be there to advise her.

Her father slept, so she left his side and wandered round the flat, which was big and spacious. She perched on the corner seat between the two windows where she and her brothers had sat looking down on the changing scenes in the street below. She climbed the narrow stairs up to the attic full of junk where they had played hide and seek. The same junk, which had belonged to her grandparents, was there, a bit more dust and decay, but the same. She would have been outraged if anything had been changed! She went into the big kitchen, once so full of life and nice smells enticing to a child, but now cold and unused. She went into the bedroom she and her sister had shared and decided at once that she would occupy the same room. But one of the beds must go up to the attic – she could not sleep with Gillian's cold, empty bed in the room. She shuddered and returned to the kitchen to make a cup of tea.

Footsteps were heard on the stairs, and a man entered. He was youngish, cleanly dressed and carried a black bag. They met in the hallway and shook hands. He introduced himself as Dr Fuller.

'And I understand from Terry, the barman, that you are Miss Masterton, my patient's only living daughter?'

Julia nodded.

'I wish we had known about you a year ago. He said his family was dead.'

Julia felt herself blush with shame, and did not know what to say. Together they went into the sick room.

Expertly he examined the emaciated body. Julia winced to see the rib-cage exposed, with barely any flesh covering the bones. The doctor felt for enlarged lymph glands and neck rigidity. He palpated the chest at various points and listened through his stethoscope to the heart and the sounds of laboured breathing. He tested for muscular strength, which was almost nil. He looked into her father's eyes, and at his fingernails, which were a curious shape, Julia noticed. He examined the sputum in the pot. He said, 'You are doing nicely. Warmth, good food, and rest are what you need. I'm glad your daughter is here.'

'Yes. She has just come for the day. It's her day off work. It's nice to see her. A nice surprise.'

'I was hoping she would be staying,' said the doctor pointedly, knowing that Julia was just behind him.

'Oh no, no. She's got her own life to lead. She's doing well as a telegraphist. I don't want to be a drag on her. She's got her own friends, her own life.'

'I see,' said the doctor with a sigh. 'Well, I will return again in a few days.'

In the sitting room, Julia informed the doctor that she did intend staying, but had not told her father of her decision. She wanted to know more about his condition, and said that her four brothers and a sister had died of tuberculosis. The doctor told her that Mr Masterton had probably had a primary infection of the tubercle bacillus for many years, which had passed unnoticed. Any symptoms, such as fever or coughing, would have been put down to 'flu. However, about a year previously, a secondary infection had probably occurred, involving the mediastinal glands. 'I'm afraid that tuberculosis is now widespread throughout his lungs.'

Julia asked what treatment was available.

The doctor explained that treatment consisted of rest, warmth, good food, plentiful fluids, inhalations, postural drainage, fresh air and syrup of codeine linctus, and that later he would prescribe morphine.

Julia asked if her father would get better. The doctor looked unwilling to reply, but she insisted.

'I must know.'

'A year ago, my partner and I advised your father to go for six months' sanatorium treatment in the Swiss Alps. But he refused. He said he could not leave the pub for so long.'

'Typical,' said Julia angrily. 'He could never leave his pub, not even to save his own life. But do go on.'

'The clean air of the Alps might have saved his life, but it is too late now. Anyway, he seemed to improve for a while, or at least stabilise, and his decision seemed to be the right one. But two months ago he deteriorated rapidly. There is no drug available at this advanced stage that will effect a cure. In some cases, injection of sodium-gold thiosulphate is beneficial in diminishing the lung deposits, but we tried the gold injections weekly, with no effect. Your father, I am afraid, has now reached the stage of advanced phthisis, from which recovery cannot be expected.'

Julia sat quietly looking at the floor. She was not really surprised, just deeply sad.

'Can he go to a sanatorium now? The air of Poplar is notoriously bad, you know.'

The doctor smiled. 'Yes, I know, but there is no evidence that the air of Poplar causes tuberculosis. People living in ideal surroundings get the disease and do not recover. But your father cannot be moved now. It would kill him.'

Julia thought of her mother, toiling across Europe, a two-day journey by boat and train, with a sick child who had died shortly after arrival, and agreed with the doctor. 'So what can be done?' she whispered.

'You can make his life as comfortable as possible. He can eat what he likes, if he can eat at all. He can get up if he feels able to. Keep him warm. Inhalations are very soothing. You will need a nurse. I recommend the Nursing Sisters of St Raymund Nonnatus, an order of nuns who have worked in these parts for many years.'

Julia set about the massive task of tuberculous nursing with no knowledge or experience whatsoever. She did not tell her father of her plan to stay because she thought his pride might make him refuse her. Instead, she told him a story about having lost her job, and being unable to find another; that she had no money to pay the rent, and had been turned out of her lodgings.

Her father immediately said, 'That's hard, girl, you can come and stay here, of course, until you get on your feet again.'

After that he accepted her continued presence without question. He provided her with money to run their small ménage, to pay Mrs Weston for her cleaning, and to pay the doctor and the nurses, and for medicines. In fact, he was very generous, saying things like, 'Get yourself something pretty, a nice blouse or something. A young girl likes pretty things.'

He still kept a strict control of pub accounts. Ill as he was, and despite the fact he never went into the bar, he seemed to know exactly what was going on. Every morning Terry had to come upstairs and go through the previous day's sales. He had to give the number of customers in the bar, the number of sales and the quantity of stock consumed, and all was reckoned against the cash in the till, which was counted and entered in the ledger. Julia watched all this and marvelled that her father was so much in command. He seemed stronger while Terry was with him, and his mind was clear and focused. She also realised that it was only by maintaining such strong control that a publican could avoid being robbed by his staff. With hundreds of glasses of liquor being sold to customers every evening, it would be the easiest thing in the world to skew the money. Her father seemed to know from the daily sales what stock remained, and he placed all the orders himself and signed all the payment cheques. He was known by everyone as the Master, and his daughter came to admire his business acumen greatly. Her father would sink back on his pillows, exhausted and sweating, after Terry had gone; frequently he was coughing and trembling all over and needed his linctus and a cooling drink to get him over the ordeal. One day he said to Julia, 'Them doctors don't know anything about business. Wanted me to go away for six months, they did. That would have been a good day for the jackals if I'd gone, wouldn't it? There would have been nothing left by the time I got back.' He chuckled at his own astuteness, although Julia wondered what there was left of him through *not* going away to a sanatorium.

The doctor had advised she contact the Nursing Sisters, and as soon as Julia saw the heavy figure of Sister Evangelina lumbering upstairs she recognised her as the nun who had come to nurse her brothers when they were ill a decade previously. Sister was out of breath and grumpy by the time she got to the flat. She went straight to the sick room, sat down and demanded a cup of tea. Julia had expected a nun to be all holy water and prayers, but her opening remarks were about money.

'I will come each day, if you want me to, but it is going to cost you something, I warn you. We are an Order who nurse the poor. The Master of the Master's Arms is not poor. If you want me, you will have to pay handsomely, so that we can treat the poor for nothing. Take it or leave it and yes, two sugars please.'

Mr Masterton chuckled, which brought on a fit of coughing. Sister Evangelina sat drinking her tea, but watching him over the top of her teacup with an experienced eye. Eventually he was able to splutter, 'I agree, Sister, name your figure and I'll double it. There are thousands round here who can't afford to pay for the medical treatment they need.'

'Thousands?' she snorted. 'Tens of thousands would be nearer the mark. We see them all the time.'

She stared aggressively at Julia, who felt very small and didn't quite know what to make of the big nun.

'I suppose you don't know anything about good nursing, or any nursing at all, for that matter?'

Julia shook her head.

'No. I thought not. Ignorant girls. Dizzy young things. It seems to be my fate always to be landed with these flib-bertigibbets. Well, I suppose you are better than nothing, so let's get on with it. Postural drainage is what the patient needs. Potions and pills and linctuses are all very fine, but they won't get the phlegm out of his lungs. Postural drainage,' she added emphatically and stood up. Julia was obliged to take a step backwards.

'In the bar I saw several trestle tables. That is what we need. Go to the bar and get the men to bring one up,' she commanded

Julia, who stood looking bewildered. 'Go on, go girl. Don't stand there gawping. And we will need a mattress.'

'A mattress?'

'That's what I said.'

'But we've got a mattress.'

'We will need another one. Now go on, go on. I haven't got all day, you know.'

Hastily Julia ran down to the bar. She was quite overwhelmed by the big nun, but she told two men to carry a trestle table upstairs, and then to fetch a mattress from the attic. The Sister looked at the equipment and grunted with satisfaction.

'Right, you fellows. Leave the table like that with the legs folded in, and lean one end against the bed, sloping gently – further up – yes that will do. Now pull that chest of drawers up to wedge it so that it can't slip. That will do nicely – now put the mattress over it. Good lads. Perfect.'

She glared hard at Terry.

'It's Terry Weston, isn't it?

He nodded.

'I thought as much. I knew you when you were about thirteen – you had eaten too much of something that didn't agree with you and couldn't get rid of it. Constipated for a fortnight, you were. I had to give you two enemas to shift it. Hope that taught you a lesson.'

Terry blushed scarlet, and the other man sniggered. Mr Masterton also laughed, which brought on the coughing again.

Sister shooed the men away, and when the coughing had subsided, she said gently, 'Now, Mr Masterton, we have to get some of that fluid off your chest. I want you to lie head down on the mattress. I am going to palpate your back, and show your daughter how to do it. I will help you to get into the right position.'

Julia marvelled at the gentleness of Sister Evangelina as she handled her patient. After behaving in such a brusque manner, it was unexpected. The nun was kind and respectful in every way as she helped Julia's father to get up and to lie face downwards on the sloping mattress. She explained that the position would drain fluid out of his lungs. 'Now I am going to palpate your back, cupping we call it, and massage from the lower lungs to the upper lobes, to try to shift some of the muck. We will need a bowl or a chamber pot for you to spit into, so fetch one, will you, nurse – I mean Miss Masterton?'

Julia did as she was bidden, then Sister began to work on her father's back. 'Watch me carefully,' she said, 'In a minute I am going to ask you to do it.' Her father coughed uncontrollably and brought up copious amounts of frothy fluid, streaked with thick ropes of greenish phlegm. 'You will feel better after this,' said Sister Evangelina to the sick man. 'Now come here, Miss Masterton. You have a go.'

Julia was terrified of touching her father's back, which looked so thin and fragile, but she could not disobey this commanding woman. 'That's right. Shape your hands like cups and slap from lower to upper lobes; keep going – round the sides also. Now some massage. You have the idea. You have a feel for it. Ten minutes is enough. Now cover your patient, he must be kept warm.' Then to Julia's utter astonishment the nun smiled and said, 'Good girl. Well done.'

To Mr Masterton she said, 'This must be done every day, twice a day. Your daughter can do it, and afterwards you must lie for about twenty minutes head down. It will make you feel a good deal better. I am going to leave you now, but I will call each day.'

Once they were in the sitting room, Sister turned to Julia and said abruptly, 'This will not cure your father. Nothing will cure him short of a miracle. But it will make him feel easier. Eventually he will drown in the fluid which accumulates in his lungs, but in the meantime it is our duty to make him as comfortable as possible. Apart from which I usually find that such drastic treatment encourages the patient into thinking that something positive is being done. This stimulates hope.'

She grunted and humphed, gathered up her things and plodded heavily downstairs. In the bar she called out, 'I'll be back tomorrow, Terry. In the meantime, keep 'em open, then you won't get bunged up again,' to the immense discomfort of the poor fellow and the hilarity of the lunchtime customers.

Julia nursed her father for three months, and during that time she grew to understand him more. His reticence and reserve appealed to her temperament; the way he shrugged off suffering won her admiration; his desire not to be a nuisance was touching; and his gratitude for the least thing she did for him was unexpected. His constant interest in and care for his pub was consistent with the man she had known throughout her childhood. She admired the huge effort he made each morning, going over the accounts with Terry, and she always stayed in the room in order to help her father, should he need help. Sister Evangelina came each day, and together they administered postural drainage and massage, and she saw the fortitude with which her father endured it. He always seemed a little better an hour later, so they continued.

He never openly showed affection, but one evening he squeezed her hand and muttered, 'You're a good girl, Julia, the only one left. Go to that cupboard and get the box out. I haven't seen it for years; we'll look at it together.'

Julia did as she was bid. Her father sat up in bed, his eyes bright, his breathing laboured.

'Open it, lass, will you? I can't any more.'

Opening the box, so long unopened, revealed more of her father than anything else could have done. Inside was a jumble of children's toys and books, colouring pencils, pictures drawn by a childish hand, a small teddy bear and a china doll. At the bottom was a wooden Noah's Ark.

'Get it out, Julie, we must look at it.'

Julia opened it up and took out the wooden animals. Her father chuckled.

'I remember you all playing with these. Do you?'

Of course she did, and the memory nearly choked her. He fingered the giraffe, and the lion, and the ghosts of her brothers seemed to enter the room.

'There's another box in there. Lift it out, will you?'

She did so, and it was full of toy soldiers. Her father handled them eagerly, his eyes bright.

'I bought these as a birthday present, once. The boys played with them for hours.'

The dying man closed his eyes.

'I can see them now, all over the floor with their soldier games.'

Julia looked at him, and a wave of tenderness swept over her. 'All gone, all dead,' he murmured, and his hand fell limply on the counterpane. But then he brightened. 'There's a little cotton bag in the bottom; pull it out.' Inside the bag were some hair ribbons and a child's bolero, the ones he had asked her to send to Gillian for her birthday when the family were in Skegness. He took the bolero, which was made of soft angora, and rubbed it up and down his cheek. 'Is there a card there? Read it to me, will you?' Julia read the card from Gillian, which said how lovely the bolero was, and how she wore it all the time and would not take it off. Her father chuckled. 'Wouldn't take it off, bless her,' but then his face crumpled, and tears started in his eyes. He turned his head away quickly, ashamed of his weakness. 'Go and get a cup of tea, there's a good girl.'

Julia left the bedroom in tears. So he had cared after all, and she had not known it. She lit the gas stove, put the kettle on and drew the kitchen curtains. The sounds from the pub were starting downstairs, but she hardly noticed them any more; they were just part of life. The singing and dancing would begin soon, but she no longer resented them. She sat down at the kitchen table and leaned her head on her arms and sobbed. Why was he dying now, just when she was getting to know him? He was the father she had never had but had always wanted, because all girls want a father to love.

The tears did her good. She stood up and washed her eyes in cold water, then made the tea and returned with it to the sick room.

Her father appeared to be asleep, with toys and books and childish things all around him, so she decided not to disturb him. She poured herself a cup of tea and sat down beside him. She took his hand, and he responded with a little squeeze; the other hand held the fluffy pink bolero. He stirred a little. 'Do you want that cup of tea, Dad?' she whispered. 'By and by,' he croaked, 'by and by,' and he drifted off to sleep again. She sat quietly beside him, as the sounds of 'Pack up yer troubles' floated upstairs. She shut the window, but he roused again. 'No, don't do that. It's nice to hear them enjoying themselves.' She opened it again and the shouts of '. . . . in yer ol' kit bag and smile, smile, smile' came flooding in. 'Smile,' he croaked. 'That's what we gotta do. It's a funny old world, eh, Julie?' And he drifted off into sleep once more.

Julia sat beside him for several hours; she couldn't bring herself to leave him. Darkness fell, and the tea grew cold. The noise from the pub ceased at closing time but continued in the street for a while. Raucous shouts and shrill cries grew fainter as the customers wandered or staggered away to their homes. A few tuneless attempts at a song, accompanied by a guffaw of laughter – and then all was quiet.

Julia fell asleep in her chair, and when she awoke the Master of the Master's Arms was dead, surrounded by children's toys.

THE MISTRESS

I saw pale kings and princes too
Pale warriors, death-pale were they all;
They cried – 'La Belle Dame sans Merci
Thee hath in thrall!'
'La Belle Dame Sans Merci', by John Keats

Julia was so accustomed to death in her family that she was neither afraid nor surprised when she found her father had died in his sleep. She waited till morning and then called the doctor. When Terry came up with the previous day's account of sales he questioned if they should close the pub for the day. She thought for a moment and then said no, her father would not have wished it – business as usual. But she told him to put a notice on the bar informing all customers and requesting quiet, out of respect for the Master.

Two days later a lawyer called. He informed Julia that she was the sole inheritor of the Master's Arms, of the buildings and all its assets, subject to a life annuity for Mrs Masterton. The will had been made six years earlier. Julia was shattered. The inheritance of the pub had not crossed her mind. If she had thought of it at all, it was only in a vague way, as though a business can carry on by itself. Her first words to the lawyer were 'What am I going to do?' He explained that she could sell the freehold to one of the big brewers, and that he would arrange the business side of things for her. 'You will be a wealthy woman,' he added.

Julia was a mere twenty-three years old, and the large inheritance overwhelmed her. When the lawyer had gone she wandered around the flat in a daze. She made her way down to the bar, and the staff and several lunchtime customers came over to her with words of sympathy. She went down to the cellar and looked at the huge barrels, the crates of stock and the bottles lining the walls. It was all hers. She felt numb with shock, and her mind was in turmoil. She returned to the flat and sat for a long time in the window seat overlooking the street. She watched the women gossiping or passing by, many pushing prams, going in and out of the little shops, some now and then making a furtive entry into a pawn-shop. Two barrow boys were arguing over a pitch. She heard children's voices from a nearby school. There was a street sweeper with his hand-cart. A woman flower-seller trundling along with her basket. A group of seamen in clogs and a Chinaman with a pigtail went past. A woman opposite was scrubbing and whitening her front doorstep. A shopkeeper in his long green apron was sweeping the pavement in front of his store. The lawyer had told Julia that she could sell and she would be a wealthy woman. But sitting in the window and watching the street scene had a calming effect on Julia, and she realised, for the first time, that she was amongst her own people, and that this was where she belonged. The memory of her father's hard work and pride in his achievement, and that of her grandparents, brought with it a proud and stubborn resolution: she would not sell, she would be the fifth-generation landlord of the Master's Arms.

The staff cheered when she told them of her decision, but were dubious, because she was a woman. They had not taken into account Julia's determination to succeed. Knowing that she was little more than a girl taking on a man's job, her instinct told her that she would have to be the undisputed boss from the very beginning.

She immersed herself in the business, taking over her father's office, and apart from cleaning it up a bit and introducing flowers and some pictures, she changed very little. She poured over the ledgers and on her own initiative drew a graph of sales and purchases throughout the year, which was pinned to the wall, giving an immediate visual record of profit and loss. She familiarised herself with suppliers and visited breweries and distilleries, causing quite a stir among the men, who had never seen a woman publican before, still less a young and pretty one. But Julia was always reserved and serious-looking, which did not invite cat-calls or lewd comments. In all this Terry was indispensable to her, and, knowing that she could not succeed without him, she raised his wages.

Each day she spent a great deal of time in the bar, watching how a pub was run, and admiring the skill and speed of the barmen. But when one of them slipped his arm around her waist and murmured that she needed a man's help now, and if they married they could make a real success of it, she slapped his face and sacked him. She also sacked one of the barmaids who took the liberty of calling her 'Julia', with the cold words 'My name is Miss Masterton.' There were no more 'Julias' after that, and the rest of the staff were quietly respectful. She had Terry's unqualified support, but she knew that she needed another man, preferably one with fighting skills, and she found one in Chubb, an ex-professional heavyweight with a broken nose and no front teeth. He was running to fat, and of limited intelligence, but the hammer fists and ingrown profile ensured that no one would knock his beer over to see how he took it. Chubb and Terry served her with dog-like devotion, and she rewarded them accordingly.

Within a few weeks she was known as the Mistress of the Master's Arms, a title in which she took great pride. Several of the big breweries offered to buy her out, but she refused them all, preferring to run a free house.

Every day she was in the bar, memorising and ordering stock, overseeing sales, bar and table service, and the hundred and one other things involved in running a pub. The local customers were intrigued by the new Mistress, who was always courteous and welcoming, but never over-friendly or familiar. She was even around during the sing-song and knees-up. She never joined in, but just stood quietly, watching and smiling. Chubb the Brawn was never far from her, and if anything got too rowdy a look from Julia and a movement from Chubb would put a stop to it instantly. In observing and analysing the people who came in, Julia realised that the pub and its atmosphere were an essential outlet for high spirits in her Cockney clients. One thing, however, had always made her unhappy, and that was seeing children hanging around the doors of the pub waiting for their parents. She was determined to do something about it. There was no point in refusing admission to the parent; they would merely move on to the next pub, and probably wallop the children as well. So she got the men to clear one of the stock rooms which was quite separate from the licensed premises, and turned it into a children's room. This was a completely new idea. A lot of people were scornful, but it worked, and sales increased.

It was 1937 when the Master died and Julia took over. Rumours of war were spreading all over Europe. No one believed, or wanted to believe, it could happen so soon after the last war, but Churchill thundered on about the dangers, and the Government dithered about rearmament. Two years passed, and in September 1939 war was declared. 'It will all be over by Christmas,' everyone said cheerfully. But it wasn't, and a year later on 30 September 1940, the bombing of London started with a ferocity hitherto undreamed of. For fifty-seven nights an average of 200 German bombers a night attacked London, aiming mainly at the Docklands. Acres of housing were destroyed, many were killed, and thousands of people made homeless. Noise, destruction, burning and death filled the streets, and each night nobody knew if they would live to see the morning.

The Master's Arms in Poplar was in the thick of it, and the chances of a direct hit, killing all inside, were pretty high. Julia felt she ought to close the pub and move to the safety of the countryside, but seeing the relief occasioned by the pub's warm and welcoming atmosphere made her hesitate. One day she was standing at the door, looking at the smoke and the devastation all around, and the rescue workers digging in the rubble for survivors, when a little old woman caught her eye. She was typical of the older generation of Cockneys – tiny, skinny, bright-eyed, toothless, with straggly grey hair beneath a greasy greyish cap and wearing a long, frowsty coat, of that indescribable colour created by age, damp and decay. She was standing in the street, smacking her lips and grunting to herself. An ambulance worker came up to her and said kindly, 'Are you all right, mother?' Quick as a flash she replied, 'All right? 'course I'm bleedin' all right! Vat bugger Hitler, 'e's bombed me 'ouse, 'ard luck, 'e's killed me ol' man, good riddance, 'e's got me boys – vey're all fightin' in ve war – 'e's got me girls, vey're somewhere, dunno where. But 'e aint got me. An' I got sixpence 'ere in me pocket, an' ve Master's Arms is open.' She grabbed his arm and grinned a toothless grin. 'So let's go in, mate, an' 'ave a drink an' a sing-song.'

That old woman banished Julia's indecision. She would not abandon her people. She would stick it out. If they wanted a drink and a sing-song, they should have it. She would not close the pub. Most of her staff were being called up into the services – all the young men went, including Terry – but she managed to keep going on a skeleton staff. Then a draft came from the Ministry requiring her services as an experienced telegraphist. She had to obey, so she worked all day in the telegraph office and all evening in the pub. Her office work was squeezed in after the pub closed. With a routine working day of about eighteen hours, she was always tired. But she survived, and the Master's Arms stayed open all through the war.

Julia had always been a remote, self-contained person, and the war years intensified this side of her personality. Life was hard, she could see the evidence all around her, and she could see little to smile about. She had loved her mother, whom she continued to meet occasionally, and her brothers and sisters, now dead; she had even grown to love her father at the very end of his life, when it was too late. But apart from that, love had not touched her and local people always said, 'She's a typical old maid.'

But one should never judge from appearances. Still waters run deep, and in wartime love affairs are intense, complicated, sometimes fleeting, but passionate.

Like a thunderbolt of God's grace, a man from RAF Intelligence Service walked into the telegraph exchange. He was twenty-five years older than she was, and married, but they loved with passionate intensity. They met seldom, and she never knew where he was stationed, because it was top security, but it made no difference. Their moments together were ecstatic and life-renewing. They gave themselves to each other, body and soul, because they both knew that they might never meet again. Death, if it came, would be swift and violent; it could come at any time, and neither would know the fate of the other.

It was 1945. Everyone knew that the war was coming to an end, and there was a lightness of heart in the air. In the Master's Arms each evening drinking and singing continued, and Julia watched her customers with quiet satisfaction. Against all odds the pub had never closed, and by a miracle it stood undamaged, alone amid streets of rubble.

And another miracle was about to happen; Julia realised that she was pregnant. At first she was fearful, but when she felt the quickening of new life within her, a thrill of unspeakable joy flooded her whole body. She was going to have *his* baby. Her love affair, lasting three years, had always been fraught with as much sorrow as joy; the stolen hours were always too brief, and the partings always agony. They both knew that, even if they survived the war, they would lose each other in the end, because he was a married man. The heartbreak was overpowering when the final parting came. But now his child was growing within her, and she could never be wholly separated from him. She

Earnest 'collectors' swapping cards on the pavement – a not unusual scene in the East End of fifty years ago. Boys collected marbles, bottle tops and cigarette cards; girls collected buttons, ribbons and cotton reels. Swapping and bargaining was a serious business © Allen Young

Men trundled barrels like this all over London in the 1950s © Allen Young

It was a sad day for the local lads when the water sprinklers were taken out of service © Tower Hamlets Local History Library and Archives

Right: A vigorous public health programme to limit the spread of tuberculosis was started around 1910 © The Stroke Association

Below: Cows were herded down Stepney High Street as late as the 1940s. Testing cattle for TB was not compulsory until 1945, and 'our own cows' probably contributed to outbreaks in the East End © Tower Hamlets Local History Library and Archives

Left: A market scene from the 1950s with a rather intriguing sign © Allen Young

Below: Preparations for war – grim days © Tower Hamlets Local History Library and Archives

Grovesnor Buildings, corner of Cotton Street. Of the Canada Buildings, only one was destroyed. The others remained, three of them completely untouched by bombs © Tower Hamlets Local History Library and Archives

A boat under construction jutting out onto Manchester Road, Isle of Dogs, around 1920 © Tower Hamlets Local History Library and Archives

Entrance lock to West India Docks, looking towards the Wood Wharves from the river side. Chummy would have entered at this point, in the dark and wind © Museum of London Port of London Authorities Collection

Children getting
a treat from an
old-fashioned
ice-cream vendor
© Tower Hamlets
Local History
Library
and Archives

Men were still
unloading timber
like this in the
1950s. They were
tough, lean and
very strong ©
Museum of
London Port of
London Authorities
Collection

Jenny Lee at the wedding, 1959

thrilled with happiness. The child would always be with her, the consummation of her first and only love.

A baby girl was born and filled Julia's life with a happiness she had never dared hope for. All her maternal instincts of love and protection were focused on the baby and her life was emotionally complete. She continued to run the pub with her usual efficiency, and she engaged a nanny each evening when she needed to be downstairs in the bar. Terry had returned from war service and resumed his job, as manager, so she had more time to spend with her baby. People talked, of course, – people always do – and a baby born out of wedlock was a juicy subject for gossip. Some said, 'She's a dark 'orse,' while others said, 'She's no better 'an she should be,' but Julia was not perturbed. People had always talked about her, and she had always been indifferent to their comments. Nothing could spoil her happiness, and her staff noticed a softening in her eyes and a radiance in her features that they had never seen before.

It was 1957 when I first saw Miss Masterton, twenty years after she had taken over the Master's Arms from her father. It was my day off, which happened to be on a Saturday, and I had been showing my West End friends, Jimmy and Mike, and some of their set, around the Docks. We ended the day in the Master's Arms. There was a pleasant, relaxed atmosphere, and we settled down for a good session. The pub filled up as the evening wore on – local people on their night out, looking for fun. The war had changed much, but not the Cockney's appetite for bawdy enjoyment. A pianist started to bang out 'Doin' the Lambeth Walk, hoi!' and within seconds everyone joined in, *con belto* style. Glasses were raised with every 'oi!' which grew louder and louder with each refrain. Bodies swayed in rhythm, and beer was spilled. Our group sat in a corner and exchanged surprised glances. 'This is going to be fun,' we muttered. Then a group of girls got up, linked arms and started a side-kick routine to the 'Lambeth Walk', which went on and on, till they sank down exhausted amid cheers and whistles. 'Run rabbit run' followed, and several old music hall songs. Someone got up and acted as chorus master with an 'all together now ...' and the pub was filled with raucous voices splitting their vocal cords. It was impossible to hear yourself speak, so we just sat back and enjoyed it.

One woman in particular caught my eye. She was standing behind the bar. She was about forty-five, was well-dressed and good-looking, but was not the typical barmaid. She was quietly pleasant to all her customers, but in a subtle way, seemingly detached from everything around her. Yet at the same time she was obviously watching everyone and everything that was going on. A group sitting by the door began to get a bit quarrelsome, one man shouting at and threatening another. The woman stepped out from behind the bar and walked towards the table. She did not say a word; she just looked at the two men and, somewhat shamefaced, they sat down. There was no more trouble. Her whole aspect exuded quiet self-confidence, but when you looked at her face there was something missing, something in the eyes that I could not define; a sort of blank, vacant expression, as though she was looking at people but not seeing them, or looking through and beyond them to something that was not there.

The boys were enjoying themselves and wanted to stay, but for me, the noise was getting a bit too ear-splitting for comfort, so I left early. As I walked back to the convent, the memory of the woman's face, and the look in her eyes, haunted me.

A few weeks later I saw her again, but it was a very different person from the woman I had seen in the pub. I was in All Saints Church with Sister Julienne. It was mid-afternoon, and the church was empty but for Sister and me. Then a woman staggered in. I did not recognise her at first, her hair was dishevelled, her eyes so red from weeping that she could hardly see, and her legs seemed barely able to support her. She looked wildly around her and clung to one of the pews for support. Sister Julienne went up to her to ask if she could help, but the woman did not answer. She took a couple of faltering steps forward and croaked, rather than spoke.

'Yes, this is the place. Six years ago it was. Here, in this church.'

She let out a low moan and staggered forward a few more steps.

'They stopped here, right here where I am standing. This is where they rested it, the little, little coffin. Six years ago to this day.'

She sank on to a seat and sobbed.

Sister asked if she could do anything to help.

'No. No one can help me. Nothing can bring her back. I just want to light a candle, and then I'll go.'

Sister helped her to the altar, and they lit a candle together and prayed. Then they sat quietly talking for a minute or two. Finally the woman stood up. She did not say anything, but she looked slightly more composed. She walked towards the spot where she had stopped before, where she said the coffin had rested. She stood silently for a few minutes and then with a firmer step walked out of the church.

I asked Sister if she knew the woman, and she told me it was Miss Masterton, owner of the Master's Arms. And then she told me the tragic story of the tuberculosis which had claimed nearly all her family, and lastly her little girl, aged six. The mother had nearly gone mad with grief, she had doted so on the child.

I told Sister Julienne that I had seen Miss Masterton in the pub, and something about her had caught my attention, perhaps the look in her eyes.

'Yes, there is something in the eyes of a woman who has lost a child that sets her apart from others. The grief and pain never go away. And for Miss Masterton it was all the more terrible because she was advised to be tested for the tubercle bacillus herself. Blood tests were taken showing that she was a carrier of the bacillus, and had been for a long time, but had never shown any signs or symptoms and had never succumbed to the disease herself. It is probable that she had infected her own daughter.'

THE ANGELS

While she could vividly remember things from long past, Sister Monica Joan's short-term memory seemed to be getting shorter and shorter. She appeared to have forgotten completely the unpalatable fact that she had been before the Court of the London Quarter Sessions on a charge of larceny only a few months previously. The prosecution had alleged that she had stolen jewels from Hatton Garden and initially all the evidence had pointed to her guilt. But a surprise witness proved her innocence. The trial had been a shock, to say the very least, for the convent, but for Sister Monica Joan it was as though it had never happened. She was her old self, delightful and entertaining, in her conversation, but in her behaviour she was becoming increasingly eccentric and unpredictable.

Sister had a niece, more accurately a great great niece, living in Sonning, Berkshire. They had not met or communicated for many years. One day Sister decided to visit her niece, and what is more she determined that a pair of fine Chippendale chairs which she had in her room should be presented to the woman as a gift. Accordingly, she left Nonnatus House early one morning while the Sisters were at prayer, and before Mrs B the cook or Fred the boiler man arrived. How she carried two chairs downstairs is impossible to conjecture, but she did.

Out in the street, she carried one chair to the corner and then came back for the other. She proceeded in this fashion to the East India Dock Road, where a policeman approached and asked her if he could help. Sister Monica Joan did not like policemen. She exclaimed, 'Tush, out of my way, fellow,' and rammed the chair leg into his stomach. The policeman decided to let her get on with it.

Sister reached the bus stop and sat down to regain her breath. A bus came, and the conductor, being a kindly soul, helped her on with her two chairs and put them in the luggage hold. When they reached Aldgate, he helped her off and pointed to where she could catch a bus to Euston, where she would have to change onto another for Paddington Station.

It was approaching rush hour when the bus trundled into Paddington. The bus stop was some distance from the railway station, so Sister left one of the chairs (Chippendale, of enormous value) at the bus stop whilst she carried the other to the station. Then she left that one in the station forecourt, and returned for the second. Once in the station things became easier for Sister Monica Joan, because she found a porter who loaded the chairs onto his trolley and took them to the train bound for Reading, were she would have to change onto a branch line for Sonning.

Meanwhile at Nonnatus House the alarm was raised. Sister Monica Joan was missing, and no one had a clue where she had got to. Mrs B was in tears. The police were informed but could offer no help. At lunchtime a phone call was received stating that a policeman had reported seeing a nun at six o'clock in the morning in the East India Dock Road, and that she had rammed a chair leg into his stomach.

'A chair leg!' cried Sister Julienne incredulously. 'What was she doing with a chair leg?'

'She was carrying a chair,' replied the duty policeman.

'But that's impossible. She is ninety, and it was in the East India Dock Road, you tell me.'

'I'm only telling you what the constable reported, ma'am. I'm not making anything up. Now, if you will excuse me, I have work to do. We'll keep an eye open for this missing nun, and if we have any more reports of her activities, you will be informed. Good day to you, ma'am.'

Sister went hastily to Sister Monica Joan's room and observed that not only one chair was missing, but two! Lunchtime conversation around the big dining table focused on nothing else, and prayers were said for Sister Monica Joan's safety.

The train reached Sonning station at about midday, and Sister Monica Joan telephoned her niece. There was no reply. So she decided to go with God and sat down on one of the chairs to have a little doze. A kindly porteress gave her a cup of tea. At about four o'clock she telephoned again, and this time she was lucky. Her niece was at home. Her astonishment at hearing from her great aunt after so many years, especially as she was waiting at the station with two chairs, can only be imagined. The niece came in her car to collect her aunt. Only one chair could be fitted into the boot, so the other had to be left on the pavement outside the station. It was still there when she returned a couple of hours later.

They telephoned the convent at about five o'clock. The niece said her aunt was tired but happy, and was welcome to stay for a few days if she wanted to. She added that she had received no warning of the intended visit, and that it was only by chance that she was at home at all, as her work often took her away for several days at a time. What would have happened to her aunt had she been away, she could not imagine. The telephone was passed to Sister Monica Joan, who in reply to Sister Julienne's anxious enquiries said, 'Of course I'm all right. Don't fuss so. Why should I not be all right? The angels look after me.'

The angels certainly had a heavy responsibility looking after Sister Monica Joan, and they could never relax their vigilance for a moment. Take the occasion when she nearly set fire to herself, for example. She had complained that the light in her room was insufficient, and that she could not see to read in bed; it was not good enough, something must be done. Obligingly, Fred, our odd-job man, ran a small cable up the wall and fixed a light just above her head. It was nothing fancy — just a bulb over which a small, fringed shade was placed. Sister Monica Joan was delighted. So simple; dear Fred — she could always rely on him, and now she could read in bed all night, if she wanted to.

She did want to, with alarming consequences. Since her bout of pneumonia, caused by wandering down the East India Dock Road in her nightie on a cold November morning, Sister Monica Joan had been favoured by being allowed to have her breakfast in bed. Mrs B usually took it up around 9 a.m., after we midwives and nurses had gone out on our morning visits. But the angels must have seen to it that Mrs B needed to be at the market by 9 a.m. that particular morning, and so she took Sister's breakfast up at 8 a.m. We were all in the kitchen having our breakfast, and the nuns were still in chapel. The house was quiet, except for the scratch-scratch of Fred raking out the boiler. A piercing scream, followed by louder repeated screams, shattered the calm. We girls and Fred rushed into the hallway, all shouting, 'What is it, where did it come from?' The chapel door opened, and the nuns ran out. (Nuns have been known to run, when the occasion demands!) The screams had stopped, but we could hear someone rushing about on the first floor. 'Stay where you are,' ordered Sister Julienne. 'Fred, come with me.' Disappointed at missing the drama, I waited with the others in the hallway. A smell of burning now filled the air. More running feet, more muffled voices, and smoke billowed along the corridor. Someone went to the bathroom, taps were turned on, windows were closed, banging and stamping was heard, and then Sister Julienne's calm voice: 'I think we have got it under control now. Thank God you came up when you did, Mrs B, otherwise I tremble to think of the outcome.'

Sister Monica Joan, protesting about being disturbed, was led out of her room and away from the smoke to the safety of the ground floor. Mrs B was in a very much worse state. She was pale and shaking, and needed several cups of strong tea fortified with whisky before she could tell us what had happened. Sister had had her new light on, with the pillows arranged so that she could sit up. The topmost pillow was touching the light bulb, and she must have fallen asleep. As Mrs B entered the room, a tiny flicker of flame no more than an inch high had leaped from the pillow. Mrs B screamed and dragged it from under the sleeping head. The open door and the movement had caused the pillow, which must have been smouldering for some time, to burst into flames. Her repeated screams brought help, and a rug thrown over the burning pillow and heavy stamping had controlled the fire. But the smoke was terrible, and they were lucky not to have been overcome by fumes. In the meantime Sister Monica Joan had sat on the bed saying, 'Gracious heaven! What *are* you doing?'

No one was hurt. The hem of Sister Julienne's habit was badly scorched, but she was not burned. They were all black with smoke and soot. But Sister Monica Joan was the least troubled of anyone. Either she genuinely forgot about it or decided that it would be expedient to do so (I could never be quite sure), but she did not refer to the incident again. When the light was removed from above her bed she said nothing, but she put on her hard-done-by look.

Then there was the occasion when Sister Monica Joan got stuck in the bath.

We girls first became aware that something was amiss when we heard movements and voices from the Sisters' floor during the period of the Greater Silence. This is the time after Compline, the last office of the day, and before Mass, the first of the new day, during which hours complete silence is normally observed in the monastic tradition. But on this occasion the Sisters were by no means observing the rule. First we heard one or two whispered words, then more, then a gaggle of anxious voices all talking at once, accompanied by banging on a door, and calls of 'Sister, can you hear us? Open the door.'

What was going on? We looked enquiringly at each other. Novice Ruth came running downstairs.

'Is Fred still here? Has he gone yet?' she called as she ran towards the kitchen. We didn't know, but then heard 'Fred, thank goodness you are still here. Come quickly to the second floor. We think you'll have to break down a door.'

Mysterious! Exciting! Thrilling! We girls looked at each other expecting more.

We heard more voices upstairs but didn't know what was going on. Fred came back down and passed us as we stood expectantly on the landing.

'What is it, Fred? What's up?'

'I'm goin' outside to see if ve winder's open.'

'The window? We thought it was a door.'

'It'll be easier.'

'Than what?'

'Than breaking ve door.'

And off he ran.

At this point Sister Julienne came downstairs and met Fred coming in.

'Yes, Sister. Winder's open. I reckons as 'ow I can do it.'

'Oh, Fred, you're wonderful. But do be careful.'

Fred assumed an heroic air.

'Don' choo worry 'bout me, Sister. I'm OK. We gotter ge' the 'ol lady safe, like. I'll get ve ladders.'

And off he ran.

Cynthia spoke. 'Sister, please tell us what is going on.'

'Well, the bathroom door is locked. It seems that Sister Monica Joan is in the bath and can't get out, but no one can get in to help her.'

Eager to get a slice of the action, I said, 'Fred's getting on a bit. I'm more agile than he is. Couldn't I go up the ladder?'

Sister looked at me knowingly.

'I have no doubt that you are more agile. But if you suggested to Fred that he was getting on and was no longer capable of going up a ladder he would be highly offended. We'll leave it to him.'

Twenty minutes later Fred came downstairs looking,

unusually for him, abashed. The fag that normally hung from his lower lip was not there. He looked different without it.

'What happened, Fred?' we chorused.

Knowing that we were agog with anticipation and that he was the only source of information, just to tease us he took out a battered tobacco tin from his pocket and started rolling another thin fag.

'Oh, Fred. Don't provoke. Tell us what happened.'

He lit his fag, scratched his head and looked at us with his south-west eye, before saying, 'Well, I reckon as 'ow I must be ve only bloke in England wot's seen a nun stark naked.'

'Ooooh!'

He was warmed to his story by our reaction.

'Well, I gets up ve ladder to ve winder, like, an' pokes me 'ead in. "Be off with you, fellow," she calls out. 'I gotta ge' in, Sister,' I says. "Come back another day, if you must; it's not convenient at the moment." And she splashes water in me face. Well, I wasn't expectin' it, an' I nearly lost me balance.'

'Oooh, Fred. Poor Fred.'

He was really enjoying himself.

'But I grabs ve sides of ve winder an' hangs on, and says, "I'm sorry, Sister, but I gotta get in. You can't stay in 'ere all night. You'll catch yer death o' cold." Nah, tricky bit is ve bath's under the winder, so I 'as ter get in an' over the bath, wiv 'er in it an' not fall in meself.'

'How did you manage that, Fred?'

'Wiv difficulty 'an injinuity. Jest bein' smart, like.'

'Fred, you are so clever.'

'Nah, nah, jest smart like,' he said modestly. 'Worse fing was I drops me fag some'ow, an it floats around ve ole lady. Then I unlocks ve door, and Sisters come in, an' now I'm goin' a put me ladders away.'

'Would you like a cup of tea before you go, Fred?'

'Well now, vat's an invitation I can't resist, if you girls will 'ave one wiv me.'

Of course we would. We would like nothing better. So we all sat down in the big kitchen for a cup of tea and some of Mrs B's cake and a good old natter.

Upstairs we heard further sounds of movement and voices, then splashing of water and the gurgling of a waste pipe. Then no more. The Greater Silence had begun.

Sister Monica Joan was found in the bicycle shed one winter's night by Chummy who had been called out at about two o'clock. Again, the angels must have arranged it. If Sister had remained in the shed until morning she would probably have died of hypothermia; she was very thin, having no protective reserves of fat to cover her old bones. Chummy was getting her bicycle out when she heard a movement in the corner of the shed and thought it was a rat – we were all nervous of rats in dark places. She shone her torch over the area and was horrified, and indeed terrified, to see an arm move. Then an imperious voice, accustomed to being obeyed, ordered, 'Don't shine the light in my eyes like that! Fetch me a pillow if you want to be useful, but turn the light off.'

Sister Monica Joan was curled up in some old camping equipment, probably dating back to someone's Girl Guide endeavours. She was very cold and very sleepy, which is a dangerous combination. She resented being disturbed and tried to push Chummy away. 'Go away with your nasty lights and bothersome noise. Why can't I be left in peace?' Chummy carried her into the house and alerted the Sisters as she had to go out to a labouring mother. The Sisters covered the old lady with warm blankets and hot-water bottles and gave her hot drinks. Astonishingly she came to no harm, not even a cold in the nose.

I was in her room a few days later and referred to the night's adventure. She dismissed it as 'a lot of fuss about nothing'.

'Well,' I remarked, 'you were lucky that there was some old

camping equipment in the shed to cover you, or you might have died of cold.'

'Camping,' she said, 'such fun! We used to love it.' Her eyes were alight and her voice animated.

'Camping, Sister?' I exclaimed. 'You can't be serious. You've been camping?'

She was offended.

'Certainly, my dear. You don't imagine I have done nothing in my life, do you? We used to go camping often, my brothers and sisters, and some friends, with the maid and the manservant. It was wonderful.'

'A maid and manservant? Camping?'

'It was perfectly proper – a husband and wife in our service.'

'I wasn't thinking of the propriety of the arrangements But servants! Camping . . .' My voice failed me.

'We needed them, my dear. We needed the man to put up the tents and fetch the water and light the fires and things like that, and we needed the maid to do the cooking.'

'Well, if you put it like that, Sister, I suppose you did.'

I chuckled quietly, but I don't think she saw the joke.

One memorable Sunday afternoon Cynthia and I took Sister Monica Joan for a walk. The weather was beautiful, and we decided to take her up to Victoria Park, where there is a lovely lake, and where East Enders would gather with their children in sunny weather. But when the bus arrived it was full, so on the spur of the moment we changed our plan and took the next bus, which was going to Limehouse, and past the canal known as the Cuts. We thought we could have a walk along the towpath. The canal was dug in the nineteenth century to connect the River Lea to the Limehouse Reach of the Thames and was much used by commercial barges until the closure of the Docks in the 1970s. It was always a pleasant area for walking.

When we got there Sister said unexpectedly, 'I don't like the Cuts.'

'Why not, Sister?'

'A grim place. Bad associations.'

'What do you mean?'

'The place of suicides. In the old days, the bad old days, when there was no money, no work for the men, no food for the children, every week a cry would be heard: "Body in the Cuts, body in the Cuts," and always it was a woman. A poor, ragged, half-starved woman, driven to the limits of despair. Once a woman with a baby strapped to her body was dragged out, I was told.'

'Sister, how terrible. Shall we go away?'

'No. I want to go and see it for myself. I haven't been here for forty years, since Beryl died.'

Cynthia and I glanced at each other. We both wanted to hear the story, but didn't want to disturb her thoughts, in case they flitted off onto something quite unconnected, and the story was lost. But the dark water, barely moving, seemed to focus her attention, and she continued.

'They told me she jumped off Stinkhouse Bridge one night, and her body was dragged out the next day. I wasn't surprised. No one was. She had a brute of a husband, seven children, another expected, no money, and a hovel to live in – the usual story. It is only surprising more women didn't do it. Every child's fear, you know, was that one day things would get so bad that mother would jump into the Cuts.'

Sister Monica Joan raised her hand, took hold of the cross that hung around her neck and held it up over the canal. She called out, 'Be sanctified, you black and wicked waters. Rest in peace, Beryl, unloved wife, weeping mother. May the lamentations of your children sanctify these turgid deeps.'

Sister was in good form and continued, 'Do you know what that brute of a husband said when the vicar informed him that his wife was dead, and how she had died?'

'No. What?' we chorused.

'He said, my dears – the vicar himself told us – the husband said, "Spiteful cat. Spiteful to the last. She knowed as 'ow today's Newmarket day, and she knowed as 'ow I'm a delicate feelin' sort o' chap, so she goes an' kills 'erself jest to put me out of sorts for the races. I knows 'er nasty ways. Spite it was; pure spite." Then he walked out. The vicar was left alone in the derelict kitchen, with seven dirty, hungry children around him, for whom he would have to make some sort of provision, if the father wouldn't. Then the man returned. But he had no thoughts for his children. He walked jauntily up to the vicar, tapped him on the chest and said, "Now you listen 'ere, mate. I wont 'ave no funerals on Friday. Vat's Epsom day, see? No funerals. I wont 'ave 'er laughin' twice."

'That was the last the vicar saw of him. He didn't turn up for the funeral, which was on a Tuesday, and he simply abandoned his children. All of them ended up in the Workhouse.'

Sister Monica Joan said no more, and we continued walking. The sun was pleasant, and the ghosts of the past seemed long since asleep. Cynthia and I talked of our plans for the future. She was hoping to test her vocation in the religious life. I knew it was a huge step to take, requiring much thought and prayer, but I had always regarded Cynthia as a saint (or very nearly) and was not surprised. We came to a wooden seat and sat down, and she asked Sister's opinion.

'Do you think I am called to be a nun, Sister?'

'Only God knows. Many are called but few are chosen, my child.'

'What brought you to the religious life?'

'The conflict between good and evil. The eternal battle between God and the devil. I tried to resist the call, but it was too strong.'

The nun sat looking at the water. I ventured the question, 'Was there no other way?'

'For me, no. For others it is different. You do not have to be a nun to be at war with the devil. To be in the fight, on the side of the angels, is all that matters.'

'Do you believe in the devil?' I asked provocatively.

'Stupid, thoughtless child, of course I do. You only have to look at the record of the Nazis during the war to see the work of the devil.' The atrocities of the war were vivid in the minds of everyone.

She turned her head away from me scornfully. I had offended her, and she muttered, 'Thoughtless, empty questions,' but then said more gently to Cynthia, 'Test your vocation, my child. Become a Postulant, then a Novice. Time will reveal if you are truly called. It is a hard life, and doubts will always plague you. Just go with God.'

Mention of the Nazis brought to mind what Sister Julienne had told me some time earlier; that there was in Germany a community of Lutheran nuns, started in 1945 or 1946, just after the war, whose vocation was contemplative prayer and repentance for the sins of their fellow countrymen. The women lived a life of extreme privation, as near to concentration camp life as they could get: minimal food (the nuns were all close to starvation), scant clothing, no shoes, no heating in winter, and no beds, just a straw mattress and a thin blanket. And this life they lived in atonement for the sins of others. I had found this story deeply impressive, though I could not really understand the spiritual side of the vocation. I was grappling in my mind with the problems of sin, guilt, atonement, redemption, religious vocation and many unfathomable subjects, when abruptly Sister Monica Joan stood up.

'The water is not very deep,' she announced, 'I don't see how anyone could drown in it.'

'It is in the middle,' I pointed out. 'It takes cargo barges.'

'But you can see the bottom. Look, you can see the stones.'

'That's only at the edges. Anyway, the water level is low at the moment. I assure you it is deep in the middle.'

'I don't believe it. We shall see.'

Before we could stop her, and she was surprisingly nimble,

Sister Monica Joan had crossed the few steps to the canal and now stood ankle deep at the water's edge.

'There, I told you,' she cried triumphantly, 'the stories about people drowning in the Cuts are just fancy.' And she took another step towards the centre.

'Come back' screamed Cynthia and I in alarm. We leaped into the water beside her, but Sister was too quick for us.

'Don't be silly,' she called out, taking another step forward. But the Cuts was cut away, and instantly she fell forward into deep water.

Cynthia and I were not the only ones to hurl ourselves in after her. As many as a dozen East Enders dived, fully clothed, into the canal that Sunday afternoon. None of us need have bothered. It was immediately obvious that Sister Monica Joan could swim. Her habit did not absorb the water at once, and it floated around her like the wings of a huge black water-fowl. Her head was held high, and her white veil floated behind her like exotic plumage.

All might have been well, and Sister might have swum back to us, had it not been for the enthusiasm of three local lads who dived in from the other bank. They grabbed hold of her and began swimming back whence they had come.

'No, not that side!' I screamed. 'Come back – this side!' Everyone around, including those in the water, was screaming instructions. We all knew that if the boys landed Sister on the opposite bank there was no towpath exit to the bridge. But the lads did not or could not understand in all the confusion. They had pulled Sister to the middle of the canal and saw themselves as heroes. A powerful man, with muscles of oak and the speed of an Olympic swimmer, reached them first. He clouted one lad around the ear, pushed the other boy under, took hold of the protesting nun and swam back with her to our side.

Do not ask me how we got Sister Monica Joan to the convent. The whole process was too complicated and confusing. My memories are hazy: getting her clothes off with modesty and decorum; dozens of wet people offering advice; wondering what on earth to put on her; someone donating a raincoat, a cardigan, a baby's shawl; trying to find her shoes. The swimmer and another man got her to the Commercial Road by giving her a chair-lift. She sat regally on their crossed hands, holding their arms with perfect composure, as though a ducking in the Cuts were a regular experience. Someone must have stopped a lorry in the Commercial Road, because I remember the two men lifting Sister up into the lorry and settling her comfortably. She thanked them with queenly grace, and two tough, strong dockers blushed with pleasure. 'No trouble at all, ma'am,' they said. 'Any time. Good day, ma'am.'

Back at the Convent she was put to bed with hot-water bottles and hot drinks. She slept for twenty-four hours, and when she awoke, she appeared to have no memory at all of what had happened. She suffered no ill. It must have been the angels again.

TOO MANY CHILDREN

'I'm sorry, Mr Harding. Nothing can be done.'

'But you says we was top of the housing list.'

'You are. But there are building delays. Strikes. An electricians' strike.'

'We can move in wivout no electricity. We got no electrics where we are, so it don't matter.'

'I'm sorry, the Council cannot allow you to move into premises that are incomplete.'

'But I tells yer, it don't matter to us. We're desperate to move, anywhere'll do. Anywhere's better'n what we got.'

'It's out of the question, Mr Harding. The law is quite clear. Council premises must be adequate and suitable for the family applying for rehousing.'

The Council official shuffled his papers. His was an impossible job. Ten applicants for every house or flat being built. A housing list of thousands, every one of them clamouring for something better than the bomb-damaged buildings, the overcrowded and insanitary conditions in which they lived. But he had to follow the rules.

'Well, when vis electricians' strike's over, how long will it be? How long, eh?'

Bill Harding leaned forward menacingly. The official leaned back defensively.

'I don't know.'

Bill thumped the desk with his powerful fist.

''ow long? You must have some idea. How long's the strike gonna last? A week? Two weeks? Then we can move – yes?'

'I'm afraid not, Mr Harding. It's not just building delays. It's a question of size.'

'Size? What size?'

'Family size, Mr Harding. You have too many children. The Council at present is building two- and three-bedroom flats. We cannot allow a family of eight to move into a three-bedroom flat. We would have to provide a four-, or even five-bedroom flat or house for a family of this size. And at present the Council is simply not building five-bedroom flats.'

'But vat's daft. Three bedrooms is a luxury. More'n enough. We only gots one bedroom, and we all sleeps in it. We'd give anything for three bedrooms.'

'I'm sorry, Mr Harding. But we have our standards and our rules. We cannot rent a three-bedroom flat or house to a family of eight. It is simply not allowed.'

Bill had lost all his aggression, and despair overtook him. He sighed deeply and held his head in his hands. He had to get back to work. He had taken an hour off to see the Council, and it was like banging his head against a brick wall.

'Bloody red tape,' he groaned.

'I'm sorry, Mr Harding, really sorry. But the rules must be obeyed.'

Bill stood up and left without looking at the Council official, who, with a depressed and weary sigh, called, 'Next please,' knowing that the next interview would be as bad, or worse, than the last.

Bill slouched down the road towards the shipbuilder's yard, where he was a welder. He slunk against the wall and kicked a stone, hard. It shot across the pavement and hit a passing lorry. The stone ricocheted off and bounced back onto the pavement. A policeman saw what had happened and came over to Bill. No real damage had been done, but the copper tore a strip off Bill for dangerous and irresponsible behaviour. The incident did nothing to improve his humour – bloody red tape, bloody law. Well, his bloody job could wait; he needed a drink. He went into a pub and drank away his lunch hour until chucking-out time at two o'clock. He arrived back at the yard at 3 p.m., having been away since 11 a.m. The foreman came down on him like a ton of bricks. Bill swore obscenely at him and walked out. He walked around the streets until opening time at five o'clock and then got blind drunk.

Hilda made herself another cup of tea, lit a fag, and sat down at the table with her *Daily Mirror* propped up against the milk bottle. The two youngest children crawled around the floor, playing – thank God the older ones were at school and off her hands for a few hours. She couldn't face what she thought she knew. She sipped her tea and stared at the cracked wall and the huge damp stain on the grey-brown ceiling. It's gettin' bigger, she thought. When's the whole damn thing goin' to fall, that's what she wanted to know. No good talkin' to that landlord – you never saw him anyway, couldn't get past his agent, who only said if you don't like it get out, get your name on the Council housing list. Well they'd been on the damned list for five years, and look where it'd got them. Nowhere. Nuffink. Sweet Fanny Adams.

She poured herself another cup of tea, and laced it with sugar. Now this. She couldn't face it. Not another. But all the signs were there. She hadn't told Bill. Hadn't dared. Perhaps she should have told him before he went to the Council, but somehow she hadn't the courage. Wonder how he got on. He'd said he would be firm, wouldn't leave till he'd got the promise of a place, and a date. A date. That's what they wanted. A date to look forward to when they could leave this falling-down dump. She could wring that agent's neck. Last time she had pointed to the damp on the ceiling and asked for repairs, he had smiled and said it was a condemned property and that the Council wouldn't permit repairs because it was condemned. That's logic for you! She had heard the dripping last night as she lay awake wondering if she should tell Bill or not before he went to the Council, and the drips seemed to be getting closer.

They knew the roof had gone, but that was two storeys up, and the floors above them kept the rain out. But if the floors went, then there would be no roof over their heads. She must get Bill to go upstairs and lay a tarpaulin over the floor above. That would keep them dry for a bit, and then they might get a Council flat. Bill would be at the Council office now. He'd tell 'em.

The children were playing boats – floating matches on a bucket of water. One of them had an empty match box which the other wanted. He grabbed at it. The child screamed and lunged at his brother. 'Mind it,' shouted Hilda. But too late. They had tipped the bucket over, and water streamed across the floor. 'You little devils,' she shouted as she jumped up, and walloped them both. 'Look at the mess. Now I've got to clear it up.' She got a cloth and wiped up the water, wringing it out into the empty bucket. Well at least it's giving the floor a clean, she thought as she wiped and wrung. 'Now I've gotta go an' get more water. An' don't you touch anyfink while I'm gone,' she said menacingly. She picked up the bucket of dirty water. Might as well empty the pot while I'm downstairs. She pulled the chamber pot from under the bed and carried it down the creaking and rickety stairs. This stinkin' stairwell's worse than our rooms, she thought. At least we've made an effort to put a bit of paint on an' I try to keep them clean. No one's repaired or decorated this landing or these stairs for years. An' as for cleanin'. Well you might as well save your effort. She went out into the yard, to the lavatory with its asbestos roof and broken door and emptied the chamber pot. She pulled the chain – well at least it still flushes, but for how long? How long? How long would they have to wait in this hell-hole? She'd murder that landlord if she could get her hands on him.

Might as well do the washin', now I've got some clean water. She filled two saucepans and lit the gas stove on the landing, then went down again for another bucket of cold water. And now, just when the little one was out of nappies. Now this! She shut her mind to the possibility of more – yet more – nappies. She filled the tin bath – the one they all washed and bathed in – with hot water, added some soapflakes and started the daily chore with her dolly-board and a bar of Sunlight. The little ones clung to her skirts and wanted to help, but she pushed them away. A couple of hours later she had finished the washing, wringing, rinsing, mangling and hanging out. Well, at least it's a fine day. It'll soon be dry. That's one comfort. The little ones were clamouring for their dinner, and two of her children, those of primary school age, would be home for their midday meal. Thank God the others get theirs at school now. Saves a bit of trouble, anyhow. She had a small cupboard on the landing where she kept some food. Not too much, or it'd get pinched in this rotten hole. She pulled out a couple of tins of baked beans and some sliced bread. The grill sometimes worked – she tried it. Yes, it was working today. They could have beans on toast. Always enjoy it, they do.

The downstairs door opened, and two grubby children tumbled upstairs, pushing, shouting, laughing. 'Now shut yer noise, an' siddown, 'ere's yer beans on toast, and don't get it all over yerselves.'

She tried to eat a bit herself, but it made her feel sick. Oh no – another sign! Can't be much doubt. She'd have to see the doctor, she would.

After she'd packed the children off to school at two o' clock, she had to get some grub in for the evening. She went to the corner shop, the one she'd known since childhood, the one her mother got tick from when there was no money and no food in the place and a brood of half-starved kids. Well at least she wasn't always living on the breadline, not like her poor mum – at least she could feed her kids and not do without herself. Bill earned a good wage, and his job was secure, thanks to the Trade Union. She bought some more bread and half a pound of bacon. They could have fried bread and bacon this evening, then on reflection she added a large tin of beans. Well, at least they get some good food, bacon's more than she ever got when she was a kid, she mused. The two toddlers were restive and excited to be out, so she took them for a bit of a walk, not too far because she was tired, and she didn't want to go past the bomb site where the meths drinkers hung out. They scared her. She went down the street where she had played as a child, but it depressed her – all the windows boarded up, signs of demolition at the far end. Wearily she made her way back home.

Four o' clock and the brood would be home. She steeled herself for the rush and the noise. She prepared a large quantity of beans and bacon and fried bread. 'Now get that inside yer, an' go out an' play. An' take ve babies with you. I've had 'em all day, an' I'm just about up to here with 'em.' She raised her hand to her neck to indicate how high. The children gobbled down their food, and rushed out.

Hilda settled down to a quiet cup of tea and *Woman* magazine. It was the only time of day she got any peace – when the bigger children took the little ones off her hands. An hour later she thought, it's getting dark. The kids'd better be in. She went to the window and yelled down the street. No children in sight. They'll be on that bomb site, I'll be bound. I've told 'em not to. It's not safe. You wait till I get my hands on 'em, little devils. Muttering and grumbling, Hilda trudged off to the bomb site and gathered up her brood, cuffing each of the bigger ones round the ear as she did so. 'You jes' wait till I tells yer dad you've been down 'ere,' she shouted. The boys grinned and made rude faces and dodged out of her reach.

It was nine o'clock by the time they were all in bed, the four little ones in the bedroom, the two older ones in the cupboard – a decent-sized cupboard, she and Bill had agreed when they took the room shortly after the war, almost as big as another room. We can put all our junk in there, they had said, laughing.

Now it was full of kids! Still no Bill. What's happened to him? She sat down with another cup of tea and another fag.

At 10.45 she heard the front door bang and heard Bill singing down below. Her heart leaped – he's got good news – she jumped up to get another cup for him. He'd like a cup of tea before his meal, and then he could tell her the news. The door opened slowly, with Bill clinging to it. He swung into the room and leaned heavily against the wall, staring vacantly at her. Oh no, not drunk, she'd have to be careful, treat him gently, no questions, no chatter, she didn't want his fist in her face. Mrs Hatterton had got her nose broken only last week. But Bill's not like that, not really. She sat him down and took off his boots.

'Like some bacon and beans, eh, ducks?'

'Nope.'

'Cup o' tea?'

'Nope.'

''Ow about a nice bacon sandwich, ven?'

'Vat's more like it.' His eyes brightened a little.

She went to the gas stove on the landing, made two rounds and brought them to him. He hadn't eaten all day and devoured the first ravenously.

'Nice cup of tea to wash it down?'

He nodded. He was beginning to look more like himself.

He'll be all right after a good night's sleep. No trouble. You just need to know how to handle a drunk man, then you get no trouble. But her Bill wasn't like that anyway, wouldn't hurt a fly, but still you never knew, when the drink was on them. She went into the bedroom and pushed two children over to the far side of the bed so that there would be space for their father to lie down. She led Bill into the bedroom, quietly undressed him and held the chamber-pot for him to have a jimmy riddle. The pot was so full she had to go downstairs to empty it, and when she returned he was sprawled sideways across the bed, his feet and legs around two sleeping children.

There was no room for her, so she spent the night in a chair, wrapped in a coat.

She roused herself at six and went down to get some water. She made a pot of tea and buttered some bread, then she quietly shook Bill. 'Come on. You've got to get off to work,' she whispered so as not to wake the children. He struggled to his feet, sober, but somewhat the worse for wear. They sat at the table together. She lit a Woodbine, stuck it in his mouth and pushed his tea and bread towards him.

'You're a good girl, ducks,' he muttered, drawing on the fag.

'Well? What happened yesterday?'

'Happened? I got pissed, that's what.'

'No, afore vat. At ve Council.'

His mind slid backwards, and he groaned.

'Nuffink. Zilch. Gotta wait.'

'Wait! We've waited five years. I thought we was top of ve housin' list.'

'We are. But we still gotta wait.'

'Why?' she said savagely.

'Too many kids, vat's why.'

'How d'ya mean? They said all the kids 'ave to move to better, 'ealthier places.'

'I know. But we got too many. Council has to provide a four-bedroom 'ouse for two adults an' six kids. An' vey only builds two and fhree-bedroom places at the moment.'

'But we can manage with three bedrooms. We've only got one an' a cupboard here.'

'I tells ve bloke vat, but it makes no difference. It's rules – bloody rules.'

'I don't believe it. Vis place is fallin' down.'

'I told 'em so, an' vey say as what it's not Council property, so it's not ve Council's responsibility. We 'ave ter ask our landlord for repairs.'

'Fat lot of use that'll be. Look, let's get vis clear. Council has three-bedroom houses, but we can't 'ave one 'cause we got six children?'

'That's abou' it. We're stuck. Now I've gotta get off. Can't be late today.' The front door slammed, and footsteps hurried down the street.

THE ABORTIONIST

Hilda sat at the wooden table and lit another fag. She was stunned. Foremost in her mind was the suspicion that had been nagging at her for three weeks. What a blessing she hadn't told Bill! Only yesterday she thought she would have to, and then go to the doctor. Not now, no siree, no bleeding doctors. She'd see Mrs Prichard, who was well thought of in the area. She'd enquire in the corner shop. Someone would know how to find her. Hilda got the children up and packed them off to school, paying little heed to their demands and squabbles. Her mind was planning what she would have to do – the sooner the better, every day would count.

Discreet enquiries led her to Mrs Prichard. She had to be very careful. Back-street abortions were quite common in those days, but the practice was illegal, and both the client and the abortionist could be prosecuted if caught and would face a prison sentence if convicted. Every precaution was necessary.

Mrs Prichard and her daughter lived in a better class of house on the Commercial Road. To the police, local doctors, church and social workers, she was a herbalist, specialising in potions, known only to the mystics, for the cure of hay-fever, gout, arthritic knees and so on. Her front room was filled with bottles and phials. Her premises had been inspected several times by the public health authorities, who had found her remedies and treatments to be harmless, if ineffectual. Evidence of the more lucrative side of her business was nowhere to be seen. She had learned her trade from her mother, who had been an abortionist since the 1880s, and when the old lady died Mrs Prichard had inherited the equipment which had been stolen from a hospital about fifty years earlier.

Mrs Prichard was a well-upholstered lady. She wore smart suits and several gold chains over her ample bosom. Her face was heavily made up, and her eyebrows, plucked until nothing was left, were replaced by a thin pencil arc, reaching high into her forehead. Her hair was a colour that no woman of her age could hope to retain and was elaborately coiffed and curled. She greeted Hilda with a smile, and listened to her story sympathetically. When she spoke her voice was falsely genteel, an accent beloved by character actresses.

'Oh, my dear, what you got is stomach cramps. I sees a lot of it these days. The doctors don't know what to do with it. Don't know nothing, they don't. I can't think why they have all that training – they don't seem to learn nothing. Can't even treat a simple case of stomach cramps. Inflammation of the intestines, I calls it, dear. Going up or going down, it makes no difference, the intestines has a lot of work to do, and they get inflammation. Now what you need is some of my special stomach cramps mixture, dear. My own remedy, known only to myself. My dear deceased mother, who was a wise woman as ever there was one, passed the secret on to me on her death-bed. "Don't let anyone get it off of you," she says as she was dyin' like. "It's more precious than gold," she says. "Them doctors don't know nothing about it," she says, and then she expired, leaving me with the secret.'

Mrs Prichard wiped her eye and sniffed sadly as she went over to a counter. She took several bottles off the shelves, and with a measuring glass and a great deal of care, and with one eye shut, squinting against the light, she filled a bottle. Hilda was most impressed.

'That will be two guineas, dear, and worth ten of anyone's money, I can tell you. Now take a tablespoonful night and morning for five days. It will make the stomach cramps worse at first, but that is a sign that the potion is working, so don't stop taking it, will you, dear? It's got to get worse afore it gets better. If you don't get any bleeding, come back to me next week. My dear mother left me on her death-bed with other secret remedies for stomach cramps, known only to myself.'

Mrs Prichard pocketed the two guineas. Smiling and solicitous, she showed Hilda to the door.

'Now remember, dear, this is for stomach cramps. Mrs Prichard treats all sorts: headaches, migraines, ingrown toenails, flatulence, tennis elbow and stomach cramps. If anyone asks you, this potion is for them stomach cramps, which you 'ave been suffering of.'

Hilda took the potion as directed for five days. The taste was so revolting that it made her retch with each dose, and the pain in her stomach was intense. The third day she developed violent diarrhoea and vomiting, and spent most of the night in the outside lavatory. She sat curled up with pain on the rough wooden seat, trying not to cry out as the fluid poured from her. This'll get rid of it, she thought, and good riddance. In the morning she looked hopefully for signs of blood – but there were none. For three more days she put up with the pain and nausea and diarrhoea, trying to pretend to Bill and the children that nothing was wrong, but by the sixth day she was forced to admit that it had all been to no avail. She had lost no blood. She was still pregnant.

Hilda felt weak and shaky when she returned to Mrs Prichard, who in contrast looked splendid. Her hair had been newly dyed and was piled up on her head in layers of curled sausages. Her make-up was even thicker than before, and her lips and fingernails were a vivid red.

'Oh, my dear. These naughty cramps. Sometimes they really have to be swept away with a new broom. My dear mother always used to say that, if the cramps don't go with the old trusty broom, you've got to get out the new. Now it's up to you, dear. Do you want me to get out my new broom to sweep them clean away? I will have to come to your place, of course. Can't be done here. I ain't got the premises. And my daughter will have to come with me. I need her as my trusty assistant, you understand. And there must be no one around, no children nor husbands nor nothing like that, you understand? The decision is yours, dear.'

Hilda gulped, and felt sick.

'Will it hurt?' she murmured.

'Hardly a prick, my dear. I will give you a potion, my mother's secret mixture what she gave me when she was a-dying. It numbs the senses.'

'Is there no other way?'

'If the potion for cramps don't work, my dear, it means it's a real sticking, stubborn sort of cramp, and the only way is a new broom.'

'All right. When can you do it?'

'Wednesday morning. And it'll be twenty guineas. Ten guineas now, and ten when I've done. You won't regret a penny, my dear.'

Hilda went to the post office and drew out twenty guineas from the War Time Savings Account she had guarded so carefully to buy new furniture when she and Bill got their new place. She returned to Mrs Prichard, who took the money with 'You won't regret a penny, my dear. Till Wednesday.'

Hilda spent the next few days in an agony of doubt and indecision. Had she done wrong? Should she go through with it? She could cancel the whole thing and just have the baby. But the thought of a seventh baby in that horrible flat filled her with such dismay that she thought anything would be better. Should she tell Bill? She didn't know. Men are so squeamish, perhaps he'd rather not know. Then again he might start blabbing to his mates at work, and then, who knows where it might get to. Next thing they'd have the Law knocking on their door. She decided not to tell him.

On Wednesday, Mrs Hatterton opposite agreed to have the two little ones for the day, and the older children had all been sent to school with instructions to have school dinners and not to come back until four o'clock. Hilda waited with pounding heart. She had carried up several buckets of water, laid out clean towels and sheets and provided a few rolls of cotton wool. She didn't know what else to do. The waiting's the worst, she thought. There was a knock on the door at nine thirty, and she nearly jumped out of her skin, though she had been expecting it.

Mrs Prichard and her daughter entered. The two women were soberly, even drably, dressed in brown mackintoshes. They both had their hair wound up in curlers with a headscarf tied over the top, which was a common sight amongst East End women. They carried wicker shopping baskets from which protruded cabbages, leeks, turnip tops and brussel tops. They looked exactly like a couple of housewives coming back from market. It was a disguise to fool the police.

'Now, dear, the sooner we get on with this, the sooner it's over. Let me see your premises.'

Mrs Prichard mounted the rickety staircase going up from the foul-smelling hallway and wrinkled her sensitive nose in disgust.

'I'm not surprised, dear, that you wants to get rid of these stomach cramps.'

She looked round Hilda's rooms with a professional eye.

'Can't use the bedroom. We'll have to do it on the kitchen table. I will need some hot water. Where's the gas-stove? On the landing! That won't do. The hot water must be ready and in here. Now, can we lock the door? No? Why not? The door must be locked from the inside. Find the key. Ah, is that it? Good. Now clear the table. Draw those curtains; we don't want any prying eyes, do we, dear? Now dear, drink this. It's my mother's potion to numb the senses – and climb up on that table. Miriam, put that bucket there, and that bowl there, put those towels here, and get those sheets under her buttocks. I wants you to hold the knees against the chest, and to keep them there whatever happens.'

Miriam was a large, silent female, and she grunted her acquiescence.

Trembling, Hilda drank the potion as instructed and shakily climbed onto the table. She lay down in what is known medically as the 'lithotomy position', with her buttocks at the edge of the table, her legs drawn upwards and spread apart. Her head was spinning. A silky voice penetrated her hazy mind.

'Have you got the other ten guineas, dear? A professional person can't be expected to carry out professional duties without due payment.'

'On the shelf, in the brown pot,' Hilda answered thickly. Miriam went to the pot and took the money.

Mrs Prichard delved amongst the leeks and brussel tops and produced her instruments. They were exceedingly old and made of rough, unpolished steel, virtually impossible to sterilise – if, indeed, Mrs Prichard ever made any attempts at sterilisation. They consisted of a few ancient surgical instruments, such as forceps, dilators, curettes and a Higginson's syringe.

'Just a little prick, dear, you'll hardly feel a thing,' Mrs Prichard cooed, as she inserted her fingers into the vagina. Hilda felt no discomfort. This is going to be all right, she thought. The drug she had taken made her feel light-headed and sleepy.

Mrs Prichard glanced at her and muttered to her daughter, 'Keep her firmly in that position and have the towels ready.' She felt with her fingers until she thought she had located the cervix. She hissed, 'Keep her still now,' and with the forceps she grabbed the cervix and pulled it towards her. Hilda felt a pain like a knife stabbing her body, but she managed to suppress a scream. Holding the cervix quite firmly Mrs Prichard took one of the dilators and attempted to force it through the closed cervix, with no success. 'Too big,' muttered the abortionist and reached for a smaller dilator, which she pushed hard against the cervical orifice. Hilda felt pain like burning knives tearing her body apart. She opened her mouth to scream, but a towel was thrust in, pushing her tongue backwards and nearly choking her.

Miriam's weight held her legs fast against her body so that she could not move.

Mrs Prichard had a curette at her disposal. So she poked with it in a blind attempt to force entry through the cervix into the uterus. When she thought she had succeeded she started scraping around and continued scraping until blood began to flow. The pain was so intense that Hilda passed out, and when she regained consciousness she was vomiting, but the towel that had been thrust into her mouth was still there so she started choking. 'Pull that towel away; we don't want her to choke on us,' muttered Mrs Prichard.

The fresh blood flowed freely, but Hilda was unaware of it. She was conscious only of the vomit that was rising in her throat and of the towel being snatched away just in time, before she inhaled her own vomit, which would probably have killed her. She was aware of a silky voice saying, 'There now. A nice flow of blood. That's all you needed, dear. A nice new broom to sweep away them stomach cramps. You'll be all right now, dear. You might feel shaky for a day or two, but it'll soon pass, and you'll be fine. Now get up, dear. Yes, you can get up all right and go and lie on the bed for an hour or two. We'll do the clearing up. It's all part of the service. I pride myself on never leaving a mess behind.'

Hilda staggered to her feet and with the help of Miriam went to the bedroom. As she passed the end of the table she saw a bowl full of blood and blood dripping off the table onto the floor. Has that all come from me, she thought and clung to the towel the women had put between her legs. She vomited again. 'Have some more potion, dear,' said Mrs Prichard smoothly. 'It will ease the stomach and help you sleep. These cramps can be real nasty, can't they, dear?' Hilda drank the potion, and lay down on the bed. She drifted again into unconsciousness, a state that kept coming and going for the rest of the day.

The two women cleared up, after a fashion, Mrs Prichard muttering 'If she expects us to clean this hovel, she's got another think coming,' then left Hilda bleeding, shocked and semi-conscious.

Mrs Hatterton brought the toddlers back at three o'clock. She saw the state that Hilda was in and put two and two together. 'You poor soul,' she murmured. She took the children back to her place and returned with clean towels and sheets and carried fresh water up, because Hilda was raging with thirst. She took away the bloodied linen and packed the clean around the injured woman. Later she took the older children to her place too, and fed them, returning to Hilda several times to change the linen and to give her a drink. When she saw Bill returning at six o'clock, she stopped him in the street and told him his wife was ill. Nothing more. She told him that she would keep the children till her old man came back, but then they would have to return home. Bill just assumed that his wife had 'flu – 'She's bin a bit off colour lately.' He had no idea, and was aghast when he saw Hilda, deathly white, scarce able to move or speak. 'I'll get a doctor,' he said. 'No, no, don't, you mustn't,' was the woman's anguished reply. She had to tell him, but he did not comprehend. 'Women's troubles,' was his reaction. No man had anything to do with women's troubles. He made his tea and went out. Mrs Hatterton brought the six children back at seven thirty and put them to bed, two in the cupboard and the others on the sofa or in the cot which she pulled into the main room. She gave Hilda some more water and changed her linen again. 'You'll have to manage,' she said. She did not suggest getting a doctor. She knew, as Hilda did, that a doctor would probably mean police involvement and prosecution. These things had to be kept quiet. 'I'll be in tomorrow,' she said as she left.

Bill returned at ten thirty. He had been drinking, but was not drunk. Hilda looked no better. 'You sure you don't want no doctor?' he asked, concerned. She had to explain to him that a doctor was legally bound to inform the police of a criminal abortion. He didn't really understand, but the mention of police kept him silent. Seeing Hilda so pale and weak stirred his old tenderness for her. 'How about a nice cup o' tea, eh, duck?' he said kindly, 'do you good.' Hilda forced a smile, 'A cup o' tea would be nice. And Bill, thanks. Thanks for everything.' The children slept on.

It took about three weeks for Hilda to recover her strength. The bleeding stopped within a few days, but the shock, the pain and the general weakness kept her in bed for most of that time. Mrs Hatterton was good to her. She came in daily and saw the bigger children off to school. She cared for the toddlers, and did the washing, shopping, cooking and carrying of water up and down stairs. Mrs Prichard was not seen again. Her professional services did not include post-operative care.

BACK-STREET ABORTIONS

A woman's right to control her own body is so taken for granted now that younger people can scarcely believe that abortion used to be a criminal offence in the UK punishable by a prison sentence for the woman and the abortionist. The Criminal Abortion Act of 1803 was law for 165 years. It was only repealed in 1967.

There have always been women who wanted or needed an abortion. For rich women it was relatively easy – a clandestine visit to a secret address, often abroad, where a doctor working in an unregistered clinic would operate illegally, and usually successfully, leaving little damage to the woman. Sometimes it was possible to procure an abortion legally if two doctors, one a psychiatrist, would testify that the woman seeking the abortion was mentally and physically incapable of carrying the pregnancy to full term. It cost a lot of money, but the risk of prosecution was removed.

For poor women it was a different story. Most working-class people lived in a perpetual state of poverty, the whole family crowded into one, two or at most three rooms, with not enough food, lighting or heating. Contraception was inadequate, and women had too many children, far more than they could decently house or feed. Another baby was frequently a disaster. For single women pregnancy was a catastrophe, and many preferred suicide to the stigma of bearing an illegitimate child.

So millions of women sought an abortion. The first method attempted was usually a simple vaginal douche. But this was unlikely to work, because the fluid has to enter the uterus to be effective. If a caustic solution was used it caused chemical burns to the vagina and cervix.

Thousands of women tried medicinal ways of evacuating the uterus. Violent purgatives, such as a pint of Epsom Salts, were used. Gin and ginger, turpentine, raw spirit, aloes and sloes were also employed. None of them worked. Disreputable newspapers and journals advertised what they called 'cures for menstrual blockage' for a sum of money. These were poisonous and sometimes fatal. Quinine was common, and some 'cures' even contained arsenic or mercury.

'Wise women' have known for millennia that the black fungal growth on rye grain will induce an abortion. It was called 'ergot', and was also known to cause the deadly disease commonly called St Anthony's Fire. When I was a young pupil midwife doing my theoretical training at a teaching hospital, a colleague was having an affair with a doctor and she became pregnant. She stole a bottle of ergometrine from the ward medicine cupboard and took the tablets over a period of days until she aborted. She became terribly ill, but such was her desperation that she continued working throughout. If Matron had discovered that she was pregnant, my colleague would have been dismissed, and if it had come to light that she had been stealing ergometrine, her name would have been removed from the register (she was an SRN) and very likely reported to the police for prosecution under the Criminal Abortion Act.

Some women tried violent methods, such as falling downstairs, or half drowning, or taking a scalding hot bath, in the hope that they would provoke a spontaneous miscarriage. If the woman survived, she would usually still be pregnant, because one would virtually have to kill the mother before the foetus could be destroyed.

Driven to extremes by despair, women would go to unbelievable lengths in trying to make themselves miscarry. Knitting needles, crochet hooks, metal coathangers, paper knives, pickle spoons, curved upholstery needles, spokes of bicycle wheels have all been forced into the uterus by desperate women who preferred to do anything rather than continue the pregnancy.

How any woman could push an instrument through the closed os of her own cervix is more than I can imagine – but it has been done, times without number, sometimes successfully.

I have given talks to women's groups on the early days of midwifery. In the course of many of these talks, some lady in the audience has told us a story about a grandmother or great aunt who had induced an abortion on herself. I have heard many such stories, and in diverse circumstances, and they are all so dismally similar that the oral evidence cannot be in doubt.

One story, related by a lady at a Women's Institute meeting, will suffice: 'My aunt was a respectable single woman of thirty-five living with her mother, who was very proud of the family reputation. While on holiday my aunt became pregnant and tried to abort herself with a crochet hook. She bled profusely, and her mother found out what was going on. The old lady was so horrified at what the neighbours might say that at first she refused to call a doctor. It was not until it became obvious that her daughter would die that, in great secrecy, she summoned a doctor who performed an evacuation of the uterus and suturing on the kitchen table of their home. Afterwards he said, "this must not go beyond the walls of this house. No one but we three will know what has happened tonight." The story was not told in the family for forty years.'

The doctor had saved the woman's life but he had risked his career in doing so. Had the story become known and his name reported to the General Medical Council he would have been brought up before a disciplinary committee for professional misconduct. He might have got away with it by pleading that it was a life-saving emergency operation, but there would have been no certainty of exoneration and whatever the outcome such an experience would have been traumatic for a conscientious doctor.

The alternative to attempting to make oneself miscarry was a visit to an illegal abortionist. Back-street abortionists favoured one of two methods: the surgical procedure or the flushing-out method. Both are highly dangerous, and only a doctor trained in surgery is competent to conduct an abortion. However, that did not stop countless numbers of women practising for a fee. They had a vague idea of female anatomy and operated with improvised instruments such as those described, or with obsolete instruments often stolen from a hospital. There was no sterility, no anaesthetic, no proper lighting, and operations frequently took place on kitchen tables.

It is easy to push a metal object into the vagina, but the cervix lies at nearly a ninety-degree angle to the vaginal wall. Without surgical knowledge the instruments could easily miss the cervix and go straight through the vaginal wall. Working blind, abortionists had been known to push a sharp object into the bladder or rectum. If the instrument did enter the uterus, it was sometimes pushed right through and out the other side. Even if all these hazards were avoided, bleeding was frequently uncontrollable.

In my book *Call the Midwife*, I recall meeting Mary, a young Irish girl who was lured into prostitution. She told me the tragic story of her only friend in the brothel, who became pregnant. The madam called in an abortionist, who used the surgical method. The girl haemorrhaged and died in Mary's arms. Her body disappeared, and no one was prosecuted.

In 2004 a film about an abortionist – *Vera Drake* – was released. It is a brilliant film exploring the social dilemmas of the time. The film is probably regarded by millions as an accurate template of back-street abortions in the 1950s, but it does contain inaccuracies.

In the film, the flushing-out method was favoured. Vera Drake was seen supposedly pumping a solution of carbolic soap and water into a woman's uterus with a Higginson's syringe. But what she was doing was no more than a simple vaginal douche, which was unlikely to have any effect on the course of pregnancy because the fluid would only enter the vagina, not the uterus.

Flushing-out may seem less traumatic than the surgical method – in the film it is made to look very simple, even gentle – but it is still fraught with danger. Firstly, the caustic solution has to be exactly right; too weak and it will have no effect, too strong and it will burn the mucosa of the internal organs. Secondly the quantity of fluid and the rate of introduction into the uterus have to be accurate. One of the most severe pains a human being can endure is the sudden distension of a hollow organ. If too much fluid is pumped too fast into the uterus it could cause shock, a sudden drop in blood pressure, heart failure and even death.

At a talk I gave to the East London History Society in 2006, a woman in the audience told us that, in the 1930s, in the small Essex village where she was born, there was a bona fide midwife who was also an abortionist. She was a good practitioner, experienced and respected. A mother in the village came to her and said that her fourteen-year-old daughter was pregnant and begged her to carry out an abortion. The woman did not want to, but the mother pleaded so earnestly that eventually she agreed. The flushing-out method was used, and the girl died on the table. Mother and abortionist were sent to prison.

As nurses and midwives we often had to clear up the mess after a bungled abortion, especially when we worked on gynaecological wards. The outcome for these women was frequently chronic ill health. Conditions such as anaemia, scar tissue with adhesions, prolapse with chronic pain, incontinence, cystitis or nephritis could be expected, along with many others. Thrombosis of the leg was not uncommon. This could lead to a clot travelling in the bloodstream and lodging in the lungs. Anticoagulants were not available until the 1950s.

I have seen much mutilation and two deaths. The first was a girl of nineteen whose internal mucosa and cervix had been burned by a carbolic acid or some other caustic solution used during a flushing-out abortion. There was little we could do, and she lingered for a while, but she was in constant agony and died after a few days.

I recall another tragic woman, the mother of five children, who developed a massive sac of pus in the peritoneum after a surgical abortion. We tried to drain it without success, and for many weeks pus oozed from her abdomen. The five children coming into hospital just before their mother died can never be forgotten.

The Criminal Abortion Act 1803 was repealed in 1967. Knowing that I had been a midwife I was sometimes asked if I approved of it or not. My reply was that I did not regard it as a moral issue, but as a medical issue. A minority of women will always want an abortion. Therefore it must be done properly.★

★ My thanks to the Marie Stopes Society for reading and approving this essay.

STRANGER THAN FICTION

Life, my dear Watson, is infinitely stranger than fiction; stranger than anything which the mind of man could invent. We could not conceive the things that are merely commonplace to existence. If we could hover over this great city, remove the roofs, and peep in at the things going on, it would make all fiction, with its conventionalities and foreseen conclusions flat, stale, and unprofitable.
The Adventures of Sherlock Holmes, by Sir Arthur Conan Doyle

A couple of months passed, and Hilda was just about able to cope with her household again, but the constant clamour of young children, incessant washing, endless meals to prepare and above all the squalid surroundings were dragging her down. She became more and more depressed, irritable with the children and quiet with Bill. He hadn't seen her like this before. They had always had fun together. Now she was a woman who hardly spoke. Sometimes he wondered what he had done wrong. He'd always been a good husband and a good father – or he'd tried to be – he'd always brought his money home, not like some of the blokes who drank all their money, and then beat their wives for not cooking a hot dinner for them.

Hilda roused herself and went to the Council. She was going to have it out with them. But she could have saved herself the effort. No four-bedroom houses or flats were available. They were scheduled for building next year, and the Hardings would be informed. Yes, they were top of the list, and they would be the first to be offered a place. In the meantime . . .

In the meantime, Hilda came close to throwing herself under a bus. But suicide is not so easy, and she balked at the actual fact of doing it. Life dragged on.

Another couple of weeks passed, and something strange was

happening in Hilda's body. At first she thought it was wind, and she took a dose of Epsom Salts. After a good clear-out, it seemed to settle down, and she thought no more of it. But a week later it came back, and then again with added emphasis. She put her hands on her tummy, and at that instant felt an unmistakable kick. With horror and disbelief the truth dawned upon her: the bleeding she had experienced must have come from a rupture to an artery, and the abortion achieved with so much pain and suffering, not to mention expense, had been a failure. She was still pregnant.

In a furious rage she took the bus to the Commercial Road and knocked on Mrs Prichard's door. The house was the same, the plush interior the same, Mrs Prichard − overdressed and over-painted − was the same, but gone the welcoming smile, the sympathetic voice, the womanly understanding.

'Well?' she demanded.

'You fraud. I'm still pregnant.'

'If you are going to descend to calling names of me, I've nothing to say to you.'

'Did you 'ear? I'm still pregnant.'

'You never was pregnant when I saw you. You had stomach cramps, if you cast your mind back, and I treated you for stomach cramps, with my dear deceased mother's secret remedies.'

'You liar. You did an abortion on me.'

'I did no such thing. And don't you call me a liar, you dirty little rat-bag.'

'You did, you stinking liar.'

'If you use that word again, you can leave my house. I'm a herbalist. I practise ancient remedies, passed on to me by wise women.'

'Then what did you do at my place, when you nearly killed me?'

'I came to your stinking hovel out of the kindness of my heart, because you kept a-pesterin' me with your stomach cramps. In the goodness of my nature, I do occasionally visit clients.'

'You nearly killed me.'

'Rubbish.'

'You did. The pain nearly killed me.'

'Well you look all right now.'

'No thanks to you, you bloody butcher.'

'Ooh, I can't stand this foul language any longer. I must ask you to be a-leave-taking of.'

'Not till I get my twenty guineas back.'

'Twenty guineas! What twenty guineas? I never heard such fairy-tales in all my life. I charged you two guineas for the secret herbal potion as was passed on to me by my dear deceased mother for the efficacious treatment of stomach cramps, remedies as what is known only to the select few.'

'Damn your dear deceased mother!'

'Oh, my poor mother. She would turn in her grave.'

Mrs Prichard took a lace handkerchief, and applied it to her mascara-ed eyes. Hilda was beside herself with rage.

'Are you goin' to give me back my twenty guineas what you took off me for a bungled abortion?'

'Excuse I, but I did not take twenty guineas off of you.'

Mrs Prichard walked swiftly to the door, her high-heeled shoes clicking as she walked.

'Miriam, dear. Come here, will you?'

Miriam entered, strong and silent, and stared hard at Hilda.

'This, er – lady, shall we say – this lady, Miriam, says that I took twenty guineas off of her. I did not. Did you receive any money, Miriam?

'No.'

'There you are, you see. Neither of us took any money off of you. You are fabricating, I'm afraid. I've met the likes of you before.'

'Then what did you do at my place, what nearly killed me?'

'Don't exaggerate. We gave you an enema for stomach cramps and left you well and comfortable.'

'An enema?'

'An herbal enema. That was all.'

'But it nearly killed me. I bled like a pig.'

'Piles, my dear. Piles. If you got piles what bleed in your – er – lower passage, you can hardly hold me responsible. Now, if you will excuse me, I have important work to do. I am expecting her ladyship, Lady Lucrecia, who won't hear of going to no one else for her migraines and dizzy spells.

'Damn you, d'you hear me, you painted ol' sow.'

'Oh, I have never been so insulted in all my life.'

Mrs Prichard patted her hair, her crimson fingernails fluttering. A gold bangle flashed on her wrist. It was an action calculated to make Hilda feel shabby.

Poor Hilda, clinically depressed, anaemic, weary, worn down by work and worry, still suffering from the pain inflicted by this woman, was suddenly made aware of her seven-year-old utility coat, her down-at-heel shoes, her straggly hair, her swollen hands and broken fingernails. The unspoken taunt drove her beyond the limits of self-control. She lunged out, trying to grab the blonde curls and pull them out by the roots, but Miriam stepped forward quickly and held her. Pinioned she screamed with frustration.

'You painted bitch, you, with yer false bloody eyelashes, and yer blonde wig and yer la-di-da accent. Yer nuffink but a sly, filthy, thieving ol' cow.'

'Oh, this is too much. If my dear deceased husband could hear you, he would defend me.'

'An' damn your dear deceased husband, an' all.'

'Now you're insultin' my hero hubby, Captain Prichard, what died an 'ero's death at the Battle of Agincourt in the last war. Miriam, show this person out.'

Miriam, strong, silent and menacing, took Hilda's arm, propelled her towards the street door and pushed her out onto the pavement. Blinded by tears, Hilda dragged herself back to her place – she always used 'place' in her mind; 'flat' was too posh a word for the dump. She bought four pounds of sausages and a couple of loaves at the corner shop. That would keep them quiet for the evening. 'Everything OK, Mrs Harding?' enquired the shopkeeper brightly. Nosy devil, always tittle-tattling, thought Hilda. 'Yes, everyfink's OK,' she said, sullenly. All that pain and suffering, all that time in bed feeling ill – and for nothing. She was back to where she started, and twenty guineas lighter.

In the evening, after the kids had gone to bed, she told Bill that the abortion had been a failure and she was still pregnant. He received the news in silence, drawing deep on his Woodbine. She'd seemed a bit off colour. So that was it.

'You're sure, are you?'

'Quite.' At least he didn't seem cross. Resentful, perhaps, but not cross.

'We've got too many kids as it is.'

'I know.'

'We can't do wiv any more.'

'I know.'

'Isn't there anyfink else you can do?' he asked hopefully, 'something what'll get rid of it?'

She sighed. If only he knew what she'd been through.

'I've tried. I've done everything I can, an' I'm still pregnant. There's nothing for it but to go through with it. I'm sorry, Bill.'

Then he did something surprising, something she had not expected. He took her hand. A simple gesture, but it made all the difference. He squeezed her hand and said, 'You don't need to be sorry, duck. It's my fault, as much as your'n. We've always had fun together, you an' me. That's the trouble – too much fun.' He grinned and winked at her. 'We'll see it through together. You'll see. As long as we sticks together, we'll see it through. There now, don't cry. Everythings gonna be OK. I'll go out and fetch a jug of ale. That'll see you right.'

When he had gone, Hilda dropped her head on the table and sobbed with relief. Just to know that she had the support of her Bill turned the tide of despair into a flood of hope. Nothing had changed, they still had too many children in a slum flat, and she was expecting another, but, as Bill had said, they would see it through together.

The story of Hilda and Bill was told to us by a friend and fellow midwife, Ena, who was attached to the Salvation Army Maternity Hospital in Clapton. The hospital had several district midwifery centres at the time, and Ena was based at the one in Hackney Road, Shoreditch, which bordered on our area. Consequently we often saw each other when we were out on our bikes. Their district was just as busy as ours, but when we had time we would meet and swap yarns. Most midwives in those days had some pretty ripe stories to tell, which provoked peals of laughter, or gasps of dismay from the rest of us, but Ena's story is the most astonishing and the most macabre that I have ever heard.

She first met the Hardings when there was a knock at the door late one afternoon. Ena opened it and a man stood before her. 'Can I help you?' she enquired. He did not say anything but just stood there, cap in hand, turning it round and round. 'Is anything the matter?' she asked. Still he said nothing. He pulled a packet of Woodbines from his pocket and with shaking fingers opened it and pulled one out. He stuck it in his mouth. 'Have you come to us for any reason?' Ena enquired, puzzled. He took a box of matches from his pocket and fumbled with it. His awkward fingers could not seem to pick one up. Ena noticed blood around the edges of his nails. 'Here, let me help you,' she said kindly, and took out a match, lit it and held the flame to his cigarette. He inhaled deeply.

'Now, can I help you?'

'Is you ve midwife?'

'Yes.'

'Well, it's come.'

'What's come?'

''Ve baby.'

'Whose baby?'

'My wife's.'

'Who is your wife?'

''ilda. Mrs 'arding.'

'Is Mrs Harding booked with us?'

'I dunno.'

'Let's get this straight. Your wife, Mrs Harding, has had a baby?'

'Yes.'

'When?'

'Abaht quar'er of an hour ago.'

'You mean it's just been born?'

'Yes.'

'Where?'

'At 'ome.'

'Who was with her?'

'I was.' He drew deeply on his fag and spat on the pavement. He seemed ill at ease and would not look at her. Ena was growing increasingly alarmed. A baby born before arrival (a BBA we used to call it) happened occasionally, but usually the midwife had been called in advance and literally could not get there in time.

'Did you call anyone?'

'Nope.'

'Why not?'

He drew on his fag again and chewed his bloodied fingernails. Ena was putting two and two together.

'Did you deliver the baby?' she enquired, incredulous.

'S'posin' I did?' he said defensively.

'Nothing. It's just unusual, that's all.'

He blew smoke into the air, still not looking at her.

'It just come. Quick like.'

'Well, I had better come if a baby has just been born. Your wife and baby will need attention. Do you think she was booked with us? If so, I'll get the antenatal notes.'

'Like I says, I dunno.'

Ena decided that looking for notes that might not exist would only be a waste of time. She went quickly to fetch her delivery bag. Many thoughts were racing through her mind: a baby just born would need attention, almost certainly the cord would not have been cut; the third stage of labour would have to be dealt with; perhaps the woman was bleeding. She returned. The man was still standing at the door. He had lit another fag.

'Where do you live?'

'Round ve corner.' He pointed to a near-derelict road where 90 per cent of the houses had been destroyed by the bombing, or had been boarded up as structurally unsafe.

'I thought no one lived in that road,' she said.

'We do, worse luck.'

'We'd better get to your wife and baby, then. Come on.'

Ena walked quickly down the road. He followed a step or two behind, dragging his feet.

'Which house?'

'Over the road. The one with the windows.'

She crossed the road and approached the front door. It was locked.

'Have you got a key?'

'Reckon so. Somewhere.' He fumbled in his pockets, seeming unable to find it.

'Oh, do hurry. You must have the key. You only left the house a few minutes ago.'

He grunted and continued fumbling. Eventually he produced it and opened the door.

Ena entered a foul-smelling hallway, and for the first time since the man had approached her, it occurred to her that this might be a trap. She felt a sharp stab of fear. Everything about the man was so strange. He had seemed ill at ease, or even shifty, since the beginning of the interview. She stifled a moment of panic when it occurred to her that perhaps the blood around his fingernails was not from the birth of a baby, but from something much more sinister. A derelict house in a bomb-destroyed street was not the sort of place in which a baby would be born. Yet the man had specifically asked for a midwife. If he had had any ulterior motive, he would have been more likely to ask for a nurse. His next words were reassuring. 'My wife's upstairs. You'll have to come up. Mind that broken step. Don't hurt yourself.' She controlled her fears and followed the man. He opened a door.

A woman was lying on the bed, staring vacantly at the ceiling. She did not speak, and neither did the man. 'Where is the baby?' asked the midwife. No one answered. 'Where is it?' she asked a second time. Panic was beginning to take hold of her once more. There was something menacing in the silence of the man and the woman. She looked from one to the other, but they both avoided meeting her eye. 'Where is the baby?' she demanded a third time, more emphatically. 'There,' said the woman, pointing to the floor.

Ena looked down and saw a chamber pot, overflowing with a gory, bloody mess, and two little white legs hanging over the side. She ran over to the pot. The mess she had seen was the placenta; the baby was head down in the chamber pot, covered by the placenta. Ena grabbed its legs and pulled the baby out. It was a little boy, quite limp and lifeless, suffocated by his own placenta.

Shock, horror and panic made her unable to speak. She was only young, scarcely more than twenty, and had seen nothing like this before. She wrapped the little body in a towel and tried mouth-to-mouth resuscitation; she tried milking the cord towards the body in a vain attempt to introduce new blood; she tried heart massage. All to no avail. The baby was quite dead.

'Why did you leave it like that?' she demanded hysterically.

'We didn't know what to do.'

'But you've had other babies? You must surely know that a baby cannot be left head down in a chamber pot.'

'No one told us what ter do. How was we to know?'

'Why didn't you call us earlier?'

'It was all so quick. There was no time.'

'Well why didn't you pick the baby up?'

Neither one answered. The woman continued to stare at the ceiling, while the man blew smoke at the window as he gazed out into the street.

'I must go and get the senior midwife. I don't know what to do.'

She left the room and ran downstairs, stumbling and nearly falling. Out in the street she had to lean against the wall for several minutes to control herself. It was only a few hundred yards round the corner, but her steps were unsteady.

The senior midwife called the police, then went to the house. Mr and Mrs Harding repeated their story to the police. The baby's body was taken for post-mortem examination.

The report stated that a normal baby at full term of gestation had been born. All internal organs – heart, brain, lungs, liver, kidneys, intestines, venous system – were well developed and normal, with full potential to support life. The lungs had expanded at birth, and the baby had taken several breaths, but the lungs were full of blood and amniotic fluid. The conclusion was that the baby had drowned in the fluids inhaled into the lungs.

A coroner's inquest was held a few weeks later, at which Ena was required to give evidence. She told them everything she knew. Mr and Mrs Harding were questioned. Hilda said that she was booked to go into the Salvation Army Maternity Hospital to have the baby. She said she had felt a few labour pains and had asked Mrs Hatterton opposite to get her husband and to look after her two youngest. Bill came back and was just getting ready to take her to hospital when she felt a bit wet, and wanted to go to the toilet. So she had sat down on the chamber pot, and it all just came away from her.

The senior midwife confirmed that this was perfectly plausible, and that occasionally a multigravid woman could feel little more than slight abdominal discomfort, and a bearing-down sensation, just as Mrs Harding had described, in which case, labour need take no more than about fifteen minutes from the start of contractions to delivery of the baby.

When the coroner asked the Hardings what they did next, both of them repeated their story that they didn't know what to do and no one was there to tell them. Mr Harding said that he'd thought the best thing would be to go round the corner to get one of the district midwives, which is what he did. By the time they got back, the baby was dead.

The coroner said that he found it very difficult to know what judgement to record. He found it hard to believe the story that the Hardings did not know what to do. On the other hand, he supposed that in the absence of a trained midwife or a doctor, two ignorant and unlettered people might really be at a loss to know how to act, especially if they were in a state of shock at the unexpected and rapid birth of a baby. Mr Harding had taken the course of action that seemed to them to be appropriate – he had gone to call a midwife. But it was too late.

In the event the coroner recorded an open verdict, which meant that the case was not closed, and that, if any further evidence came to light, it could be reopened and re-examined. But no further evidence was forthcoming.

THE CAPTAIN'S DAUGHTER

It was well that Chummy was on first call. Who else would have had the grit, the stamina and the sheer physical strength and courage to do what she did in the Docks that night?

Camilla Fortescue-Cholmeley-Browne came from a long line of 'Builders of the Empire'. District Commissioners and Colonels were her forebears. All the women seemed to be Lady This, That or the Other, and could not only run a garden party or a county ball for thousands but could also live in torrid isolation, maintaining the Hill Stations for their husbands the District Commissioners, who single-handedly governed areas the size of Wales. Whatever one may say about the British Empire, it certainly bred self reliance and courage in its administrators.

Chummy was typical of her family in this respect. In other ways, though, she was a misfit, because she was gauche, awkward and shy. Roedean and expensive finishing schools had been a failure. Chummy possessed no social graces whatsoever – a fact of which she was quite unaware – and she was always surprised and hurt when her mother let her know that she was an embarrassment to the family. The fact that she was over six feet in height and that she could not seem to control her long limbs did not help. She was always falling over or bumping into things, and after several disasters in public places her parents decided they could not take her anywhere. Many genteel and ladylike occupations were proposed, but after a fair trial, it had to be admitted that she was no good at any of them. 'Whatever are we to do with Camilla?' her mother would ask despairingly. 'She can't do anything, and no one is going to want to marry her.'

Demoralised and bewildered, Chummy accepted her role as the family failure. But the ways of man and the ways of God are not the same thing. Quite suddenly she found her vocation. Chummy was going to be a missionary. For this purpose she trained as a nurse and was an instant and brilliant success. Then she trained as a midwife, which is how we came to meet at Nonnatus House.

And, as I said, it was well that Chummy was on first call that night.

The telephone rang at 11.30 p.m., getting her out of bed.

'Port-of-London-West-India-Docks-nightwatchman speaking. We needs a nurse, or a doctor.'

'What's the matter? An accident at the docks?' asked Chummy.

'No. Woman ill, or somefink.'

'A woman? Are you sure?'

''Course I'm sure. Think I can't tell the difference?'

'No, no. I didn't mean that. No offence, old chap. But women are not allowed in the Docks.'

'Well, this one's 'ere all right. Captain's wife or somefink, the mate says. Least, that's what I think he's tryin' 'a say, because he can't speak no English. Just rolls his eyes and groans and rubs 'is tummy – vat's why I called ve midwives.'

'I'll come. Where do I go to?'

'Main gate. West India.'

'I'll be there in ten minutes.'

Chummy dressed in haste and went out into the night. It was windy. Not cold or raining, but a strong head wind made cycling slow, and it took Chummy nearly twenty minutes to reach West India Dock. The nightwatchman was sitting by the burning brazier next to the gate, which he unlocked.

'You bin a long time. Bloody wind, I s'ppose. Don't like ve wind.'

Chummy had never been inside the Dock gates before, and the place seemed eerie and alien in the darkness. The stretch of water in the basin looked vast, as she gazed down it, and the hulks of huge cargo boats loomed over the oily water. On the skyline numerous cranes criss-crossed each other. Some of the boats were dimly lit, but others were completely dark. The night watchman's coke fire glowed on the quay. The wind caused the water to splash and the rigging to tremble, making hollow moaning sounds.

'Swedish timber carrier on South Quay. Woman got a belly ache or somefink. Shouldn't be there, I told the mate, but I reckons as 'ow he never understood.'

Reluctantly he hauled himself up, left his comfortable little hut and tipped some more coke onto the fire.

'This way,' he sighed mournfully. 'Bloody women. Shouldn't be 'ere, I says. I've go' enough 'a do, wivout all vis.'

They made their way to the South Quay.

''ere we are. The *Katrina*. Yer rope ladder's there and yer guiders.'

He grabbed a rope, pulled it and shouted. A faint sound was heard about forty feet up. The watchman was thinking of his fire, and his cosy hut, and the sausages and fried bread he was going to cook. 'Bloody women,' he muttered, 'no offence to you, nurse.'

A head appeared over the side of the boat.

'Ya?'

'The nurse.'

'Bra. Valkommen. Tack.'

'Yer'll 'ave to climb ve rope-ladder. It's leeward o' the wind, an' won't rock too much. You can climb this, can't yer?'

Most women would have taken one look at the bulk of the ship towering above, at the slender rope ladder swinging dizzily in the wind, and said 'No'. But not Chummy.

'Right,' she said, 'Jolly-ho. But I think they will have to haul my bag up separately. I'm not sure I could carry it, and climb the ladder one handed.'

The watchman groaned, but tied the handle of the bag to a

rope and shouted to the men above to start hauling. Somehow they understood him, and Chummy watched it swinging upwards.

'Now for it,' she said, taking hold of the rope ladder.

'Ever done this afore?'

'We had a tree house when we were children, so I suppose you could say I've had some practice.'

'The 'ardest part is when you jumps off, because you're goin' to 'it the side of ve boat. But just hold steady and yer'll be all right. Ven you can start climbing.'

'Good egg. Thanks for the tip.'

The wind was blowing Chummy's gabardine raincoat in all directions. It was a heavy garment, and long, as required by nursing uniform standards.

'This bally thing's going to be a nuisance.'

She took it off. The nightwatchman looked at her. He was beginning to respect her, and his sausages and fried bread seemed less important.

'Yer skirts too long. You might catch yer foot in 'em.'

'Not to worry.' Chummy pulled her skirt up above her waist, and tucked it into her knickers. 'No need for false modesty,' she said cheerily.

She took hold of the ladder again and put a foot on the first rung.

'Go up a rung, so you pull ve ladder taut. Grab 'old of a rung above head height. Don't try holdin' the sides of ve ladder.'

'Thanks. Any other tips?'

'No. Just keep yer nerve, an' keep climbing. Don't look down or up. Keep a steady climb, and whatever yer do, don't stop. Jes keep it steady, an' you'll be all right.'

Chummy put one foot on a rung. 'Wizard show. Here we go,' she said, cheerily, feeling upwards for the next rung. She hauled herself up.

'Only another fifty to go,' she called out to the man watching as she reached upwards for another rung.

'I only 'ope to Christ them Swedes know 'ow to make a rope ladder,' he muttered to himself, 'a weak link could be ve death of 'er.'

'What did you say? I couldn't hear for the wind,' she called.

'Nuffink important. Jes' keep going, one hand, one foot. Keep it steady, and don't stop or look down.'

Chummy kept going. The wind was rocking the boat, and every now and then a sudden gust caught Chummy and blew her a few feet to one side. But she kept her nerve. She would have tougher things than this to face when she was a missionary. She remembered Miss Hawkins, a retired missionary and Matron of Queen Charlotte's, where she had done her early training. Matron Hawkins had taught all her students as though they were going to be up a creek without a paddle. Just keep going, old girl, thought Chummy.

She reached upwards and there was nothing. She groped around with her fingers, but no, nothing. Then she felt the wood of a broken rung swinging loose against her arm. Panic hit her, and she froze, leaning her head against the side of the ship. To be paralysed with fear can mean death, because the muscles are unable to respond. Chummy listened to her heart pounding and knew her breathing to be shallow and irregular. Her whole body was stiff. She sensed her danger. She was a sensible and highly trained nurse and knew that, if she could control her breathing she would begin to regain control of her muscles. She knew the breathing that she had taught others in ante-natal classes would help. Gradually she felt she could move. She brought her foot up to the next rung, which gave her a longer reach, and was able to grab the one above her head with her outstretched hand.

'That was a close shave,' she muttered to herself.

The nightwatchman had seen what had happened, and his heart was in his mouth.

'She's got guts, vat girl,' he thought. The men above were commenting in Swedish.

Chummy did not know it, but she had not far to go. She felt exhilarated now. Having successfully negotiated the danger of the missing rung, she felt she could tackle anything, and she even enjoyed the rest of the climb. Suddenly she heard voices close to her ear, and her hand touched the metal bars of the bulwarks. She climbed over the edge and stood flushed and breathless on the deck. For once in her life she was not confused or embarrassed to be surrounded by men, even though she was standing among them in her knickers.

'Whoops, cover your legs, old girl,' she said to herself as she let her skirt fall. They all laughed and clapped and cheered.

One of the men handed her the bag then another took her down to a cabin on the middle deck. He knocked and spoke in Swedish. The door opened, and a tall, bearded man appeared. He spoke rapidly to Chummy in Swedish, as though he expected her to understand him. A female voice from within the cabin called out in English, 'Don't try to explain, Dad, I can.'

Chummy entered the cabin, which was very small. A hurricane lamp swung from a hook and the atmosphere was suffocatingly hot. The woman, who was lying on a small bunk bed, was positively huge and not only filled the bunk but spilled out over the edge. She was sweating and dry around the mouth. Her eyes looked gratefully at Chummy. 'Thank God you've come,' she breathed, 'these men will be the death of me.'

The woman lay back and closed her eyes. Heavy blonde hair fell over the grey pillow. Beads of sweat covered her fat features, her chin was indistinguishable from her neck, which in its turn blended into a vast and pendulous bosom.

A small wooden crate in the cabin obviously served as both stool and table. Chummy sat down and took out her note-book.

'I'm glad you can speak English, because I need your case history.'

'My mother was English, my father Swedish. My name is Kirsten Bjorgsen. They call me Kirsty. I am thirty-five.'

'What is your address?'

'The *Katrina*.'

'No, I mean your permanent address.'

'The *Katrina is* my permanent address.'

'That is not possible. This is a trading vessel. It cannot be your permanent home. In any case, I'm told women are not allowed on the ships.'

Kirsty laughed.

'Well, you know, what the eye doesn't see . . .'

She laughed again.

'How long have you lived on the boat?'

'Since I was fourteen, when my mother died. We had a home in Stockholm, and I went to school there. But when she died my father brought me onto the *Katrina*. He is the captain.'

'I was informed that you were the captain's wife.'

'Wife? Who told you that? He's my dad.'

Chummy said no more on the subject, but enquired about the woman's condition.

'Well, I have a pain in my belly. It comes and goes.'

Chummy was beginning to put two and two together. 'When was your last period?'

'I don't know. I don't really take much notice of that.'

'Can't you remember at all?'

'Perhaps a few months. I'm not sure.'

'I need to examine your stomach.'

Chummy palpated the mountainous abdomen, which was all flesh and fat. It was quite impossible for her to tell whether the woman was pregnant or not. She took up her Pinards foetal stethoscope, but it sank about six inches into the abdomen, the flesh virtually covering it, and all that Chummy could hear was the gurgle and swish of intestinal movements.

The woman groaned – 'Ooh, you're hurting me. It's making the pain come back. Please stop.'

But the pain got worse. Chummy felt the lower abdomen and felt a hard round sphere beneath the flesh. When the pain had passed she said, 'Kirsty you are in labour. Didn't you know you were pregnant?'

Kirsty raised herself on her elbow. 'What?' she demanded, her eyes round and incredulous.

'You are not only pregnant. You are in labour. That's what your stomach pains are.'

'I can't be. You're wrong. I'm always so careful.'

'I'm not wrong.'

Kirsty lay back on the pillow. 'Oh no! What's Dad going to say?' she murmured.

'Which of the men on board is your husband?'

'None of them. And all of them. They are all my boys, and I love them all – well nearly all, anyway.'

Chummy was shocked. Kirsty read her thoughts and laughed a great belly laugh, which set all her flesh rippling.

'I'm what you call the "ship's woman". I keep the boys happy. My dad always says there's no fighting on a ship when the boys have a nice woman to go to. That's why he brought me here when mother died.'

Chummy was deeply shocked.

'You mean to say your father brought you here when you were only fourteen to be ...' she hesitated, 'to be the ship's woman?'

Kirsty nodded.

'But that is shocking, disgraceful!' exclaimed Chummy.

'Don't be silly. Of course it's not. After my mother's death I couldn't stay in Stockholm by myself, and Dad was always at sea. So he took me with him. He explained what was expected of me. He couldn't keep me for himself, because that would cause trouble with the crew – so it had to be fair all round.'

Chummy felt she was choking.

'Your dad explained to you ...?' Her voice trailed away.

'Of course. He was always fair, and he still is. But he's the captain, and he always goes first. The other boys have to wait their turn.'

'Your dad goes first?' said Chummy weakly.

'Well, he *is* the captain. It's only right.'

Chummy was thinking about the headmistress of Roedean, and what she would have said about the situation.

Kirsty continued, 'And I never have two at once. Dad wouldn't allow that. He has very high standards.'

'High standards!' Chummy gasped, and the standards enshrined on the coat of arms at Roedean School flashed through her mind – *Honneur aux Dignes*, 'Honour to the Deserving'. But Kirsty was happily babbling on.

'I love my father, I do. He's a lovely man. He has, how do you say it, the best bugger's grips you've ever seen.'

'Bugger's grips?!' Chummy felt weak from shock. This was a different world.

'You know, whiskers on his cheek bones. They're called bugger's grips. I like to brush them when he's relaxed, after he's done with me. Then he goes to sleep, often. It's like having a baby in my arms.'

Another contraction came, and Chummy sat with her hand on the lower abdomen until it passed. She could scarcely believe what she had heard and needed a few seconds to adjust. Kirsty chatted on.

'That's better. I feel all right now. I thought it was stomach cramps. I was eating green apples yesterday.'

'No, I assure you. You are in labour and you're going to have a baby.'

'But the boys always wear a rubber when they are doing it.'

'A rubber?' repeated Chummy enquiringly.

'You know – French letters, they call them in England, or *capotes anglaises*, as they say in France. Anyway, the men always wear one. Dad insists, and they wouldn't disobey the captain. And anyway, I make them put one on, or I put it on. Dad gets a great box of them. Five hundred at a time, when we come to a port. He's most particular.'

Chummy felt light-headed.

'Five hundred?' she murmured and stared aghast at Kirsty.

'And they are never reused – Dad insists on that – in case one splits, and I wouldn't know. So you see, I can't be pregnant. It must have been those green apples.'

Chummy couldn't reply to that, but was murmuring, 'Five hundred! How long does a box last you?'

'Oh, a few weeks. Dad would never let me run out. If it's a long voyage, he'll buy in two or three boxes. We always need them.'

'Always?'

'Well, the boys need me, and I'm always here for them. I'm the most important member of the crew, Dad tells me, because I keep the men happy, and happy men work hard. And that's what every captain needs – a hardworking crew.'

Chummy swallowed. She had entered a different world of morality and did not know how to respond. Kirsty must have read her thoughts because she patted her hand kindly.

'There now. Don't worry. You're only a young girl, and I can see you come from a different class. But it's all quite natural, and I've had a good life. I've travelled the world. Sometimes they can smuggle me ashore and I can have a look round the shops. I like that. I can buy a few pretty things, because Dad gives me money.

'Don't you do anything else – the cooking, or sewing, or something?'

'Oh no.' Kirsty squawked with laughter and slapped Chummy's shoulder. 'Don't you think I have enough to do with a crew of twenty? Sometimes it's one after another for hours on end. Do you think I could work after that? In any case, we have a ship's cook. He is the one who gave me those green apples yesterday. Oh . . .'

She doubled up with pain. Chummy felt the uterus; it was harder and more prominent. She had timed ten minutes since the last contraction. Labour was progressing.

Chummy had other things to worry about than Kirsty's

position on the boat. She was alone, in the middle of the night, on board a ship with no telephone and with a woman in labour. Furthermore the woman was a primigravida of thirty-five, who had had no antenatal care. She should go to hospital at once. But how? In the unlikely event of an ambulance arriving, the woman would be in no condition to climb down the rope ladder! If a doctor was called, would he climb *up* the rope ladder? Chummy remembered her climb, and the missing rung, and knew that she could not expect anyone else to do it. She was alone, and a cold hand gripped her heart. But in the same instant a voice whispered to her that she was going to be a missionary, and that this was just God's way of testing her. She prayed.

The contraction passed, and a new, strengthened Chummy spoke.

'You must stop all this nonsense about green apples. You are in labour, and your baby will be born within the next hour or two. I have to examine you vaginally, and I must have clean cotton sheets, cotton wool and something to act as absorbent pads, a cot to put the baby in, and hot water and soap. Now, where can I get all these things?'

Kirsty looked dumbfounded.

'You must call my father,' she said.

Chummy opened the door and called, 'Hi there!'

The big, bearded man entered, and Kirsty explained. He let out an oath and looked savagely at Chummy, as though it were her fault. But Chummy was taller than him and looked down on him with new-found confidence. The captain turned to go, but Chummy stopped him with a light touch on the arm. She said to Kirsty, 'Would you also tell your father that this cabin is quite unsuitable for the delivery of a baby, and that I will need somewhere better.'

Kirsty translated. The captain no longer looked savage. He looked at Chummy with respect. Then his whole expression changed, and his eyes filled with anguish. He kneeled down beside his daughter, took her huge body in his arms and rubbed his beard into the folds of her neck. He stood up with tears in his eyes and fled from the cabin.

Two more contractions came and went. They are getting stronger and more regular, thought Chummy. I hope the crew can get something sorted out quickly, because I need to move her, and she has to be able to walk.

The captain returned and said that the best cabin was ready. Kirsty sat up and heaved her great bulk off the bunk. With enormous difficulty she squeezed herself through the narrow doorway and along the gangways. Several men looked out of their cabins and patted her arms or shoulders. One man gave her a crucifix. They all looked anxious. The ship's woman was not only well used, she was well thought of.

The captain led them to a much larger cabin that was more appropriate in every way. Kirsty gave a cry when she saw it and embraced her father. He kissed her and turned to leave, but first he saluted Chummy in military fashion and bowed to her.

When the door closed, Kirsty said, 'This is the captain's cabin. He's so good to me, I tell you. What other captain would give up his cabin?'

'Well, under the circumstances, and considering he might be the father of the baby, I think it's the least he could do,' retorted Chummy dryly.

The captain's desk and all other naval paraphernalia had been pushed to one side. A large folding bed had been placed in the middle of the cabin, covered with clean blankets and linen. Kirsty looked at it and said, 'I didn't know they had these nice things on board.' A bowl was standing on a small table with jugs of hot water beside it, and soap and clean towels.

Another contraction came, and Kirsty grabbed the edge of the desk and leaned over it. She was panting and sweating. When it passed, she grinned and said, 'You must be right, nurse; this is more than green apples.' She went over to the bed to lie down.

'I still don't know how it happened. I'm so careful. Do you think one of the boys didn't put his rubber on, but told me he had?'

'I don't know. I haven't any experience in your line of business,' said Chummy truthfully, and they both laughed. A bond of female friendship and understanding was developing between them.

Kirsty said, 'You are nice. I'd like you to be my friend. I haven't had any girl friends since I left school, and I miss them. It's men, men, all the time. I never have the chance to talk to another woman. When I go ashore, which isn't very often, I look at the other women in the streets and think, "I'd like to talk to you and see how you live." But then it's back to the ship and off to sea again.'

'Do the lads ever talk to you?' asked Chummy, who was beginning to sense loneliness.

'Oh yes, some of them tell me all their troubles, they tell me about their wives and girl friends, and some tell me about their children. It's nice to hear about their children – it makes me feel part of the family.'

Secretly Chummy wondered if the compliment would be returned, but Kirsty was still speaking. 'But I must say most of them just want to be quick and have done with it. I don't mind, if that's what they want, but it's tiring, especially if I get ten or twelve who've only got half an hour before the next shift.' She puffed at the memory. 'You need some strength in my job, I can tell you. These men will be the death of me. Oooh, no, not again!' She threw her body back in pain and cursed in Swedish.

Chummy watched her carefully and made a note that contractions were now coming every seven minutes and lasting for approximately sixty seconds. She could feel the uterus firmly just above the pubic bone, but nothing higher, because abdominal fat occluded it. She longed to be able to hear the foetal heart and reassure herself that the baby was healthy, but it was impossible. She was going to make a vaginal examination. Perhaps that

would reveal something. Suddenly she remembered the obligatory enema – that monstrous practice, sacred to midwifery –
and abruptly forgot the idea. How absurd on a ship, and
surrounded by men! She wrote in her notes: 'Enema not
given'.

The pain passed, Kirsty relaxed with a sigh, and Chummy
gave her a drink of water.

'I've got to examine you internally,' she said. 'That means I
have to put my fingers into your vagina to assess where the baby
is lying, and how close to birth it is. Will you allow me to do
that?'

'Well, I'm used to that sort of thing, aren't I? But not for the
same reasons!'

Chummy placed her delivery bag on the captain's desk and
opened it. She scrubbed up and extracted a sterile gown, mask
and surgical gloves and put them on. While she was doing so,
it occurred to her that Kirsty had probably contracted syphilis
during her career. Chummy had no practical experience of
venereal disease, but from her classroom work she remembered
that syphilis can usually be diagnosed by the hard, rubbery
chancre on the vulva, whilst gonorrhoea is manifested by profuse
greenish-yellow vaginal discharge. She recalled the midwifery
tutor saying that a syphilitic woman very seldom carries to full
term, because the foetus usually dies within the first sixteen
weeks. She also remembered the next part of the lecture: that
in the event of the baby going to full term, it was likely to be
stillborn and was frequently macerated. Chummy felt queasy at
such an idea. A macerated stillbirth could leave a midwife feeling
sick and depressed for days, or even weeks – let alone the effect
it had on a mother.

Chummy quickly put the thought from her. Another contraction was coming. She timed it to be seven minutes since the
last one. Full dilation of the cervix was getting closer, and as she
had been unable to assess the lie of the baby from external
palpation, a vaginal assessment was imperative. When the

contraction had passed, she said 'Now I want you to draw your knees up, put your heels together and then let your legs fall apart.'

Kirsty did this with great agility. Her lower limbs were surprisingly flexible. Her massive thighs not only flew apart, but her knees touched the bed on either side, revealing a vast, moist purple-red vulva. Chummy was a bit taken aback at the speed and efficiency with which the exercise was undertaken, and Kirsty must have seen her expression because she laughed. 'You seem to forget I do this all the time,' she said.

Chummy examined the external vulva carefully. She could neither see nor feel syphilitic chancre, nor was there any evidence of a foul-smelling and profuse vaginal discharge. Against all the odds, it seemed that Kirsty did not have venereal disease. It must have been her father's gifts of boxes of 500 rubbers at frequent intervals that had protected her. 'Bully for the captain!' thought Chummy.

Chummy did as every good midwife would do. She prepared to place two fingers gently in the vagina, but without the slightest effort her whole hand slid in. 'Great Scott! You could get a vegetable marrow in here,' she thought.

With easy access she could feel the cervix. It was three-quarters dilated, a head presenting, fairly well down, waters intact. She breathed a sigh of relief that the baby was lying in a good position for a normal delivery.

Then she felt something very strange. At first she thought it was part of the soft, undulating vaginal wall. She moved it with her fingers. It was not part of the vaginal wall. 'What on earth is it?' she wondered. It was attached above, and seemed to be hanging freely beside the baby's head. She palpated it with her fingers, and it moved a little. Chummy was feeling this strange thing and moving it about with her fingers, when she realized with horror that it was pulsating. She froze, and blind panic overtook her for the second time that night. She looked at her watch and saw that the thing was pulsating at 120 beats per minute. The pulsation was the baby's heartbeat. The cord had prolapsed.

Chummy said afterwards that in all her professional career she had never known a moment of such terror. She went shivery all over but could feel the sweat pouring out of her body. She withdrew her hand, and it was trembling. Then her whole body began to tremble. 'What can I do? What should I do? Oh please, God, help me!' She nearly sobbed aloud but controlled herself.

'Everything all right?' enquired Kirsty cheerfully.

'Oh, yes, quite all right.'

Chummy's voice sounded far away and faint. She was thinking back to her midwifery lectures: 'In the event of prolapse of the cord, an emergency Caesarean section is necessary.' She looked around the cabin, with the hurricane lamp swinging from the beam; at the portholes, black against the night sky; at the jugs of hot water and towels so thoughtfully provided; at her equipment laid out on the captain's desk, adequate for a normal birth, but no more. The ship moved in the wind, and she remembered her isolation and the impossibility of getting help. She trembled at her own inexperience and thought, 'This baby will die.'

Yet something else was stirring in her mind. The lecturer had not ended with 'a Caesarean section is necessary', but had continued. What else had the lecturer been saying? The pulsating cord, and the knowledge that a living baby depended on her for life, forced Chummy's mind back to the classroom. 'Raise the pelvis by instructing the mother to adopt the genupectoral position and sedate the mother. If the amniotic sac is unbroken it is sometimes possible to push the baby's head back a little and move the cord out of the way.'

Good midwifery is a combination of art, science, experience and instinct. It used to be said that it took seven years of practice to make a good midwife. Chummy had everything but experience. She possessed intuition and instinct in abundance. The amniotic sac was not yet broken. There might still be time to attempt the replacement of the cord. She must have a go. She could not sit and do nothing, knowing that the cord would be crushed as labour progressed, and that the baby would die.

'Raise the pelvis', the lecturer had said. Chummy looked at the massive thighs and buttocks of Kirsty, who probably weighed about thirty-five stone. A crane would be needed to raise her pelvis. The genu-pectoral position would be possible in a smaller woman, but Kirsty could no more roll over onto her front than a beached whale could. But only raising the pelvis would take pressure off the cord, and Chummy was resourceful. She remembered that a folding bed had been provided. If she folded up the legs at the head of the bed, but left the foot end standing, perhaps her patient could lie with her head and shoulders on the floor and her buttocks resting on the higher end of the bed. It was worth a try.

She explained what she wanted to Kirsty. She did not say anything about the cord or the gravity of the situation, because there was no point in alarming her unnecessarily. She merely explained about the bed, as though it was the usual way to deliver a baby.

With great difficulty Kirsty got to her feet, and Chummy crawled under the bed to collapse the legs so that the head dropped to the floor. That was easy; the difficult part would be getting Kirsty back onto it in the required position. The problem was solved by Kirsty. She calmly went to the raised end of the bed, sat on it, leaned backwards, then rolled her back down the bed. 'I do this all the time,' she said, splaying her legs apart.

Pressure would now be off the cord, Chummy thought with satisfaction – gravity would pull the baby back into the uterus, allowing a little extra space for the cord. But the advantage would not last for long, because the inexorable process of uterine contractions would push the baby forward. Time was short, and running out. Contractions were already coming every six minutes.

Chummy weighed in her mind whether or not to give pethidine to sedate her patient. It would relax her and might help when it came to replacing the cord. But on the other hand it would also sedate the foetus, and delivery was imminent. She decided against sedation. Kirsty seemed relaxed enough and would just have to bear the pain. The life and health of the baby were Chummy's main concern, and pethidine in its bloodstream would be an additional hazard.

A contraction was coming, and Kirsty groaned with pain. She threw her head around and tried to move her legs up to her body. 'Whatever happens, don't roll out of that position, Kirsty. It's perfect,' said Chummy.

'I must try to replace the cord before the next contraction,' she thought. The time between each would soon be only five minutes. The contraction passed, and Chummy said a quiet prayer for what she was about to do. She had never seen it done before and had received only one lecture on the subject, but it had to be enough, and with God's help it would be.

'I'm going to push you around a bit, Kirsty. Hook your knees over the edge of the bed, and hold on, so that you don't slip backwards with the pressure.'

Chummy slipped her gloved hand into the vagina. There was no perineal resistance, something she knew she could be thankful for. She felt the partly dilated cervix again, the forewaters protruding and the pulsation of the cord within. With her forefingers she felt around the baby's head – there must be no pressure on the fontanelle, she thought, because that could kill the baby at once. Her fingers were placed ready to push when the ship moved, causing them to slip. She had to find the correct position a second time. When she thought her fingers were rightly placed she pushed hard, but the head did not move. She felt the sweat running down her face and neck. 'It's got to,' she thought, 'it's got to go back.' So she pushed again. This time the head retreated slightly but not enough for the cord to be replaced behind it.

After the second unsuccessful attempt Chummy paused, trembling.

'Pressure, that is the only thing I've got to help me, massive pressure, and God be with me that I do no harm.'

Shaking all over, she leaned her head on the soft cushion of Kirsty's enormous thigh, trying to think clearly. The wind groaned outside, and the ship moved in sympathy. Her fingers slipped, and she withdrew her hand. If the amniotic sac broke, that would be the end: nothing could save the baby. Only the fact that the cord was still floating freely in the amniotic fluid made replacement a possibility.

Another contraction came. 'Five or six minutes can't have passed,' she thought. 'I can't have spent all that time achieving nothing.' She looked at her watch – it had been five minutes. Contractions were getting closer, and time was rapidly running out.

She saw the uterus heave with the muscular pressure of the contraction, and a plan formed in her mind. Looking at the uterus, her instinct told her that, if she applied reverse pressure externally, and internal pressure on the baby's head, she might be able to move it sufficiently to replace the cord. It was not a procedure that had been taught in the classroom, but something told her that it might work. With only five minutes, perhaps four, before the next contraction, she had to be successful, or the baby would surely die. The ship lurched as a great gust of wind hit the side, and Chummy prayed for calm during the next few minutes.

When the contraction passed Chummy said, 'Kirsty, I want you to listen carefully. Grip your knees over the edge of the bed again, and hold on. Just concentrate on holding your body still, because I am going to push hard, and you must *not* allow me to push you downwards.'

'I'll do my best, nurse. I have to be strong in my job. I don't suppose you can push any harder than a fifteen-stone first mate. I'll be all right.'

Chummy took her at her word. She inverted her left hand over the upturned uterus, just above the pubic bone. Being able to insert her whole hand into the vagina was a huge advantage. She cupped the palm of her right hand over the baby's head, stood up and took a deep breath.

'Hold on, Kirsty, don't let yourself slip. I'm going to push now.'

Chummy was tall and strong. She exerted massive downward pressure internally and externally. The baby shifted two or three inches from her internal hand, but still she kept up the external pressure on the uterus. When she felt it was enough, she relaxed.

'That was hard! I don't know if I've had it harder than that. But I didn't move, did I?' said Kirsty.

Chummy did not reply. Her job was not done. She still had to replace the cord into the uterus. She felt for the cord, but it was not there. She stretched her finger inside the os and ran it around the rim, but could feel only the smooth, round surface of the baby's head. The cord had disappeared. Internal fluid suction, caused by shifting the baby, must have withdrawn the slippery cord without any further action being required from the midwife.

Chummy felt giddy with relief and leaned her head on Kirsty's capacious thigh. She giggled weakly.

'It's done, it's done, thanks be to God! And thanks to you, Kirsty. You didn't move. I couldn't have done it without you.'

'All in a day's work,' observed Kirsty casually.

The whole operation had taken only about thirty seconds. But Chummy sat trembling with relief for another two or three minutes, until her more practical side took over. Now that the baby was safe, how was it to be delivered? All sorts of questions tumbled into her mind. Kirsty looked quite comfortable, but could a baby be delivered in an upside-down position? She wondered what the midwifery tutors would say about that! On the other hand, moving this massive female might be a problem. Kirsty had rolled down the slope of the bed, but would she be able to roll up? The third stage of labour, the delivery of the placenta, was vitally important, and Chummy was not confident about the mother expelling a placenta upside-down. Kirsty would have to be moved. Then the cord came into her mind. Reverse pressure had made it withdraw into the uterus, but if Kirsty stood up, as she would have to, would the downward pressure displace the cord and make it slip forward again? Chummy could not be sure, but it might. The risk was too great. Kirsty would have to remain in her present position.

Chummy sat beside the labouring woman, listening to the wind and feeling the ship move beneath her. She was not really surprised by the extraordinary situation in which she found herself; after all she was going to be a missionary and she would have to be prepared for anything. She was a thoughtful, prayerful girl, and she thanked God she was being tested in this way.

She pondered the ugly situation in which Kirsty had been placed. First abused, probably raped, when she was fourteen by her father, and then confined to a ship for the pleasure of all the men, including her father. Yet, Chummy reflected, she seemed happy and content. Perhaps, as she had known no other life, it all seemed quite natural to her. The men were obviously fond of her – their concern as she struggled down the gangway was evident – and she was not ill-treated. Common prostitutes, pushed onto the streets by pimps and beaten up if they protested, had a much worse life, she thought.

Another contraction came, and the waters broke. Thank God I was able to replace the cord, she thought; it was only just in time. Labour was progressing fast, and Kirsty was wonderful. She had had no sedation but had barely murmured at the pain. Chummy could feel the head well down on the pelvic floor. 'It won't be long now,' she said aloud.

Kirsty groaned and pushed. When the contraction had passed she said, 'I've been thinking about this baby. I'm so glad now. I never thought I'd have one, because Dad always gave me the boxes of rubbers and said the boys must always wear them. So they did. But now I'm having a baby. And I'm glad.'

'I'm sure you are. A woman may not want a baby, but she's always happy when it comes,' said Chummy.

'I hope it's a little girl. I'd like a little girl. I have enough men. But I don't want her to have my life. It wouldn't be right for a young girl. I think Dad will understand if I talk to him. What's your name, nurse?'

'Camilla,' said Chummy.

'Oh, what a beautiful name. I want to give her your name, nurse, may I?'

'Of course. I should be honoured.'

'Baby Camilla. That's a lovely name.'

Another contraction came, only two minutes after the last, fiercer and longer. Kirsty had no vaginal or perineal resistance, so the head was able to descend quickly and easily. She gripped her hands until the knuckles showed white and pushed hard, forcing the weight of her buttocks against the end of the bed. In protest, the bed trembled and collapsed with a crash onto the floor.

The problem of an upside-down delivery had been solved! Mother and midwife were now on the floor, Kirsty floundering and pushing, Chummy desperately trying to control the situation.

Poor Kirsty was bewildered. 'What happened?' she kept asking. Chummy, who had narrowly missed having her hands crushed, tried to calm her.

'The bed broke, but the baby is all right, and if you are not hurt, no harm has been done. In fact it's a good thing, because delivery of your baby will be easier.'

Chummy's concern now was that the baby's head might be born too quickly. The slow and steady delivery of the head is what every midwife hopes for, but with no perineal resistance, this baby could well shoot out with the next contraction.

Another contraction came, and Kirsty raised her knees and braced herself to push, but Chummy stopped her. 'Don't push,

Kirsty, don't push. I know you want to and feel you must, but don't. Your baby's head will be born with this contraction, but I want it to come slowly. The slower the better. Concentrate on *not* pushing. Take little breaths, in–out, in–out, think about breathing, think about relaxing, but don't push.' All the time she was saying these words Chummy was holding the head, trying to prevent it from bursting out of the mother at speed. The contraction was waning, Chummy eased the slack perineum around the presenting crown, and the head was born.

Chummy breathed a sigh of relief. She had been concentrating so hard that she had not noticed the cramp in her legs as she squatted on the deck of the cabin; had not noticed the poor light cast by the hurricane lamp as it swung from a beam; had not noticed the movement of the ship, nor the occasional lurch as the wind hit it. All that she knew was that the miracle of a baby's birth would shortly take place, that the safe delivery was in her hands, and that the head had been born. Chummy kept her hand under the baby's face in order to lift it away from the hard floor and waited. Another contraction was coming. Chummy felt the face she was holding move.

'It's coming, Kirsty. You can push now. Hard.'

Kirsty drew her legs upwards and pushed. Chummy eased the shoulder out and downwards. The other shoulder and arm quickly followed, and the whole body slid out effortlessly.

'You have a little girl, Kirsty.'

Emotion flooded over Kirsty with such intensity that she could not speak. Tears took the place of words. 'Let me have her. Can I see her?' she spluttered, still floundering with her head on the deck, unable to lift her shoulders. Chummy said 'I am going to lay her on your tummy while I cut the cord, then you can hold her in your arms.'

The baby sank into the soft cushion of her mother's stomach. She was slightly blue around the mouth and extremities, but otherwise she seemed to have suffered no harm from the drama of labour. Chummy severed the cord and then held the baby upside down by the heels. Kirsty gasped and held up her hands protectively.

'Don't worry, I'm not going to drop her,' said the midwife, 'this is done in order to drain the mucus out of the throat, and to help breathing.'

Then she gave a short, sharp pat to the back of the baby, who at once gave a shrill yell. 'That's what I like to hear, let's have another one.' The baby obliged, crying lustily, and from outside the door a chorus of men's voices were heard cheering, shouting, whooping and whistling. They started to sing, in a united and raucous male voice. Kirsty called out to them in Swedish, but they were making so much noise they could not hear her. The captain's daughter was obviously very popular, and the men responded in their own way. 'I expect they will all get drunk now,' she said dryly.

Chummy wrapped the baby in a towel and placed her in the arms of her mother, who was weeping with joy. 'Are you all right on the floor like that?' Chummy enquired with concern.

'I've never been better in my life,' answered Kirsty. 'I would like to stay here for ever, cuddling my baby.' She gave a sigh of contentment.

Chummy now had to deal with the third stage of labour. In retrospect she would say that it was not the most comfortable third stage she had conducted, sprawled as she was across the floor, but at least it was uneventful.

Chummy washed Kirsty and cleared up the mess as best she could under the circumstances. The problem of how to get Kirsty up off the floor was her next concern. The mother obviously couldn't care less. She was cuddling, and cooing, and whispering sweet nothings to her baby. Calling the captain was Chummy's only option, but Kirsty was stark naked. Chummy's modesty shrank from the thought of exposing her patient, naked, to a crowd of men, until she remembered Kirsty's profession. She explained to Kirsty that help was needed and opened the door.

A dozen or more bearded faces appeared at the door, all

peering in. At once they started cheering and clapping again. Chummy beckoned to the captain, who strode in, shutting the door behind him. She indicated what was necessary, and he nodded. She took the baby from her mother and retired to a stool in the corner.

The captain was a big man, and strong, but for sheer body weight his daughter could easily have doubled him. He took both of her hands and pulled – the bulk shifted a few inches. He stood astride her body and pulled again; no result. He went to the door, shouted, 'Olaf, Bjorg!' and two massive men entered. He explained, and they nodded. He took her hands again, and one man stood behind each shoulder. As the captain pulled each man heaved until Kirsty was sitting upright. They gave a cheer. This is obscene, Chummy thought, I can't bear to look at that poor woman sitting there with her huge breasts swinging on the floor, and these men cheering. They were obviously debating how to get Kirsty onto a chair. The debate was long and contentious; each man had his own ideas. A chair was solemnly brought forward and placed behind the woman. The three men grabbed her torso and heaved once more. 'That's not the way to do it,' thought Chummy, who had been taught how to lift a heavy patient, 'you'll never get her up like that.' They didn't. After another debate, they tried again, the two men locking their arms under Kirsty's armpits, and the captain ready with the chair. 'That's more like it,' thought Chummy.

I have said that Chummy had cleared up the mess as best she could under the circumstances. But resources were minimal, and the deck of the cabin was still slippery in patches.

The two men lifting Kirsty nodded to each other, took a deep breath and heaved. Her bottom lifted about six inches from the deck. Olaf, on her left, moved his foot and trod on a slippery patch. He hurtled forward across Kirsty's body and Bjorg was thrown backwards. In his fall he flung his arm upwards and hit the hurricane lamp with such force that it shattered, plunging the cabin into darkness.

In the meantime Kirsty had acted. A desperate mother can do anything in defence of her child. As the lamp shattered she screamed, 'My baby,' pushed Olaf, who was lying sprawled over her, to one side, scrambled to her feet, and ran over to the corner where Chummy was sitting. She took the baby, enfolding her protectively to her bosom. When another hurricane lamp was brought in she could be seen by all the men sitting quietly on a chair, rocking her baby, with a sheet modestly draped around her.

When the cabin was cleared of men, Chummy set about making it into a suitable lying-in room for mother and baby. The bed was not broken, the legs had merely folded in on themselves so she fixed it up again for Kirsty. But there was no clean linen left after delivery, and her patient had no nightie. There was no cot for the baby, no means of bathing her, and no clothes for her. She explained her needs to Kirsty, who was not really listening, so she went to the door, opened it, and shouted, 'Olaf!' The biggest of the bruisers entered and stood to attention, looking ill at ease.

'Tell him I need more clean linen, two more pillows, some nightdresses and a dressing gown for you. Also I need some more hot water and more clean towels for me to bath the baby; a box or basket which I can make into a cot, and some soft linen or cloth that I can tear up and make into cot blankets.' She considered there was no point in asking for baby clothes.

Kirsty translated, and Olaf looked mesmerised. She repeated the instructions two or three times, and Chummy could see him desperately trying to activate his brain and memorise the list, which he was counting off on his fingers. He left the cabin, and Chummy set about clearing things up a little more and packing her delivery bag. She was beginning to feel tired. The drama of the night had kept the adrenalin pumping through her body, but now that all danger for mother and baby had passed, her limbs felt heavy and slow.

Olaf reappeared with an armful of stuff, and a second man brought in a jug of hot water. Chummy was able to bath the baby, with Kirsty eagerly watching and commenting at every stage. A basket, which smelled of fish, had been provided, and this Chummy transformed into a crib. She made up the bed with clean linen – but still there was no nightie. Chummy could not allow her patient to remain naked, so summoned Olaf again.

Kirsty explained what was wanted, and the man turned bright red. How very extraordinary, thought Chummy, that this man, who has regularly been having intercourse with this woman, should be embarrassed to have to fetch her a nightie!

He went away and came back with a bag full of women's clothing which he handed to Chummy without looking at her.

Breastfeeding was the next thing for Chummy to think about. One really wants to establish breastfeeding immediately after delivery and ensure that the colostrum is flowing and that the mother has, at least, a vague idea of what she should do. Kirsty's breasts were so huge that they rested on the bed on either side of her. The baby could easily be suffocated by these mammoth mammaries, Chummy thought, as she expressed some colostrum. She tried the baby at the breast, and the child, surprisingly, opened her mouth, latched on and sucked vigorously a few times. Kirsty was in an ecstasy of delight. Flushed, with sparkling eyes and radiant features, she looked quite different. She must have been a pretty young girl, thought Chummy, before she became the inert, sexually active queen bee in this hive of males.

By now, Chummy was so tired that she could scarcely stand. She sat down on a chair beside Kirsty, who was examining the baby's fingers and toes.

'Look. She has little fingernails. Aren't they sweet? Like little shells. And I think she's going to have dark hair – her eyelashes are dark, have you noticed?' Kirsty looked up. 'Are you all right, nurse? You don't look too good.'

Chummy muttered, 'I'll be all right. Do you think someone

might bring us a cup of tea? You could do with a cup also.'

Kirsty called out, and Olaf entered. She gave her instructions, and five minutes later he reappeared carrying a tray laden with good food and fresh coffee. He placed it on the captain's desk and then, rather sheepishly, took a quick look at the baby and sidled out.

'Did you see that?' said Kirsty incredulously. 'They're treating me like a lady.'

Chummy poured the coffee. The caffeine perked her up a bit, and she began to feel stronger. She knew that she would need to, because one more task faced her. She had to get down the rope ladder. She had another cup of coffee and a sweet pastry, which gave her some energy. She left, telling Kirsty that she would return later in the morning.

Up on deck the dawn was breaking. The wind had dropped, and thin shafts of red-gold sunlight filtered through the grey clouds. Seagulls were swooping and squawking. The docks looked beautiful in the half light, and the fresh, cold air stung her cheeks. One of the men was carrying her bag, and they all clustered around, cheering and clapping. Chummy walked to the side and looked over the edge. It looked a long, long way down, and the rope ladder looked flimsy. If I can do it once, I can do it again, she said to herself, putting her foot on the rail. Then she remembered her skirt, and the danger it presented. So without any inhibition – she who was chronically inhibited in the presence of men – she pulled it up, tucked it into her knickers and climbed over the side. Her main anxiety was the missing rung, but she knew roughly where it was, and was prepared for the gap. When it came it was not as hard to negotiate as she had expected, and with a sigh of relief she continued to the quayside. One of the men tied her bag to a rope and let it down for her. She untied it, released her skirt, waved to the men above, and set out for the dock gates, her body tired, but her whole being exhilarated with the joy of having successfully delivered a healthy baby to an eager and loving mother.

*

The nightwatchman was preparing to go home for the day. He collected his supper box, put away his frying pan, doused his fire and was sorting out the key to lock his hut, when two policemen approached the dock gates.

'Morning, nightwatch. Fair morning after the storm.'

The watchman turned. His fingers were stiff, and he was fumbling with the key, unable to find the keyhole.

'Dratted key,' he muttered. 'Fair morning? Fair enough. Don't like the wind.'

'Quiet night for you?'

'Quiet enough. Would 'ave been quiet, 'cept for bloody women gettin' in the way.'

'Women?'

'Yes, women. Shouldn't be 'ere, I say.'

The policemen looked at each other. They knew that the Port of London Authority was very strict on women entering the docks, especially since the previous year when a prostitute had slipped in the dark from a gangplank and drowned.

'Which vessel?' The policeman took out his notebook and pencil.

'The *Katrina*. Swedish timber merchant.'

'Did you see the women?'

'Saw one of 'em. A nurse. Her bicycle's over there. Don't know what to do wiv it. An' 'er coat an' all. Don't know what to do wiv it, neither.'

'A nurse?'

'Yes. Woman ill on the *Katrina*, so I calls ve Sisters, and a nurse comes.'

'You had better tell us what happened.'

'About eleven thirty. A deck hand, 'e comes to me, saying, "Woman, woman," rollin' his eyes an' rubbin' 'is stomach, an' groanin'. So I calls a doctor, but 'e's out, so I calls ve Sisters, an' a big lanky nurse comes, an' I takes her to the *Katrina*, South

Quay. Right plucky girl, she was. Climbs up ve rope ladder an' all.'

'What! A nurse climbed the ship's ladder in that wind?'

'I'm tellin' yer. Big plucky girl. Climbed up, she did. And a rung was missing near the top, an' all. I saw it wiv me own eyes, I did.'

'Are you sure?'

'Course I'm bleedin' sure. Think I'm bloody daft?' The nightwatchman was offended.

'No, of course not. What happened next?'

'Search me. She climbed on board, an' she's still there, for all I knows. Leastways she hasn't collected 'er bike, nor 'er coat, neiver.'

The two policemen conferred. This was a matter for the Port of London Police. The Metropolitan had no authority inside the ports. But was it true? Nightwatchmen, due perhaps to their solitary calling in the darkest hours, were known to fantasise.

The man was fumbling with his key again. He turned and glanced down the quay. 'There she is. That's 'er. Told yer, didn't I? Big lanky girl.'

The two policemen saw a female figure wandering towards them. Her footsteps were uncertain, and she staggered rather than walked. The ordeal of climbing down the rope ladder had taken the last reserve of Chummy's strength. One of the policemen stepped forward to meet her and took her arm. She leaned on him heavily, murmuring, 'Thank you.' He said, 'Haven't we met somewhere before?' She looked at him vaguely.

'I'm not sure. Have we?'

He smiled. 'It doesn't matter.'

She walked towards her bike. He said, 'I don't wish to be rude, nurse, but are you fit to ride a bike?'

She looked round and slowly gathered her thoughts.

'I'll be all right. I must admit I feel a bit queer, but I'll be all right.'

The bike was a big, heavy Raleigh, iron framed and ancient.

She took hold of the handlebars, but it felt so heavy she could barely move it. The policeman said 'Nurse, I really do not think you should ride that cycle, especially down the East India Dock Road just as the ports are opening and the lorries are coming in. In fact, in the name of the Law, I am telling you *not* to ride it. I am going to call a taxi.'

'What about my bike?' she protested. 'It can't stay here.'

'Don't worry about that. I will ride it back for you. You are going to Nonnatus House, I think. I know where it is.'

In the snug comfort of a London taxi Chummy fell sound asleep. She was confused and barely articulate on waking, so the driver had to help her out and then rang the bell for her. The Sisters were just leaving the chapel when it sounded. Novice Ruth opened the door to see a cab driver supporting Chummy and holding her bag. Her first reaction was to think that the nurse was drunk. 'Sit down here,' she said to Chummy. 'I'll fetch Sister Julienne.'

Sister Julienne came quickly, paid the cab driver and turned her attention to Chummy, who seemed unable to move.

'What is the matter, my dear?' She did not smell of drink. 'What has happened to you?' Perhaps she had been beaten up.

Chummy mumbled, 'I'm all right. Just feel a bit funny, that's all. Don't worry about me.'

'But what happened?'

'A baby.'

'But we deliver babies all the time. What else happened?'

'On a ship.'

'A ship! Where?'

'In the docks.'

'But we never go into the docks.'

'I did. I had to.'

'I don't understand.'

'The baby was born there.'

'You mean that a baby was born on a merchant vessel?'

'Yes.'

'How extraordinary,' exclaimed Sister Julienne. 'This requires further investigation. Do you know the name of the ship?'

'Yes. The *Katrina*.'

'I think you had better go to bed, nurse. You don't look yourself. Someone else can clean and sterilise your equipment. I must take your record of the delivery and look into this.'

Chummy was helped upstairs to her room, and Sister Julienne took the midwife's record to her office to study. She could scarcely believe what she read. She rang the doctor, and they agreed that they must examine the mother and baby on board the ship, and have them transferred to a maternity hospital for proper post-natal care.

They met at ten a.m. at the gates of the West India Docks. Sister looked very small and out of place. She explained to the porter that they must go aboard the *Katrina*, where a baby had been born during the night. He looked at her as though she were mad, but said that he would inform the Harbour Master.

A short time elapsed, and the Harbour Master arrived with the docking book in his hand. A berth had been reserved for the *Katrina* for three more days, but she had pulled anchor and sailed at eight a.m.

Sister was horrified. 'But they can't do that. There is a mother and baby on board, just delivered. They will need medical attention. It's the height of irresponsibility. That poor woman.'

The Harbour Master gave her a very dubious look, and simply said, 'Women are not permitted in the docks. Now, excuse me, but I must ask you to leave.'

Sister would probably have said more, but the doctor led her away.

'There is nothing you can do, Sister. They have gone, and if the captain has done a runner, frankly, I am not surprised. A ship's woman, as they are called, contravenes all international shipping laws. If a mother and baby were found on board the captain would be arrested. He would certainly be dismissed from service, he would be heavily fined and might have to face a prison sentence. It is no surprise that he left port three days ahead of schedule. By now the *Katrina* will be well out in the English Channel.'

ON THE SHELF

A knock at the door. Sister Monica Joan was in the hallway. I was just coming downstairs. She opened the door, then banged it shut and started to draw the bolts across. I went up to her.

'Sister, what's the matter?'

She did not answer coherently, but muttered and clucked to herself as she fumbled with the bolts; but they were large and heavy, and her bony fingers had not the strength with which to draw them.

'See here, child, pull this one, pull it hard. We must firm up the battlements, lower the portcullis.'

Another knock at the door.

'But Sister, dear, there's someone at the door. We can't keep them out. It might be important.'

She continued fussing.

'Oh, drat this thing! Why won't you help me?'

'I'm going to open the door, Sister. We can't keep people out. There might be someone in labour.'

I opened the door. A policeman stood there. But Sister was in readiness. She had her crucifix in her hand and held it forward with an outspread arm, thrusting it in his face.

'Stand back, stand back, I adjure you. In the name of Christ, retreat!'

Her voice was quavering with passion, and her poor old arm was trembling, so that the crucifix was rocking and shaking a few inches from his nose.

'You shall not enter. You see before you a Soldier of Christ, girt with the Armour of Salvation, 'gainst which the Jaws of Hell shall not prevail.'

The policeman's face was a study. I tried to intervene.

'But Sister, dear, it's not . . .'

'Get thee behind me, Satan. Like Horatio I stand alone on the bridge to face the Midian hordes. Lay down thy sword. Desist, thou Scourge of Israel.'

With that, she shut the door, then turned to me and gave me one of her naughty winks.

'That will see them off. They won't try again.'

Poor Sister. I understood her aversion to policemen and sympathised. But perhaps the policeman had called about something to do with our work. It would not have been the first time that a Bobby on the beat had been asked to 'go an' call ve midwife, deary. I reckons I'm in labour'.

'I'll go and see what he wants. But I won't let him in. I promise you, Sister.'

I opened the door a few inches and slipped out. Sister Monica Joan banged it shut behind me, nearly catching my ankle.

The policeman was standing in the street, looking as though he did not quite know what to do next. A bicycle was propped against the railings.

'You must excuse her. She does not like . . .'

Then I recognised him. It was the copper whom Chummy had knocked over when she was learning to ride her bicycle and who had also accompanied the police sergeant in his investigations about the stolen jewellery. I burst out laughing.

'Oh, it's you. We seem to meet a lot. What do you want this time?'

'I'm not here on police business. You can tell Sister and calm her fears. I've brought a bicycle back, that is all. I told the nurse I would.'

'Which nurse?'

'I don't know her name. The very tall one.'

'Chummy. What are you doing with her bike?'

'I sent her back by taxi, because I did not think she was in a fit condition to ride.'

'What?' I exclaimed, thinking he meant that she was drunk. 'When?'

'This morning at about six o'clock.'

'Good God! Where did you find her?'

'In the Docks.'

'In the Docks! Drunk and incapable in the Docks, at six o'clock in the morning! My God! This is a side of Chummy we knew nothing about. She's a dark horse. You wait till I tell the girls. Was it a wild party, or something?'

He was smiling. He was an interesting-looking man who was probably younger than he appeared. He had an ugly-attractive sort of face, and a scar ran up the side of his cheek almost to the cheekbone. This might have made him look grim, but as he smiled his dark eyes danced with humour.

'No. It was no party, and she was not drunk. I am not sure of the details, but apparently a baby was born on one of the ships, and your nurse Chummy went to deliver it.'

I knew nothing about the drama of the night and stared at him in amazement.

'I saw the nurse staggering along the quayside as my colleague and I were talking with the nightwatchman. It had been a stormy night, and he said that she had climbed up the rope ladder. So presumably she had to climb down again. When I saw her, she looked as if she were on the verge of collapse. She hardly knew where she was going. So I told her not to ride the bike and ordered a taxi. I am now returning the bike,' he added more formally, 'and would like you to sign for it.'

I signed, and he thanked me and turned to go. But then he hesitated and half turned back.

'I was wondering . . .' And then he stopped. Silence.

'Yes? Wondering what?'

'Oh, just thinking . . .' Another silence.

'Well, unless I know what you are thinking, I can't help you, can I?'

'No, of course not.' More silence. 'How is she?'

'Who? Chummy?'

'Yes.'

'Well, I don't know. I didn't know there was anything wrong with her.'

'I'm not sure. I hope not. She looked all in when I saw her, and . . .' His voice trailed off.

'Oh, that's nothing, I assure you. We are frequently "all in". Sometimes the work gets very heavy, and we are often out for long hours. It can be quite exhausting, sometimes. But we get over it. Chummy will, you'll see.'

'I hope so.' Another long silence, in which he looked as if he wanted to say more. I waited.

'Look, tell her I brought back the bike . . .' He stopped again; ' . . . I felt responsible for her in a way this morning, when I saw her staggering along the quayside. She hardly knew where she was going and would have killed herself on a bike in the East India Dock Road. I suppose I just wanted to reassure myself that she is all right now.'

'Well, I honestly don't know. And if you will excuse me, I have to go. I have the morning visits to make, and it's getting late. If you want to know how she is, you had better come back later.' He nodded. 'But come back when you are not on duty, and not in uniform. You might meet Sister Monica Joan again!'

A few days later we were relaxing in our sitting room. The pressure of work had subsided. Then there was a knock at the door. Trixie groaned.

'Here comes trouble. Someone in labour. Who's on call?'

She came back a few minutes later with a wicked grin on her face.

'There's a young man to see you, Chummy.'

'Oh whoopee! It must be my brother, Wizard Prang ! He's on leave from the R.A.F. Pilot, you know. Commissioned officer and all that. Don't know what he does, actually, now that the war is over, but he seems to enjoy it. Ask him to come up, old girl. Not too fast. We'd better tidy up, eh, girls?'

Cynthia, Chummy and I set about clearing away the dirty mugs, plates, papers, magazines, shoes and bits of uniform that were lying around the place. If Chummy's brother, Wizard Prang, was anything like his sister, and from the name it sounded as if he would be, this was going to be a rare treat.

A tall man entered the room. I recognised him at once as the policeman, in plain clothes. Chummy, who couldn't handle men, instantly went bright red and started spluttering. Trixie, who always liked to stir things up, said innocently, 'This is David, and he wants to see you, Chummy.'

'Oh, great Scott! Me? There must be some mistake. It can't be me.'

She swallowed hard, and her arm jerked sideways, knocking over a table lamp, which fell onto the record player, where our favourite 78 was spinning round. There was a ghastly screeching sound as the needle dragged across the record.

'Oh, clumsy clot! Oh silly me! Now what have I done?' Chummy's voice was distressed.

'You've ruined the Eartha Kitt, that's what you've done, you chump.' Trixie sounded cross. 'That was "Take It Easy", something *you* need to learn to do, you idiot.'

'Oh, sorry girls. Frightfully sorry and all that. I know I'm a liability. Here, I'll stop the dratted thing.'

Chummy moved, and there was another crash as she knocked over a table of coffee mugs.

'Lawks! What next?' was her anguished cry.

There was a guffaw of masculine laughter.

'David is the policeman you knocked over last year,' said Trixie wickedly. 'He wants to see you.'

'Oh, crikey! Not that again! I didn't mean ...'

Chummy's voice trailed away into nothingness. Her embarrassment was all-consuming. David looked abashed, in the presence of four girls and a chaotic situation that somehow – he did not know how – he seemed to have provoked. Cynthia came to the rescue, her low voice easing the tension. She picked up the coffee mugs and scooped up the instant coffee from the carpet.

'Nonsense. Of course David hasn't come about last year's accident. Would you like a cup of coffee? There may be some bits of fluff in it, but you can pick them off when they float to the top.' With a few words she put everyone at their ease. 'We were talking about Chummy's extraordinary adventure in the Dock the other night.'

'That is why I came.' He turned to Chummy. 'It was a very brave thing you did. Are you all right now?'

'Lawks, yes. Nothing wrong with me. Bounce up like a cork, I do. But how did you know about it, actually?'

'I was there. I saw you coming along the quayside. Don't you remember?'

'No.' Chummy looked vague.

'Well, I do. I think I will always remember the way you looked when you got off that boat. You deserve a medal.'

'Me? Why?'

'For all that you did that night.'

'Oh, fiddlesticks. That was nothing. Anyone would have done the same.'

'I do not think so. I really don't.'

Chummy could not be induced to say anything more. She sat on the edge of her chair, stiff and awkward, looking as though she wished herself a thousand miles away.

The evening passed pleasantly. Policemen and nurses always have a lot in common. I had found from previous experience, living in nurses' homes, that if we wanted to throw an impromptu party, we only had to send an invitation round to the nearest police station, and we would be flooded with healthy young coppers, eager to try their chances. David certainly enjoyed himself, being the centre of the attention among four young girls, even though one of them was too shy to talk.

Inevitably, the conversation turned to Chummy's experience in the Docks, and in particular to the ship's woman, who held a morbid fascination for us. We were agog to hear more about the life of such a woman and tried to get Chummy to talk about her. But it was no use. Poor Chummy might have been able to be expansive with us girls, but in mixed company she was speechless with discomfort. In those days, it must be remembered, even amongst midwives who saw just about everything, sexual matters were either unmentionable, or referred to obliquely and with exaggerated delicacy. And the life of a ship's woman was in no way delicate!

We asked David if he had heard of such a character. He assured us that, although every crew might wish to have one, a ship's woman was pretty rare, because of the strict controls on trading vessels. 'But they do exist, as you have found out.' He looked sideways at Chummy with an amused grin. She persisted in looking at the carpet, biting her lips and chewing her fingernails.

The clock struck eleven. David stood up to leave. Cynthia said, 'This has been so nice. We do hope you will come again. Chummy, would you show David out, while we tidy up?'

Chummy reluctantly stood up and cast an appealing glance at Cynthia, who refused to notice her distress. In silence they left the room, and a few minutes later we heard the front door close.

Chummy reappeared, looking pink, giggly and bewildered.

'Well?' we all said in chorus.

'He has asked me to go out with him.'

'Of course. What did you expect?'

'Nothing.'

'Nothing?'

'No.'

'Well why do you think he came here, all dressed up in his best suit with a clean shirt and a new tie?'

'Was he? I didn't notice.'

'Of course he was. Anyone could see that.'

'But why? I don't understand.'

'Because he likes you. That's why.'

'He can't do. Not in that way, anyway. I'm not pretty. I'm not even attractive. I'm too big, and I'm clumsy and awkward. My feet are too big. I fall over things. I never know what to say to anyone. My mater can't take me anywhere. She says I'm on the shelf.'

'Well, your mater is an ass.'

David had been in the Arnhem debacle during the war. He had been in the Paratroop Regiment, which was a crack division. In the autumn of 1944, 30,000 troops were flown behind the enemy lines to capture the bridges spanning the canals and rivers on the Dutch/German border. At the same time, British tanks and infantry were mobilised to push through from the Allied front in Normandy to relieve the airborne troops. But things did not turn out as planned, and consequently the advance airborne divisions were cut off in enemy territory without supplies or reinforcements. David was one of the lucky ones who survived. Exhausted, filthy and half-starved, he and a handful of men had made their way through the woods to the British and American occupied territory. He had been in the war only for two years, from age eighteen to twenty, but the experience had left a lasting mark on his mind and character, as well as giving him the scar on his face.

After the war, he couldn't settle down in civilian life. He had scarcely had time before call-up to decide what he wanted to do, and after the danger and drama of the war everything seemed rather tame at home. He tried factory work, and a milk round, he worked in a garage and in a pub, but found satisfaction in none of these. His mother was worried, and his father impatient. 'Chopping and changing jobs all the time won't get you any-where. You want to settle down. A nice steady job with a pension, that's what you want.' David privately thought that a steady job with a pension would be worse than death, so he changed his job again.

He had always been a quiet boy who read a lot. He was not particularly good at school, because none of the things the school taught seemed important to him. But he read voraciously, and his young mind and soul thrilled to tales of faraway places with strange-sounding names. He wanted to go to them all and learn about the people and their customs. The army had given him the chance to get away, but the horrors of war had shattered many of his romantic dreams.

But he did not like peacetime either, and the new job – assistant in a hardware shop – was worse than all the others. His father said, 'Stick to it, boy, you've got to learn to stick with things. When I was your age ...'

But David was not a boy. He was twenty-five and more disturbed than he or anyone else had realised. One of the older men in the shop, a man who had been through the First World War, gave him the help he needed. They were sitting in the back of the shop eating their packed lunches, and David must have looked particularly down that day. They started talking and reminiscing. David spoke of the perilous crawl through the forest after Arnhem, and the man said, 'It's funny how times like that can be the best times of your life, in a twisted sort of way. It's the excitement, the adrenalin rush, the danger, the uncertainty. All these things make for intense living. You can't carry on here like this, weighing half a pound of six-inch nails and sharpening a chisel. You need more activity, or you'll go bonkers. Why not try the police? The Metropolitan are looking for recruits.'

David was twenty-seven when he entered Police Training College, and it was the best thing he could have done. He left home, leaving his mother fussing and worrying and his father criticising, and lived in the police hostel, where there were other young men who had been through the war. The training was harder than he could ever have imagined. There were hours of lectures on every aspect of crime, including assault, larceny, forgery, bribery, traffic offences, drink driving, rape, sodomy, buggery and much, much more. He had to be familiar with the Betting and Gambling Act, the Licensing Act and the Prostitution Act, to mention but a few. His head was spinning as he tried to take it all in. But an indifferent schoolboy who didn't find his lessons important turned into a police cadet who found everything meaningful, and he passed top of the examination. He then had two years on the beat as a probationer, during which time he was always with another constable, assigned to a section or a division. He found life on the streets even more fascinating than the college. It was a tough period, but he revelled in the challenge and determined to become a sergeant and inspector, with his ultimate sights set on chief inspector.

His parents were delighted. His father commented, with a chortle, that he not only had a steady job, but also a good pension. His mother started getting broody, and coyly mentioned that a 'nice girl' was what he needed.

But girls were as big a failure for him as all the dead-end jobs he had undertaken. He was quiet and rather shy and always conscious of the scar on his face. 'No girl will want me,' he thought. Also, a few unsatisfactory affairs had convinced him that girls were basically silly and self-obsessed. He wasn't interested in their preoccupations, and they weren't interested in the things that absorbed him. A few of the policewomen seemed interesting, but they were either married or going steady with someone else. He wanted a girl who could get her mind off her fingernails or her hair. One girl said to him archly, 'Do you like the way I have plucked my eyebrows?' He was aghast. Eyebrows? He had never noticed them. The girl was offended and provoked a quarrel. He wasn't really cross or disappointed. The incident confirmed in his mind that girls were a bit empty, and a man couldn't expect anything else.

That was until he saw Chummy staggering along the quayside. He had met her a few times before and he recalled with amusement the day she had propelled her bicycle into him and knocked him over, knocking herself out at the same time. She was a big, strong girl, but, as she weaved her way uncertainly towards the three men standing at the dock gates, he could see she hardly had the strength to carry her bag. His protective instincts were aroused. He had heard the extraordinary, garbled story from the nightwatchman about her going to see a woman on a boat and climbing the rope ladder, and he hadn't known what to make of it. At the time he knew nothing of a baby being born, nor of the perilous circumstances of the birth. He just thought, this is a girl who is different, whose main preoccupation is not her eyebrows or her fingernails, and after he had put her in a taxi, he determined to see her again.

His first visit left the convent in a flurry of excitement. Even the sisters were twittering with interest. It was the last thing anyone had expected. The evening of Chummy's first date was the occasion for unsolicited advice and useless assistance. First, what should she wear? She produced a few clothes from her wardrobe, none of them very attractive.

'You must have something new.'

'But what?'

We all borrowed and swapped each other's clothes, but nothing that we wore fitted Chummy, so in the end we sighed hopelessly and loaned her a pretty scarf. She was also in a dither over what she should talk about.

'I'm no good with boys. I have never been dated by a boy before. What am I going to say?'

'Look, don't be daft. He's not a boy, he's a grown man, and he wouldn't have asked you out if he hadn't any reason to think you are interesting.'

'Oh lawks! This is going to be a disaster, I know it. What if

I fall over, or say something bally silly? My mater says you can't take me anywhere.'

'Well, your mater's not taking you out, is she? Forget "mater". Think of David.'

The doorbell rang, and Chummy fell over the doormat, crashing into the door.

'Enjoy yourself,' we all whispered in chorus, but she didn't look as though she would.

We didn't see her when she came in, but after that first evening David's visits to the convent became more frequent, and Chummy went out more. She didn't say anything, to our keen disappointment, but became quieter and less of a good-old-chum, jolly-old-chum type of girl. We tried probing, of course, but the most we could get out of her was that 'Police work is very interesting. Much wider and more varied and interesting than you would think.'

'Anything else?' we asked, eagerly.

'What else?' she enquired innocently.

'Well . . . anything . . . sort of . . . interesting?'

'I've told him about my plans to be a missionary, if that's what you mean.'

We sighed deeply. It was hopeless. If all they ever talked about was the Metropolitan Police and missionaries, what future could there be? Poor old Chummy. Perhaps her mater was right, and she really was on the shelf.

It was another of those rush times. We were flying about. Eleven deliveries in two days and nights, post-natal visits, an ante-natal clinic, lectures to attend, and the telephone constantly ringing.

I was on first call, and thankful to be resting after a hectic night and day with no sleep. The phone rang. Wearily I picked it up.

'My wife's in labour. She told me to call the midwife.'

Hastily I collected my bag and looked at the duty rota to see who would now be on first call. Chummy's name was at the top of the list. I ran to her room and banged on the door.

'Chummy! I'm going out. You're on first call.'

There was no response. I banged again and burst into the room.

'You're on first . . .'

My voice trailed away, and I backed off, abashed, guilty of an unforgivable intrusion – it was one of those things you should never, ever do. Chummy was in bed with her policeman.

THE WEDDING

Chummy married her policeman and she also became a missionary. Mrs Fortescue-Cholmeley-Browne, her mater, tried to organise a society wedding, with a reception at the Savoy Hotel, but Chummy refused. 'You owe it to your family dear,' she said applying the pressure. Still she refused. She wanted a simple wedding in our local church, All Saints, to be conducted by our local rector, with a reception in the church hall. 'But we cannot announce in the *Times* that the reception will be in a church hall in the East India Dock Road!' Mater exclaimed in alarm. 'And what about photographs? I will have to inform *Tatlers* and *Society News*. The family expect it. We can't have the reporters and photographers coming to a church hall, of all things.'

But Chummy was adamant: no announcements, no photographers.

Next came the issue of a wedding dress. Mater wanted to take her to Norman Hartnell, the Queen's dressmaker, for a wedding gown. Chummy refused, even more emphatically. She wasn't going to be dressed up like a Christmas tree fairy. 'But you must, dear. We are all dressed by Hartnell.' No, she wouldn't budge. She would wear a tailored suit. 'But you must wear white, dear. Virginal white for a wedding.' 'I'm not entitled to,' replied Chummy wickedly. That put a stop to any further entreaties.

The wedding party left from Nonnatus House, and I am not at all sure that the Reverend Mother would have approved of the disruption it caused had she seen it. But she was far away in Chichester, so it did not matter. The Sisters were in a real flutter of excitement because nothing like this had ever happened in the convent, and we girls were in a state bordering on panic trying to get ready. Mrs B had been baking all week and was putting the finishing touches to delectable dishes on the last morning, but Fred the boiler man had to go into her kitchen to attend to the boiler, which nearly drove her wild, and we all thought she would walk out. Sister Julienne sorted them out and calmed the cook, which was just as well, because without her the reception would have been a flop.

Amid all the flurry of preparation the routine work had to be dealt with. We each had our usual list of ante- or post-natal visits, babies to bath, feeding to be supervised, and so on. In addition the general district nursing, especially the insulin injections, had to be attended to.

The day started badly for Trixie because she had washed and set her hair first thing and had then gone out on her bike to do her visits, so her hair was blown about, and when she got back it looked a mess. She kept wailing, 'What am I going to do with my hair? It's all over the place, and I can't do a thing with it!' Cynthia advised Vitapointe and gave her a tube, but Trixie in her hurry picked up a tube of foundation cream, which she smothered all over her hair. So then her hair was covered in grease, which looked a great deal worse. Cynthia advised washing it again.

'But it's too late. I can't go to a wedding with wet hair,' Trixie cried.

'Well, you certainly can't go to a wedding with pink face cream on your hair!'

Preparations started in earnest. A face pack was essential, then toning lotion; nails buffed and polished. Stockings were missing, or not matching, or laddered. A skirt had to be ironed.

'Be careful. It's too hot.'

'But I can't turn it down.'

'You'll have to leave it to get cooler.'

'I haven't time.'

'You'll have to. It will ruin the skirt if it's too hot.'

'Stupid thing. Why don't we get a better one?'

Hair clips had to be found, curlers taken out, lipsticks swapped, perfumes sniffed.

'I think I like the Musk.'

'The Freesia is more suitable for a wedding.'

'It's too light.'

'Well, the Musk is too heavy.'

'No it's not. Don't be such a misery.'

Eyes are the window to the soul, they tell us. But that was not good enough for us girls. Eyes needed serious embellishment. Eyebrows had to be plucked, eyelashes curled, eyeshadow blended, eyeliner drawn with trembling haste, mascara . . .

'Damn!'

'What's up?'

'This mascara's dried out.'

'Spit on it, then.'

'That's disgusting.'

'No it's not. Keeps it moist. Here have some of mine.'

'Not if you've been spitting on it, thank you very much.'

'Please youself.'

Trixie had decided that the only thing to do was to wash her hair again, and now she was frantically trying to dry it.

'This stupid dryer is useless. Haven't we got a better one?'

'I'll get mine.'

'Yours blows too hard. I tried it before.'

'Beggars can't be choosers.'

Accessories required careful thought. A brooch was pinned on, then taken off, a necklace tried, earrings swapped, bracelets considered. Scarves had to be compared.

'That one matches your dress, you know.'

'I think I prefer this one. It's a contrast.'

'No. Bit too dominant. Try that one over there.'

'How does that look?'

'Better, much better. I like it.'

'OK, then I'll wear it. No I won't. The silly thing will only get in the way. I won't wear a scarf at all.'

The only person who wasn't rushing wildly around preparing for the wedding was the bride herself. Chummy was perfectly calm and composed, and quietly smiling at the rest of us in our excitement.

'You sort yourselves out,' she said. 'I'm all ready. I will just go along the corridor and spend half an hour by myself in the chapel until it's time to go across the road to the church.'

One thing that had to be resolved was who should remain behind to be on call. Sister Julienne was adamant that we girls should all attend the wedding ceremony *and* the reception, so then came the discussion about which of the Sisters should remain at Nonnatus House.

'Weddings are for the young,' said Sister Evangelina. 'I'll stay behind.'

'No, no. That wouldn't be fair,' chorused her Sisters. 'We know you would like to go. We'll do a rota, and take it in turns.'

So that is what they did.

We left for the church, walked down the war-damaged road, past the bomb site that had been St Frideswide's church, round the corner, across the East India Dock Road to All Saints church on the south side of the road. No cars, no flowers, no bridesmaids – nothing like that. We could have been going out for an afternoon stroll. Chummy was wearing a simple grey suit, flat shoes, no make-up, no hat. She looked her usual self, but somehow more than herself, more than the Chummy we had grown to love.

The social division in the church was conspicuous. The Fortescue-Cholmeley-Brownes, oozing class, sat on one side of the aisle, and the Thompsons, shouting suburbia, sat on the other. We sat on Chummy's side with the nuns and several nurses from St Thomas's Hospital. On David's were half a dozen strapping young policemen. The policemen only came because David was popular, and for the chance of free beer. Also, they were intrigued. What on earth was a girl who wanted to be a missionary going to be like? And what, in the name of all that was holy, could they expect of a wedding party put on by a group of nuns.

They entered the church and were directed to David's side, where they sat self-consciously among the Thompson relatives. But when a crowd of young nurses entered in their wide skirts, their tight waists and high-heeled shoes, and sat down on Chummy's side, their spirits soared. They couldn't believe their luck and tried leaning sideways in the pews to make eye contact with nods and grins. But the girls ignored them, of course.

The nurses from St Thomas's had come because they found it hard to believe that Chummy was getting married at all. They had been convinced that she was firmly on the shelf, destined for a worthy spinsterhood. They were also, I'm sorry to say, condescending. 'Is it true that she's marrying a policeman, my dear? With all her connections, surely she could have done better than that? She must have been desperate, that's all I can say.' They sat demurely among the Fortescue-Cholmeley-Brownes, aware that a group of young men on the other side were trying to attract their attention, but deliberately turning their pretty heads to study the Stations of the Cross adjoining the opposite wall. The air was charged with testosterone, but the flirting had to be suppressed when Chummy entered on the arm of her father.

The wedding ceremony was beautiful, the love between these two like-minded young people filling the church with a golden light. Before God, and the present congregation, they pledged their life-long vows to each other and stepped out into the sunshine as man and wife.

At the reception the policemen made straight for the young nurses, who rapidly forgot their hoity-toity airs and graces. Everything looked set fair for a good old party. The Fortescue-Cholmeley-Brownes lined up for the ceremonial hand-shaking and introductions, but the Thompsons didn't know what to do and stood around looking sheepish, until Chummy rescued them with 'Oh come on, Mater, let's not bother with all that. Let's just mix. It will be much nicer.'

Mater's face, half-hidden by an exquisite hat, looked a trifle sour. She approached Mrs Thompson, David's mother.

'Are you related to the Baily-Thompsons of Wiltshire?'

'No.'

'Ah! Well-er-perhaps to the Thompson-Bretts of India?'

'I don't think so.'

'Well, you might be, you know. It was a large family.'

'I couldn't rightly say, madam. I don't know that any of my relations has been abroad. We come from Battersea, and we were all in trade.'

'Oh, really? How very interesting.'

'Yes. We have a nice little place, with a nice garden. Just right for a little child to run around in. You must come and have tea with me some day.'

'Enchanted.' With a pained smile, the lady inclined her head.

'And when we have grandchildren, we'll see a lot more of each other, I'm sure.'

'Oh, no doubt, no doubt. Delightful talking to you, Mrs Thompson.'

And the poor lady crossed the social divide to talk with her own set about the shortcomings of the other side.

Colonel Fortescue-Cholmeley-Browne, in grey tails and topper, opened conversation with Mr Thompson, in Moss Bros wedding hire and trilby.

'I say, old chap, let's have a snort together.'

'Don't mind if I do. You're paying for it.'

'Well, er, yes. Customary, you know. Noblesse oblige. Father of the bride, and all that.'

'And I'm father of the groom, so that makes us related, in a way.'

'Related!'

'Well, in a way.'

'I hadn't thought of it like that, I must say. Tell me a bit about yourself. I'm India, ex-army. Were you in the services?'

'Well yes, sir. I was staff orderly to the officers of the Third Riflemens' Division, East Sussex, in the First World War.'

'Staff orderly?'

'Yes, sir.'

'How interesting. How frightfully interesting.'

The colonel did not look at all interested. Soon he crossed the room to join his wife.

'Not a pukka sahib in the whole room. No one worth talking to.'

'She's really let us down. We never could take her anywhere, and I'm quite sure we never will. I suppose I must go round and "mix" with her friends as she puts it, but it will be the last time, I assure you. I think I will talk to that old lady sitting by herself over there.'

The old lady was Sister Monica Joan, who was fully absorbed with a dish of jelly and blancmange. Mrs Fortescue-Cholmeley-Browne approached her graciously.

'Can I introduce myself?'

Sister Monica Joan looked up sharply.

'Induce yourself? What! Induce yourself? My good woman, let it be known that I do not at all approve of inducing. A baby should come naturally, and the vast majority will, without the need for all these inductions. And what is a woman of your age doing being pregnant? It's indecent. And now you are asking me if you can induce yourself. Are you planning an abortion? Is that what? I tell you, it's illegal, and I'll have nothing to do with it. Be off with you.'

Poor Mater, shaken to the core, returned to her husband's side.

'I'm never going to get over this, never,' she murmured.

'Stiff upper lip, old girl,' retorted the colonel. 'This can't last for long, and then they're going to Sierra Leone, I understand.'

'Thank God for that. Best place for her,' said Mater emphatically.

Sister Julienne was quietly thrilled at the way Chummy had developed. Many girls had come to Nonnatus House aspiring to be medical missionaries, but somehow Chummy would always stand out in her mind. She gazed at the tall, happy girl standing at the other side of the room and fondly remembered her awkwardness when she first came to the convent, falling over things or walking into stationary objects. Above all she remembered Chummy learning to ride a bike with that nice boy Jack helping her. That was when the girl's true mettle first became apparent – she was indomitable. Sister Julienne chuckled to herself as she looked across the room at David, the policeman Chummy had somehow managed to run into and almost knock unconscious. So this was how the good Lord had planned it!

Sister Julienne was a deeply romantic soul, and she smiled to herself again as she remembered Jane and the Reverend Thornton Applebee-Thornton. Perhaps God had needed a bit of help there! She had never tried matchmaking before, but when the reverend gentleman had come from his mission in Sierra Leone to study the midwifery practice of the Sisters as a model for the medical services he wanted to introduce into his mission, she had shamelessly thrust Jane into his company. The success of her little plan had been spectacular. And now Chummy was going out to join them in Sierra Leone as the first trained midwife, while David had applied to the police force there.

Sister Julienne smiled around her at the happy faces, at Mrs B, in her element amid all the catering, Fred ambling around, moving chairs, clearing up, and obviously making wisecracks for the benefit of all. She looked across at the nurses from St Tommy's, who were roaring with laughter at the policemen, and thought how delightful it was to see young people enjoying themselves. And then her gaze fell on the frigid face of Mrs Fortescue-Cholmeley-Browne. This isn't right, she thought. I must go over and have a word with her.

After the usual pleasantries, Sister Julienne went straight to the point.

'Mothers and daughters seldom understand each other.'

'What makes you say a thing like that?' said Mrs Browne guardedly.

'Experience.'

'Experience? You have no children.'

'No, but I have a family. I am one of a family of nine, and I saw the tension between my mother and her five daughters. None of us lived up to her expectations. She did not attend any of their weddings. Not one! And when I took religious vows, she was outraged. I was embarrassing the family, she said. So you see, I know all about misunderstandings between mothers and daughters.'

Mrs Browne sat silent. She was not going to be drawn. After a moment's pause, Sister went on.

'Camilla is a fine young woman. You can be very proud of her. She has the makings of nobility in her. She has strength of character, steadfast pursuit of her goal and above all mental and physical courage. These are the qualities that built the British Empire.'

Sister Julienne had scored a goal. Mrs Fortescue-Cholmeley-Browne came from a colonial family. Her father had been official adviser to the Raj and administrator of Bengal. Her husband, the Governor of Rajastan. She knew all about the qualities that had built the British Empire. After a pause, she said, 'Well, I wish I could see it.'

'You will, I assure you. Mothers and daughters always draw closer to each other as the years pass. Camilla and David . . .'

Mrs Browne butted in: 'This David! This fellow she is marrying. A common policeman. I ask you! What sort of marriage is that?'

'He may be a common policeman, but I have every reason to believe he is a fine young man and will make a good husband. He has a heroic war record. He flew and landed behind the

German lines at Arnhem, you know, and not only survived, but helped others to survive.'

'I didn't know that.' The lady's face softened.

'No. Probably not. It is not the sort of thing he talks about.'

The time for speeches was drawing near. Sister Julienne felt she had no more than a few minutes alone with the mother of the bride, and must introduce some humour into the situation.

'Another thing. For years after he was demobbed from the army David's father (she pointed to Mr Thompson) strongly disapproved of his son. Nothing the boy could do was good enough for Mr T. So you see, the same misunderstandings and tensions can arise between fathers and sons. Often worse. The son does not live up to the father's expectations and earns his reproaches. And when he does succeed very often masculine rivalry can set in as the father desperately tries to beat his son at the very game he has initiated.'

For the first time that day Mrs Fortescue-Cholmeley-Browne burst out laughing. Chummy, who had been watching her mother apprehensively, looked across the room with amazement.

'Oh, how true. I know that syndrome all too well. My own husband shows a deadly rivalry with our son over sculling. The boy's far better than him, but he can't or won't see it. He is taking extra training courses and comes back exhausted, hardly able to move a muscle, and needs physiotherapy. He'll injure his back, or something, before he will admit defeat. I can't tell you what the atmosphere is like in our house sometimes with these two men competing against each other.'

The two ladies looked at each other, nearly creasing themselves with laughter but suppressing their giggles because the speeches were just about to start. Sister managed to whisper, 'I know *exactly* what you mean.'

The wedding speeches were predictable and charming. The colonel spoke with affection of his only daughter and said he was proud of her nursing career. We girls clapped and shouted,

'Hear, hear!' The best man said that David was a credit to the force, and Sierra Leone would be lucky to get him, and the policemen stamped and cheered.

The boys from the South Poplar Youth club band arrived and with them came a wedding guest who had been invited to the church, but had not come. We had all wondered why. This was Jack, a local lad of about thirteen who had been instrumental in teaching Chummy to ride a bicycle when she first came to Nonnatus House. He had turned up early and late, guiding her around the roads, helping her to steer and balance, shouting instructions as he ran along beside her until she had mastered the art. Then he had appointed himself to the position of bodyguard to keep away the local kids who teased her. As a 'thank you' the Colonel had given the boy a bicycle.

A close bond had developed between Chummy and Jack, and she had been surprised and a little sad that he had not come to her wedding. When he walked in, slightly behind the other boys, she shouted out, 'Jack! You've come – I'm so glad,' and rushed over to him. In her exuberance she would probably have taken him in her arms, but he quickly backed off with a 'Steady on, miss, steady on.' So she shook hands in the manner that boys of that age prefer. It would not do to shame him in front of the other lads.

Mrs B had held back a substantial part of the feast for the boys from the SPY club, knowing that it would be necessary, and while they were all tucking in, Chummy managed a few words with Jack.

'Well, I wouldn't miss your weddin', miss, but I didn't wanna come wiv all them toffs, like, so I comes wiv the lads, like, an' I gotta presen' for yer, miss. I made it in metalwork at school.'

He pulled a brown-paper package from his pocket and thrust it furtively into her hands, making sure that his back was turned to the others so that they couldn't see. 'It's fer you, miss.'

Then he turned quickly and blended in with the other lads.

Chummy returned to her husband and opened the parcel. It

was a tiny bicycle, carefully constructed out of wire and metal.

The SPY club band started up, somewhat out of tune but with plenty of rhythm, and the happy couple led the dancing. At seven o'clock they left to get the night train to Cornwall, where they were spending their honeymoon. A taxi came to take them to Paddington station, and a big crowd gathered outside the church hall to wish them well and see them off. Jack didn't stand waving with the rest of us. He ran round to the back of the hall, grabbed his bicycle and gave chase to the taxi, with Chummy and David looking out of the rear window in astonishment. He was a strong boy and a fast cyclist. He followed the taxi all the way and was on the platform to wave them off as the train steamed out of Paddington station.

TAXI!

Sister Monica Joan had recovered from pneumonia caused by wandering down the East India Dock Road on a raw November morning wearing only her nightie; had lived triumphantly through the shock, trauma and humiliation of having been accused of shop-lifting; had survived the ordeal of prosecution and a court case before judge and jury; and now, at the age of ninety-two, looked set for another decade.

It was a fine summer, and Sister Monica Joan had a number of relatives whom she decided she must visit. I have described earlier the niece living in Sonning-on-Thames, to whom she bequeathed two fine Chippendale chairs. Another niece and nephew with their three children lived nearer, in Richmond, which was still a tidy distance for a very old lady to travel alone by bus. But, undaunted, she set out.

I am not sure whether she told anyone where she was going (probably not), but once again there was general anxiety in the convent, because Sister Monica Joan was missing, it was eight o'clock and time for Compline. No doubt prayers were said for her safety, which must have caught the ear of the Almighty, or whoever oversees these small matters, because at that moment the telephone rang, and the niece in Richmond said that her aunt was with them, enjoying the company of the three children. Asked whether she could stay the night, the niece said it would be difficult, because they had only a small house, and there wasn't a spare bed, but her aunt was welcome to sleep on the sofa. At this point Sister Julienne made a tactical error, which she freely admitted later. A night on a sofa would have done Sister Monica Joan no harm whatsoever, but Sister Julienne hesitated and said she really ought to come back to the convent.

Thinking that it was too late in the evening to ask them to put her on a bus, Sister told them to put her in a taxi, which would be paid for on arrival.

It was a grave mistake, which in subsequent days and weeks led to a series of incidents that spun out of control. Sister Monica Joan had probably not been in a London taxi-cab since they were horse-drawn. As a professed nun she was vowed to a life of poverty, and if she travelled anywhere she took the bus or train, the cheapest available route. A modern taxi was a new and delightful experience.

At lunch the next day, Sister was full of her niece and nephew in Richmond, and their three delightful daughters. 'Such pretty gels, don't you know, so engaging.' She couldn't remember their names, but one of them, poor child, had spots. Such an affliction at that age. She would go that very afternoon to Chrisp Street market, to find something suitable for the one with spots.

She sailed around the market, oblivious to sideways glances and whispered warnings that went before her from the costers, who all kept a wary eye on her since they had been frustrated in their charge of petty theft.

She homed in on a new stall run by a woman with beads and flowers around her neck and in her hair, who sold herb and flower remedies and potions in pretty pots with exotic sounding names, guaranteed to cure anything. Ingrown toenails, gastric ulcers, piles, failing eyesight, toothache – all could be cured by her remedies. Sister Monica Joan was in a delirium of delight. This was what she had been looking for, all her life, she assured the woman behind the stall – an essence of marigold, a tincture of dog daisy, an infusion of dandelion, and all so simply explained in the little booklet. She poured over the booklet and compared it with her notes on astrology and life forces and earth centres and came to the happy conclusion that all had been revealed. Not only would the one with the spots, sweet child, be cured, but her future would be luminous.

★

The next day Sister Julienne had a rather nasty telephone call from the nephew, who said that his aunt had woken the whole house at three o'clock in the morning with a garbled story about flower essence, and if you have a bad toe rub it on your toe and it will get better, and if you have a tummy ache rub it on your tummy and the ache will go away, and if the one with the spots rubs it on her spots they will go away, and wasn't it wonderful? The nephew had replied that it was not at all wonderful. He and his wife had to go to work the next day, and the children had to go to school, and did she realise what time of the night it was? Sister Monica Joan had replied that yes, she thought she knew, but she was so sure the one with the spots ought to hear the good news straight away, so could she speak to her? The nephew had replied certainly not, it was ten past three, and the girl had to go to school. She was doing her O-levels and needed her sleep.

Sister Julienne was apologising and saying that she had no idea Sister Monica Joan was active in the middle of the night, when the nephew interrupted to say that that was not the end of the story by any means. About an hour later they were all woken again, and Sister Monica Joan explained that she didn't want the one with the spots to think she was being specially favoured, but spots were such an affliction at that age, didn't he know, nor did she want the two younger gels to feel left out, so she had a little present for them also, which she would give to them personally.

After that, the nephew said, he had disconnected the telephone, and Sister Julienne agreed that under the circumstances it was the best thing he could have done.

The following Saturday Sister Monica Joan decided to go to Richmond again. She discussed it fully with everyone around the big dining table. She must be sure to see those dear gels again, and how exciting to discover you have young and pretty great-nieces that you didn't know you had, and it reminded her of her own young days with her sisters in the big house and all the fun they used to have.

Sister Julienne was glad to know at least where she was going on this occasion, and telephoned the nephew to tell him to expect his aunt. She made quite sure that Sister Monica Joan had enough money for the bus fare.

But a humble London double-decker was not part of Sister Monica Joan's plans. Having once experienced the delights of a London taxi-cab, buses were out of the question. Oh, the pleasure and the grandeur of sitting alone in the spacious interior while a competent driver weaves his way through the streets. None of the awful business of having to get off one bus and wait anxiously for another. No standing around – just go straight from Poplar to Richmond (about fifteen miles through Central London). Sister Monica Joan was delighted with her new-found ease of transport. No fussing, looking for your bus pass. No fumbling for pennies and shillings to pay the bus conductor. And it didn't seem to cost anything. You just had to say, 'Payment will be met on arrival,' and off he went, dear man.

The nephew did not complain the first two times he was expected to finance the taxi-fare, but after the third occasion he put through a gentle phone call to Sister Julienne asking her, as tactfully as he could, if she could provide his aunt with sufficient money to pay for her own taxi. Sister, who with mounting alarm at the depletion of the convent's petty cash had paid for four return taxis, agreed that things were getting out of hand, and that she would have to do something, although she was not sure what. The nephew was particular to say that they were all delighted with his aunt's visits, and the girls adored her and would sit listening to her for hours. She was enchanting. It was just the taxi fares ...

There was considerable discussion amongst the nuns as to how best to control the mounting problem. Sister Julienne had a very serious discussion with Sister Monica Joan about the vows of poverty, the need to economise for the sake of running the convent, the expense of taxi fares, and the need to take the bus wherever possible. Sister Monica Joan was very amenable and fully understood that she had been extravagant, so she agreed to take the bus in future. But perhaps she forgot. Or perhaps she could not resist the temptation when she saw a shiny black taxi-cab in the street. Or perhaps her intentions were good, but it was raining, and Sister Monica Joan could not abide the rain. Whatever the reason, the situation continued as before. Sister Julienne felt obliged to refund to the nephew all the taxi fares incurred to date, because a nun is the responsibility of the convent, and not of her family.

The Sisters had further discussions. At the start of her next journey Novice Ruth took Sister Monica Joan to the bus stop, put her on the correct bus, paid the bus conductor, and told him where she was to get off. But Sister Monica Joan was crafty, and she always got what she wanted. She thanked Novice Ruth kindly for her assistance, sweetly waved goodbye and quite simply got off at the next stop and took a taxi.

Things were going too far. Sister Julienne was obliged to inform the Reverend Mother Jesu Emanuel. Large sums of money were regularly leaking out of the convent funds, and she could not seem to control it. A Chapter meeting of all the Sisters at the Mother House in Chichester was convened, and the financial adviser was requested to be present. Thirty-two Sisters who worked in the Mother House attended, and many of them were very critical of Sister Monica Joan. Her behaviour was outrageous. She had first brought scandal to the Order through a court case for alleged theft, and now, instead of being humble and contrite as any other nun would be, she was spending money with reckless abandon. Why should they have to skimp and save and live a life of poverty while she was riding around London like a duchess?

The Reverend Mother pointed out to the younger Sisters that Sister Monica Joan had given over fifty years of dedicated service to the poorest of the poor, in conditions of unimaginable squalor, and it was the policy of the Order to allow privileges and comforts to elderly Sisters who had retired from nursing. Two or three of the elderly Sisters spoke up to say that they had also given lives of dedicated service to the poor and needy, and that they defined 'comforts and privileges' as jam on Sundays, or an occasional cup of tea in bed. They could not approve of taxis all over the place. It was a question of what was reasonable.

The Reverend Mother sighed; Sister Monica Joan had never been reasonable. She asked the financial adviser, an independent auditor and accountant, for his opinion.

The accountant said that he had carefully studied the finances of the Order, and had observed that Sister Monica Joan's dowry to the Order in 1906, when she made her life vows, was greater than that of all the other Sisters put together. In addition, a very large inheritance which she had received in 1922 on the death of her mother had immediately gone into the convent funds. Had it not been for these two large deposits of money, the accountant questioned whether the Sisters would have been able to continue their work at all.

That settled it. The Chapter ruled that finances should be made available to Sister Julienne to use at her discretion. There were still a few sour faces and mutters of 'not fair', which the Reverend Mother dispelled by saying that she was sure that all the Sisters would be relieved by the decision, as many would be anxious at the thought of an old lady roaming alone around London by bus – especially as her mind was wandering, as had been made clear by the recent scandal. 'Let's face it. She's senile and shouldn't be let out,' muttered one of the younger Sisters. To this the Reverend Mother replied sharply that the remark was uncharitable, and she would not countenance the thought of Sister Monica Joan being confined to the house like a prisoner.

Sister Julienne was relieved by the decision of the Chapter and was able to finance several more taxi fares to and from Richmond with no further anxiety. Nonetheless, she had another little talk with Sister Monica Joan about limiting the number of visits, the need for economy and the vows of poverty. Sister Monica Joan must have taken this to heart; perhaps her conscience had been pricked by the reminder of her life vows, or perhaps she just wanted a bit of diversion. After all, she had always been an adventurous soul, seeking out a challenge. The next thing we heard was that she had been seen by many witnesses standing at the traffic lights by the Blackwall Tunnel. When the lights turned red and the traffic stopped, she would totter into the road, round the front of the cars and lorries, tap on the window of a car, and ask the astonished driver to take her to Richmond.

Whatever might be said of nuns, thumbing lifts from strange men is not the way they are expected to behave. The reaction of the drivers can only be imagined. Sister Monica Joan would have been wearing the full monastic habit of her Order. If you were a businessman going to your next appointment, such an apparition weaving its way unsteadily into the road must have looked like a visitation from God – or perhaps the devil. When the apparition tapped on your window and started a long, convoluted yarn about pretty nieces in Richmond, and how she had got a new lotion from the woman in the market for the one with spots, but she suspected blackheads really, guaranteed to make them go away, and that was why she needed to get to Richmond, but buses were so difficult, you would probably have thought you were going a bit mad, particularly if the business lunch had been of the liquid variety.

Without exception the drivers refused, but Sister Monica Joan persisted in what to her mind was a perfectly reasonable request. The man had a car, and she did not, she would point out. It would surely be no inconvenience to him to make a small detour to Richmond? She knew the address – what was the difficulty? She was a lady inclined to become extremely cross and snappish if she did not get her own way, and many of the conversations ended in acrimony.

Several times, while she was still talking, the lights turned green, and the traffic started up again. Lorries in the free-moving lane passed alarmingly close as she stood in the road. The car driver, who would still be trying to reason with her, could not start, and there would be honking and hooting and shouts from frustrated motorists piled up behind. Eventually (and this happened several times) she would accept that the car driver was not going to Richmond and would not divert his journey to take her, and she would totter back to the pavement, only to try again when the lights turned red and another car stopped on the nearside lane.

After half a dozen such attempts she was caught in the act by two policemen, who observed her actions for a few minutes and then apprehended her for causing an obstruction to the traffic and for endangering her life and that of others. Sister Monica Joan was very sensitive about policemen and protested violently at finding herself between two of them, and being escorted back to the convent.

After this little escapade, Sister Julienne begged her to take taxis, and hang the expense.

A printed letter arrived for Sister Monica Joan from Wandsworth Borough Council, stating that a lady's hand bag containing a little money, a prayer book, a pair of spectacles and a set of false teeth had been found and awaited her collection at a lost property office in West London. Sister Julienne was taking no chances. A taxi was ordered to collect Sister Monica Joan, to take her to the address on the letter and to return her to the convent.

Four hours later the taxi returned. The driver said that when he reached West London, she said that she had forgotten or lost the piece of paper giving the address. She knew she should be going to a lost property office but she was not sure which one. So she had instructed him to drive to all the lost property offices in the area, which amounted to fifteen throughout Fulham, Putney, Chelsea, Wimbledon, Kingston, Twickenham and as far west as Hampton Court. No handbag was reclaimed. He must have missed the one where it was, he said. Anyway, the old lady seemed to have enjoyed herself. She'd had a nice day out. She had enjoyed going over Hammersmith Bridge so much that she had instructed him to go back, and then to go over it again, he said. He had looked after her and brought her home safely. The cost was so astronomical that Sister Julienne thought she would have to consult the Reverend Mother again. Where would it all end?

Novice Ruth was the first person up that morning. She was approaching her first year professional vows and wanted an hour of private devotion alone in the chapel before her Sisters joined her. The time was four a.m., and it being summer, the dawn was breaking and light was returning to the world. She walked quietly along the passage, turned the corner and found Sister Monica Joan lying on the floor. She was breathing, but her eyes were wide open and staring, her pulse was bounding and she was twitching intermittently. She had wet herself and could not be roused. Novice Ruth fetched a pillow and placed it under her head and wrapped a warm blanket around her. Then she telephoned the doctor and woke Sister Julienne. Together they carried the unconscious figure back to her room and laid her on the bed. Twenty minutes later the doctor arrived, examined the patient and confirmed what they had both suspected: Sister Monica Joan had had a stroke. She did not regain consciousness and died that evening, at the hour of Compline. The last words of the last office of the day are: 'Lord, grant us a quiet night and a perfect end.'

Peace at the hour of death is one of the greatest blessings that God can give. Death can be very terrible, but peace can transform it. Sister Monica Joan received no intrusive medical treatment, no drugs, no investigations into the cause of the stroke, no attempts to prolong her life or to delay her death. She received loving nursing care from her Sisters and was able to die in peace. This is the perfect end.

Her body lay at rest for two days in the convent chapel, and local people came to pay their respects. Then she was taken to the Mother House in Chichester for the funeral service.

The death of Sister Monica Joan affected me deeply. I had not expected her to die; I had somehow believed that she was indestructible. I could not reconcile myself to the loss. The magic and mystery of that extraordinary woman haunted me. Suddenly, all the beauty and fun and bewitchment that she encapsulated was gone, leaving me utterly bereft.

Aware of my state of mind, Sister Julienne said to me one day, with her usual twinkle, 'I was thinking about Sister Monica Joan this morning in chapel. Perhaps it was rather naughty of me, but the Old Testament reading about Elijah going up to Heaven in a fiery chariot prompted the thought. Don't you think perhaps that Sister Monica Joan went straight to Heaven by taxi?'

ADIEU

David and Chummy went to Sierra Leone. Chummy opened the first midwifery service at the mission station and ran the small hospital. David joined the police and became a senior officer in the force. They found the work harder and more demanding than they could ever have imagined, but they had the strength of youth and idealism to carry them through. Above all, they had the love to support and sustain each other in times of crisis. They stayed in Africa throughout their lives, and Chummy and I corresponded for a few years. They had a family, but she continued her work in a teaching capacity. She must have been desperately busy, and in the circumstances it is not easy to continue writing letters indefinitely to an old nursing colleague. We exchanged Christmas cards for a few years, but eventually they petered out. She was a unique character, and it was a happiness and a privilege to have known her.

Trixie was the only one of our small circle who did not continue nursing. She married a young man who had both feet firmly planted on the civil service ladder. He entered the diplomatic service, and Trixie went with him. I have often wondered how she managed, because diplomacy had never been her strong suit! I just could not imagine her in one of Her Majesty's Embassies. When I knew her, she was fun, quick-minded and clever, but sharp-tongued and brutally blunt. Perhaps she introduced a breath of fresh air into the unctuous atmosphere of the diplomatic service. She travelled with her husband to many of the big capitals of the world and became quite sophisticated, but cutting comments delivered with lightning rapidity remained her trademark.

I did not see much of Trixie during these years. It was not until the couple had retired to Essex, by which time we were both grandmothers, that we met again. I noticed a small grand-daughter who looked exactly like Trixie when she was young. The little girl was about ten years old and had an answer to everything. She was an experienced manager already and bossed her three younger brothers around with consummate skill.

Trixie took me to the street market in Basildon, where we witnessed the daughters of Megan'mave at work selling their fruit and vegetables. Later, her comment was 'We never change, do we? And what is more, our children and grandchildren don't change.'

Trixie had certainly mellowed with the years.

Cynthia felt called to the religious life and was accepted as a Postulant and Novice in the order. She was a working Novice, as she was already a trained nurse and midwife. But the religious life is hard, and much is demanded spiritually and physically of any Novice. Cynthia's goodness and purity had always impressed me and had influenced me more than she ever knew, but perhaps her mind could not stand the strain. She had shown signs of clinical depression around the time of puberty, and this was a state of mind that beset her for many years. She left the order and became a hospital staff nurse, then returned to the convent to resume her life vows, but left again. Why does God so often cause good people to suffer so greatly? It is a question I have often asked myself. Sister Julienne turned the question the other way, and said, 'God loves greatly those whom he requires to suffer greatly.' This is a riddle wrapped in a mystery we cannot comprehend.

Cynthia limped through life for many years, in and out of psychiatric hospitals. Many drugs were prescribed, and also electric shock therapy. A true depressive lives a life of inner hell, which little or sometimes nothing can alleviate. My heart bled for gentle Cynthia, but there was nothing I could do to help.

At the age of thirty-nine she met a clergyman who was a

widower and had a son. They married, and his needs, mentally, were even greater than her own. Somehow the necessity to look after him and organise his life became the focus of her existence and cured her. We none of us can understand the complexities of the human mind. She became a very happy and successful vicar's wife and a health visitor. Her husband Roger was also a classical scholar. At the age of sixty-five he retired from the ministry, and for several years they lived like a couple of hippy teenagers. With no more than a rucksack each, and a budget of £3 a day, they roamed hundreds of miles across Greece, Israel, Jordan and Turkey, examining the architectural ruins of ancient civilisations. They slept in little cafés, on buses, under the stars on beaches, in fields, in olive groves and lemon orchards. They planned nothing, but simply went where the fancy took them.

After retirement, Cynthia's husband joined the Church of England World Mission Association. This meant that he could be asked to act as a locum for any church, at home or overseas, which was temporarily without a priest.

The couple were both about seventy years of age when the telephone rang one evening.

'This is the World Mission Association. Could you go to Lima? The vicar has just been shot.'

'Sounds nasty. Well yes, certainly. When do you want me?'

'The week after next.'

'I dare say we could go. I must ask my wife.'

Aside: 'Cynthia, could we go to Lima the week after next? The vicar has been shot.'

'Where's Lima?'

'Peru. South America.'

'Well, yes, I should think we could. A fortnight is enough time to pack things up here. For how long?'

To the telephone: 'Yes, we could go. For how long?'

'Three months. Six, perhaps. Not really sure.'

'That's all right. Send us details, flight tickets, etc., and we'll go.'

Cynthia – quiet, sensitive, depressive – led a life of high romance and breathtaking adventure in her old age that few of us would have dared contemplate, still less had the courage to carry out.

Some people have described my first book *Call the Midwife* as a spiritual journey, and they are correct – it is. I owe to the Sisters more than I could possibly repay. Probably they do not know how great is my debt. The words 'if God really does exist, then that must have implications for the whole of life' could not be dismissed. Sister Julienne and I spent many hours discussing these subjects, and the influence of her goodness has shaped my development. We corresponded, and I visited her all through my life, and I took my own children with me to the Mother House; we stayed in the caravan in the grounds of the convent.

I remained very close to her and always sought her prayers and wisdom at any difficult point in my life. She always guided me well. In 1991 Sister Julienne developed a brain tumour, and for the last three months of her life I visited her every Friday. It was an enriching experience, even though, or perhaps *because*, she was deteriorating week by week. Time was short, and getting shorter, in which to convey, if not in words, then in silent empathy, my love and gratitude. On the last Friday she was deeply unconscious, and it was obvious that her life was drawing to its end. She died two days later on Sunday morning – a beautiful day in June at the hour when her Sisters were saying Lauds, the first monastic office to greet the dawn.

It was a singular honour to be invited to attend her funeral at the Mother House. The service was the Requiem Mass for the dead as ordained by the Book of Common Prayer. The funeral of a nun is very quiet and reverent. Her Sisters do not mourn and grieve; they are more likely to express joy that a life given in the service of God is fulfilled. For them death is not an enemy. Death is seen as a friend.

At the end of the service, while plainsong was being chanted, one of the Sisters took up a pile of folded garments that had been lying on the altar throughout. The Reverend Mother came towards her with hands outstretched, palms facing upwards. The Sister placed the garments on the hands of the Reverend Mother, who turned and walked slowly towards the coffin. She placed the small burden on the centre of the coffin and turned and bowed to the altar. It was the folded habit, surmounted by the gold cross and rosary that Sister Julienne had worn all her professed life, and they went with her to her grave in the Sisters' cemetery in the convent garden.

Rest eternal, rest in peace, beloved Sister Julienne.

Sister Evangelina died some years ago. At her own request she was buried in Poplar, and not in the Sisters' cemetery at the convent. She had always been one of the people, and that is how she wished to be remembered.

Novice Ruth took her final vows and practised her calling for about twenty years. But in the mid-1970s she encountered a spiritual crisis, which in religious language is called 'the black night of the soul'. It is a most terrible experience, probably more shattering than the worst kind of divorce. It is well known and documented in monastic literature, and is a spiritual phenomenon to be dreaded, yet in some ways welcomed, as it is a testing of the soul and suffering can lead to an enriched spiritual experience. Sister Ruth was tormented for years with no respite and eventually renounced her life vows and left the order.

Sister Bernadette, an inspired midwife from whom I learned all the practical skills of the profession, also left the Order but for a very different reason. She worked faithfully all through the 1960s and '70s as a midwife. In the 1980s, when the HIV virus infected the Western world and when medical and nursing staff were vulnerable to being infected, she nursed AIDS patients at a time when the mortality rate was close on 100 per cent. Throughout the 1980s there had been debate in the Church of England about the ordination of women, and in 1993 the

General Synod voted that women could be admitted to the priesthood. Sister Bernadette could not take this. Deep religious conviction based on theology and history told her that it was wrong. She was in her seventies and crippled with arthritis, but she had the courage of her convictions to leave the Anglican Church. This meant that she would have to leave the Sisters with whom she had shared her life. She was accepted into a Roman Catholic order, where she lived the strict life of a solitary contemplative, devoting her time to prayer and meditation

Ambition is a double-edged sword. One side will cut through stagnation and lead to a new life; without ambition, mankind would still be living in caves. But the other side can be destructive, leading to feelings of loss and regret. I was ambitious, and my sights were set high. I was planning to be a hospital matron or at the very least a sister tutor, and I would have to climb the ladder of the nursing hierarchy. A district nurse and midwife was only a lower rung on that ladder. I did not really want to leave the Sisters, but I knew that, if I stayed with them, I would stagnate. I loved the Sisters and their devotional life, and I loved the fun and freedom of district work in the docklands, but to continue would have rendered me unsuitable for the discipline of hospital work, which was very strict indeed in those days. I left the Sisters in 1959 to become a staff midwife at the London Hospital, Mile End Road, where I enjoyed seeing more of Cockney characters. But it took a long time to settle down to the rigours and discipline of hospital routine. Eventually the move paid off, and after a couple of years I obtained my first junior sister's post at the famous women's hospital, the Elizabeth Garrett Anderson in the Euston Road (now sadly closed). Later I became night sister there, which in those days meant being in overall charge of the hospital throughout the night. Then I became ward sister of the Marie Curie Hospital in Hampstead.

I was climbing the ladder, as anticipated. But then I met a certain young man, and ideas of becoming a hospital matron seemed rather irrelevant. We have been happily married for about forty-five years at the time of writing. After our children were born I gave up full-time nursing, but continued part-time.

In 1973, after a twenty-year nursing and midwifery career, I left nursing altogether. All my life I had been a frustrated musician, and with intensive study, supported by my husband, I achieved a Licenciate of the London College of Music and later a Fellowship and started twenty-five years of music teaching.

IN MEMORIAM CYNTHIA

This book was dedicated to Cynthia as early as 2004, but she never read it. In June 2006 Cynthia died. She had had cancer six years previously, which had been successfully treated, and she and Roger had continued their adventures, but in 2004 he developed congestive heart failure, from which he died about eighteen months later. Clinical depression returned to cloud Cynthia's mind during his last illness, and then there was a recurrence of the cancer.

She died as she had lived, quietly, peacefully and with no fuss. Gently she let go of life, and had said to many people that death was what she wanted. She knew it was approaching, and was content. 'I hope I have been useful,' she whispered to me a few days before her death. Cynthia received her last communion and she, who was virtually sinless, made her confession and received Holy Unction.

Her stepson, her sister and I were with her during the last five days of her life, and on the final day, when to all appearances she was unconscious, I said to her slowly and clearly, 'I am so thankful I have been with you.' Her eyelids flickered, and she breathed rather than spoke the words, 'And so am I.' In my experience the dying always know who is with them and need the love they bring.

Cynthia was Godmother to my elder daughter, Suzannah,

who had sent a card to her during that week. It was a complete surprise to me, and I read it aloud to Cynthia. The words were so beautiful I cried as I read them, and Cynthia smiled her slow, sweet smile, and whispered, 'I remember too.'

It may seem pointlessly sentimental to those who do not know either character, but for me a testimonial to my dear friend is necessary, and so I quote my daughter's card in full:

Dear Cynthia,

I am thinking about you a lot at the present time, but most especially I am remembering past times and what you have meant to me over the years.

When I was a little girl, I remember dropping a bowl of jelly on the floor twice, and the second time the bowl broke! I was so upset I cried, but you didn't get cross.

I remember what fun it was when you took us up into the bell tower of Roger's church. You let us ring the bells – you said it wouldn't matter if all the people in the village thought it was the wrong time.

I remember sleeping in the caravan and being kept awake all night by the owls and the bells. More recently I remember visiting you when our girls were little. You took us for a lovely walk along the coast, and you made them a special pudding with smiley faces on.

Most recently you sent me some of your jewellery, and you patched up my old bear, which you made for me when I was christened.

All these things are memories I will treasure forever – they remind me of you, my Godmother. Over the years I have come to realise that you are essentially what a God-mother should be. Thank you for being you. Bless you, now and always.

Your loving God-daughter
Suzannah XXX

FAREWELL TO THE EAST END

The Sisters had opened Nonnatus House in the 1870s to meet the needs of women living in dire poverty. However, during the 1960s things began to change rapidly, and the old way of life vanished.

One by one the docks closed; air freight had replaced the old cargo boats, and the dockers became redundant. At the same time demolition of bomb-damaged and slum property started, and people were rehoused out of London in the new towns. For many this was life-shattering, particularly for the older generation who had lived their entire lives within a radius of two or three streets, close to their children and grandchildren. The rehousing programme tore apart the extended family, which had provided the unity and been the strength of East End life for generations. Families in the suburbs started a new, more affluent life, and began to feel ashamed of their old Cockney dialect with its distinctive accent, its idiosyncratic grammar, its delicious word order, its double and triple negatives, its back slang and rhyming slang. Sadly the old Cockney lingo virtually disappeared.

In the 1960s vast areas of London were torn down, and with them went the Canada Buildings. The heart went out of old Poplar.

I wandered around the Buildings after they had been evacuated. Where little girls had played hop-scotch and skipped, where boys had played football or marbles, where women in curlers and head scarves had gossiped and men exchanged racing tips, where teeming human life had been lived in all its rich fecundity was now a ghost town. Hollow sounds echoed up the walls of the high buildings, a dustbin lid rolled across the cobbles, a broken door swung against a wall. In the court, where costers had once trundled their barrows, stood rows of municipal rubbish bins. Where once there had been washing lines festooned with clean washing, broken lines now trailed in the dirt. Where the coalman with his horse and cart had sauntered in stood a notice – NO ENTRY. Stairways up which women had heaved everything, including a baby in its pram, were barricaded with the notice DANGER. Dark corners, where giggling and kissing had once been heard, were now filthy, piled high with detritus blowing in from the yard. Windows, where net curtains had fluttered, were boarded up. Doors that had always been open were now permanently closed. No movement, no life, no humanity. I left the Buildings and never went back.

IT IS FINISHED

The exodus of the traditional Cockney people affected the Sisters' practice, especially when the docklands became 'smart'. Newcomers did not know, nor particularly want to know, about the nuns. The National Health Service and the fashion of going into hospital to have a baby reduced their midwifery practice considerably. The advent of the Pill in 1963 brought it to an end altogether. Women, for the first time in history, had control over their own fertility, and the birth rate plummeted. Throughout the 1950s the Sisters had delivered around 100 babies per month. In the year 1964 that number had dropped to four or five.

The Sisters, who had done so much to help the very poor in the slums of Poplar, were no longer needed.

They had come to Poplar in 1879, when there was virtually no medical or nursing care, and their dedication and self-sacrifice had saved the lives of thousands of poor women. They were known and loved by everyone living in the area, but in the brave new world of modern technology, the nuns suddenly seemed absurdly old-fashioned. The history of these heroic women was forgotten.

This may seem a sad outcome. But the Sisters were first and foremost a religious order living under monastic vows in the service of God, and they did not look at it that way. A century earlier they had been called to nurse the sick and deliver the babies of those who could not afford medical attention. This vocation they had faithfully carried out for nearly 100 years. If the poor no longer needed them, they had fulfilled their mission and they were well pleased. 'It is finished,' were Christ's last words from the cross. A life's work fulfilled and finished is a triumph.

The nuns closed their nursing and midwifery practice and turned to other work – drug abuse, shelter for the homeless, working with the deaf, helping Asian women to integrate into British life, and in the 1980s they started working with AIDS patients. They continue to do these and other tasks into the new millennium.

In 1978 Nonnatus House was closed after ninety-nine years of service to the people of Poplar. The Sisters removed to the Mother House, to await God's calling for work – they knew not what or where. They left quietly and with no fuss. Perhaps only the local clergy and a handful of older people were aware that they had gone.

And here my tale ends, with the closure of Nonnatus House.

THE END

GLOSSARY

This glossary by Terri Coates MSc, RN, RM, ADM, Dip Ed.

Afterbirth. Also known as the placenta (see below). It is called the afterbirth because it is expelled from the womb after the baby has been born.

Amniotic fluid. The water that surrounds a baby in the womb.

Antenatal. The term used to describe the whole of pregnancy from conception to the onset of labour.

Anterior presentation. The back of the baby's head in labour will normally be in the front or anterior part of the mother's pelvis. The anterior presentation is the most favourable for the baby to adopt for a normal delivery.

Asphixia pallida. A newborn baby that has become very pale (grey/white) because there is no attempt to breathe and the heartbeat has become dangerously slow.

Atelectasis. An incomplete expansion of lobules (clusters of alveoli) or lung segments may result in partial or complete lung collapse. The collapsed tissue, unable to perform gas exchange, allows unoxygenated blood to pass through it unchanged, producing hypoxemia (deficient oxygenation of the blood). Atelectasis can be present at birth (incomplete expansion of the lungs), or during adulthood (from a collapsed lung). Prognosis depends on prompt removal of any airway obstruction, relief of hypoxia, and re-expansion of the collapsed lobule(s) or lung(s).

b.d. The medical shorthand used as an instruction on prescriptions to mean twice a day. From the Latin *bis die*.

Cervix. The cervix is the neck of the womb or uterus.

Caesarean section. An operation to deliver a baby through an incision in the mother's abdomen

Chloral hydrate. Chloral hydrate was a mild sedative and analgesic used in the early stages of labour. The drug was given as a drink with either water and glucose or fruit juice. Chloral hydrate is an irritant to the stomach and often caused vomiting, so is no longer used.

Contraction. A contraction is the intermittent tightening of the muscles of the uterus (womb) which are painful during labour.

Cord presentation. The cord is palpable at cervix through the intact membranes.

Crown. The top of the baby's head, usually the first part of the head to emerge. When the top of the head emerges it is said to crown.

Crowned. When the widest diameter of the baby's head is at the vaginal opening during delivery the head is said to have 'crowned'.

Curette. A surgical instrument that comes in different sizes and shapes that is used to scrape away unhealthy or unwanted tissue.

D and C. Dilatation and curettage (D and C) is an operation to remove any pieces of placenta or membrane from the uterus to prevent further bleeding or infection.

Dates. The date that the baby is due.

Eclampsia. Eclampsia is a rare and severe consequence of pre-eclampsia. It is characterised by convulsions and is an infrequent cause of death of a mother and unborn baby.

Ergometrine. Ergometrine is an oxytocic drug which makes the muscle of the uterus contract after delivery.

Eve's rocking. An outdated method of resuscitation. Chest compressions are more effective and are used with mouth-to-mouth resuscitation.

External Cephalic Version (ECV). Rotating the unborn baby or foetus into a position more favourable for a normal delivery.
Exsanguinate. Extensive blood loss. Possibly fatal.

First stage of labour. The first stage of labour is from the start of regular painful contractions until the cervix (neck of the womb) is fully open.
Forceps. Forceps are used to gently hold tissue during an operation or surgical procedures.
Full term. The length of a pregnancy is nine months (forty weeks). Full term is considered to be thirty-eight to forty-two weeks of pregnancy.
Fundus. The top of the uterus.

Gamgee. Absorbent tissue.
Gas and air machine. Gas and air was a popular form of pain relief for labour. The air has now been exchanged for oxygen, but the term 'gas and air' is still used. The 'gas' too has changed over the years: the 'gas' in current use is nitrous oxide.
Gestation. The gestation is the number of weeks of pregnancy.
Gluteous muscle. The gluteous or gleuteous maximus muscle is the large muscle in the bottom.

Higginson's syringe. A type of flexible syringe with a long nozzle usually used to administer enemas.

IM. Intra-muscular or into the muscle.
IV. Intra-venous or intra-venous infusion may be more commonly known as a drip (in this case blood).

Lobeline. A respiratory stimulant.
Left side. Positioning women on their left side for delivery was popular for a while. Women are now encouraged to choose the position for delivery that is most comfortable for them. The left side or left lateral position is rarely used.

Menorrhagia. Excessive menstrual blood flow.

Nurse. Title of nurse is now rarely used for or by midwives. Midwifery is an entirely separate profession. Many midwives were trained as nurses, but this dual qualification is now less common.

Obstetric forceps. Forceps used to grasp the foetal head to facilitate the delivery in a difficult labour.
Occipital protuberance. Or occiput is the back of the baby's head.
Os. The opening of the cervix which leads into the womb.
Otitis media. Inflammation or infection of the middle ear.
Oxytocic drugs. Drugs such as Oxytocin or Ergometrine that make the muscle of the uterus contract after delivery and are used to either assist the delivery of the placenta or control bleeding after delivery of the placenta.

Paediatrician. A doctor who specialises in the care of children.
Peritoneum. The lining of the abdominal cavity.
Pathology lab. Laboratory where samples of blood would be sent for confirmation of infection.
Pethidine. A drug used for pain relief in labour.
Perineum. The area of skin between the vagina and the anus.
Phthisis. Tuberculosis of the lungs. No longer in scientific use.
Pink eye. Conjunctivitis is also known as 'pink eye', an inflammation of the conjunctiva of the eye. The conjunctiva is the membrane that covers the eye.
Pinards. A simple trumpet-shaped stethoscope used by the midwife to listen to the baby's heartbeat before birth.
Pitocin. An early proprietary brand name for an oxytocic drug used for induction of labour or treatment of uterine inertia.
Pituitrin. A hormone produced by the pituitary gland, which helps enable lactation. The hormone also stimulates contraction of the uterus and was formerly used to help to induce labour.

Placenta. Also known as the afterbirth. The baby's life-support system supplying the baby with oxygen and nutrients and removing waste products while he/she is growing in the womb. The placenta also produces essential hormones during the pregnancy.

Postnatal. The time immediately following a birth when a midwife would continue to care for the mother and baby.

Post-partum delirium. A postnatal mental condition now known as puerperal psychosis. The less severe form is called postnatal depression.

Pouch of Douglas. A small pouch-shaped area situated behind the uterus and in front of the rectum.

Pre-eclampsia. A disease that is peculiar to pregnancy. The symptoms are: high blood pressure, protein in the urine and oedema (swelling).

Primigravida. A woman pregnant with her first baby.

Prolapsed cord. Occurs after the membranes have broken and the cord is found outside the uterus.

Restitution of the head. A normal corrective movement of the baby's head during delivery to bring it back into natural line with the shoulders.

Second stage. The second stage (of labour) is the time when the neck of the womb or uterus is fully open, and the mother starts to push until the delivery of the baby.

Special diet. It was thought that a restricted diet and restricted fluid intake would improve the symptoms of pre-eclampsia. It has now been proved that these restrictions had no effect upon the course of pre-eclampsia and are no longer practised. Pre-eclampsia is treated with rest and drug therapy.

SRN. State Registered Nurse.

Staphylococcus aureus. A bacterium that is commonly found on human skin and mucosa (lining of mouth, nose, etc.). It lives completely harmlessly on the skin and in the nose of about one-third of normal healthy people.

Staph infection. Staphylococcus aureus can infect wounds during or after childbirth or during surgical procedures. These infections may become serious.

Third stage. The third stage of labour is the time from the delivery of the baby to the end of the delivery of the placenta (afterbirth) and control of bleeding.

Transverse lie. Where the baby lies across the mother's womb (instead of parallel to the mother's spine) and so cannot descend through the pelvis for a normal birth.

Unstriped muscle. An outdated term for smooth muscle.

Volsellum forceps. Forceps designed to hold the cervix during gynaecological procedures.

BIBLIOGRAPHY

Sources for the 'Lost Babies' chapter
Booth, Charles, 'The Life and Labour of the People of London',
vols. I–IX, *The Journals of the Royal Statistical Society*, 1887.
Booth, General William, *In Darkest England*, 1890.
Fishman, Professor W. J., *East End 1888*, Duckworth, 1988.
Fishman, Professor W. J., *The Streets of East London*, Duckworth,
1979.
Jordan, Jane, *Josephine Butler*, John Murray, 2000.
Keating, P., ed., *Into Unknown England 1866-1913*, Fontana, 1976.
Mearns, Andrew and Preston, William, *The Bitter Cry of Outcast
London*, 1883.
William, A. E., *Barnardo of Stepney*, Allen and Unwin, 1943.

Sources for the 'Nancy' chapter
Jordan, Jane, *Josephine Butler*, John Murray, 2000
Moberly Bell, E., *Josephine Butler*, Constable, 1962.
Petrie, Glen, *A Singular Iniquity (Campaigns of Josephine Butler)*,
Macmillan, 1971.
Stafford, Ann, *The Age of Consent*, Hodder and Stoughton, 1964.
Williamson, Joseph, *The Forgotten Saint*, The Wellclose Trust,
1977.

Sources for the glossary
Ballière's Nurse's Dictionary, 7th edition, ed. B. Cape, Ballière
Tindall, 1968.
Myles, M., *Text Book for Midwives*, ed. V. Ruth Bennett and L.
K. Brown, Churchill Livingstone, 1999.
Stables, D., *Physiology in Childbearing with Anatomy and Related
Biosciences*, Ballière Tindall, 1999.

Now, discover more
wonderful stories of everyday
heroism and triumph over adversity.
Available in paperback,
audio and ebook only from Orion.

**Go to
www.orionbooks.co.uk/truetales
to read extracts
and find out more**